KT-362-609

A BRIEF GUIDE TO

# STAR TREK

## BRIAN J. ROBB

ROBINSON

RUNNING PRESS
PHILADELPHIA · LONDON

Constable & Robinson Ltd
55–56 Russell Square
London WC1B 4HP
www.constablerobinson.com

First published in the UK by Robinson,
an imprint of Constable & Robinson, 2012

A copy of the British Library Cataloguing in
Publication data is available from the British Library

ISBN 978-1-84901-514-1

3 5 7 9 10 8 6 4 2

First published in the United States in 2012 by Running Press Book Publishers,
a Member of the Perseus Books Group

US ISBN 978-0-7624-4439-7
US Library of Congress Control Number: 2011933252
E-book ISBN 978-1-84901-822-7

9   8   7   6   5   4   3   2   1
Digit on the right indicates the number of this printing

Running Press Book Publishers
2300 Chestnut Street
Philadelphia, PA 19103-4371

Visit us on the web!
www.runningpress.com

For Paul Simpson,
whose valuable feedback and *Star Trek* brainstorming sessions
helped immensely to focus and shape my thinking.

# Contents

# Introduction

## The Storytellers

*'The job of Star Trek was to use drama and adventure as a way of portraying humanity in its various guises and beliefs.* Star Trek *is the expression of my own beliefs using my characters to act out human problems.'* Gene Roddenberry

Whether you are relatively new to *Star Trek*, having enjoyed the J. J. Abrams blockbuster movie from 2009 or the sequel, or a fan of the show who's been following the various series and movies since the US debut of the original in 1966, it is clear that this iconic television show that struggled through its first three years on air has – to adapt the worlds of the Vulcan Spock – 'lived long and prospered'.

The phenomenon of *Star Trek* has been much studied, from features in the popular media and in-depth academic analysis to fan commentary and internet flame wars. The forty-five-year history of the 'franchise' has been dissected every which way in an attempt to discover the reasons for its success, longevity and cultural impact – why has *Star Trek* been so long-lasting when other science fiction TV series have fallen by the wayside, and why have its various iterations on screens large and small been so popular?

This is not an academic tome, but a critical cultural history of *Star Trek*. It's an in-depth look at how the various series and movies were made, the creative forces driving them, what their cultural impact was and what it all means. The book will examine how *Star Trek* changed through the decades and how it perhaps eventually failed to change enough with the times to escape ossification and irrelevance, requiring a dramatic re-invention to save it. It will also look at what the future might be for the *Star Trek* concept, assess what the series' impact has been on viewers, and consider the unstoppable growth of *Star Trek* fandom.

*Star Trek* now spans five distinct television series (six, if you include the often overlooked early-1970s *Star Trek: The Animated Series*) and eleven movies, from 1979's *Star Trek: The Motion Picture* to J. J. Abrams' 2009 reinvention, which has led to a new series of movies to take the franchise through the next decade and maybe beyond.

While many have pointed to the way *Star Trek* has reflected and critiqued the ethical, social and philosophical issues of our times and attempted to depict progressive gender, class and racial representations – so offering a hopeful and positive vision of the future of humanity – the secret of the success of the series is much simpler: it's all down to great storytelling.

The genius of Gene Roddenberry in creating *Star Trek* was to tackle those serious and important issues through well-told science fiction action-adventure tales that appealed to a mass audience. It was the unusual stories and unforgettable characters that first attracted curious television audiences in the 1960s, while the forward-looking ideas presented by the series turned many of those viewers into lifelong fans.

Legend elevates Roddenberry – known to fans as the Great Bird of the Galaxy – to the status of sole creator of *Star Trek*. However, while his important role as the instigator of the series and author of its concept should not be undervalued (three times, no less: in its original 1960s incarnation, its reinvention as a series of movies and its return to television in the 1980s), Roddenberry himself wasn't necessarily the most successful *Star Trek* storyteller. In fact, *Star Trek* has enjoyed more success when under the control of other storytellers, as this book sets out to demonstrate.

Among the host of others who have put their stamp on the concepts of *Star Trek*, some have honoured them (perhaps a bit too much), while others have bent them all out of shape (almost beyond recognition). Significant among them are Samuel A. Peeples, David Gerrold, D. C. Fontana and Gene Coon on *The Original Series* in the 1960s; Harve Bennett and Nicholas Meyer on the original cast movies of the 1980s; Rick Berman and Michael Piller on *The Next Generation*; Ira Steven Behr, Robert Hewitt Wolfe and Ronald D. Moore on *Deep Space Nine*; Brannon Braga and Jeri Taylor on *Voyager*, all in the 1990s; and Manny Coto on *Enterprise* in the twenty-first century. Some of them outstayed their welcome, while others had far too short a run, but each of these creators brought something unique to their respective attempts to create a new spin on Gene Roddenberry's *Star Trek*.

The story behind the *Star Trek* phenomenon is one of inspiration, struggle and good luck. Following a less than stellar career as an episodic television writer, Gene Roddenberry pitched a series he dubbed '*Wagon Train* to the stars', which was taken up by Paramount and ran for three seasons between 1966 and 1969 on NBC. The central trio of characters – headstrong Captain Kirk (William Shatner), inscrutable alien Spock (Leonard Nimoy) and McCoy (DeForest Kelley), the humanist doctor – rapidly became familiar to viewers. However, the series failed to capture a large enough audience to stay on air, narrowly escaping cancellation twice before the axe finally fell, following a lacklustre third season, in 1969. The show found new, unexpected success during syndicated reruns throughout the 1970s (and thanks to daily exposure, sealing the iconic nature of the central trio of characters in pop culture in the process), giving rise to a short-lived animated spin-off and – more importantly – a big-budget movie in 1979 intended to compete with the success of *Star Wars* (1977). While that film met with a mixed reception, it led to a successful series of movies, including the acclaimed *The Wrath of Khan* and *The Voyage Home*, which ran throughout the 1980s.

A return to television was inevitable for *Star Trek*, with Gene Roddenberry at the helm once more (for the first few years). Between 1987 and 2005 *Star Trek* would be in constant production, spanning *The Next Generation*'s new journeys where no man had gone before, through the 1990s' ethnic war dramas of *Deep Space Nine*, the exploration-driven *Voyager* and into the twenty-first century, with post-9/11 prequel series *Enterprise*. Franchise fatigue – too much mediocre *Star Trek* 'product' flooding the market at the same time – led to the cancellation of *Enterprise* and the curtailment of *The Next Generation* movie series. The second batch of movies had produced one bona fide summer blockbuster in 1996's *First Contact* (featuring *The Next Generation*'s signature antagonists, the Borg), but had crashed to Earth with the dismal *Nemesis* in 2002.

A rescue mission for *Star Trek* was necessary. It fell to filmmaker (*Mission: Impossible III*) and cult TV producer (*Alias, Lost*) J. J. Abrams to rise to the challenge of reinventing *Star Trek* once more for a whole new generation. Alongside screenwriters Alex Kurtzman and Roberto Orci, Abrams returned to the very beginning, rediscovering the iconic characters of Kirk, Spock and McCoy.

*Star Trek* has been acclaimed as utopian science fiction. Arriving at the end of the 1960s, Roddenberry's space opera tapped into real-world social and political movements, presenting a vision of the future that offered infinite diversity in infinite combinations (IDIC) and the non-interference rule of the Prime Directive. Aspects of the world of *Star Trek* were obviously contradictory: these people of the future espoused clearly liberal values, but did so while encased in a military outlook. This was a future that displayed great advances in communications and medical science, but also offered similar advances in weaponry, such as photo torpedoes and phasers.

Each version of *Star Trek* reflected the times in which it was made. The movies of the 1980s featuring the cast of *The Original Series* tackled issues of ageing and rebirth through the core trilogy of *The Wrath of Khan*, *The Search for Spock* and *The Voyage Home*. By the time of *The Next Generation*, the self-absorbed 'Me generation', who came to adulthood in the 1970s, were running things, so alongside the tactical officer and science officer, the bridge team of the new *Enterprise* for the 1980s featured a touchy-feely psychologist in the shape of Counsellor Troi. *Deep Space Nine* turned darker for the 1990s, a time when ethnic strife tore up central Europe and the Middle East erupted in conflict that continues today. The post-colonial world of Bajor and the United Nations-style peacekeeping crew of the space station *Deep Space Nine* dramatised issues of war, sacrifice and conflict in a way unthinkable in the comparably anodyne *Star Trek* of the 1960s. On the other hand, the next series, *Voyager*, reflected a somewhat blander, safer 1990s as the twenty-first century loomed; it also featured a failure of the imagination on the part of those creating *Star Trek* to genuinely escape from the past and boldly go into the unknown. They became trapped within the formula that *Deep Space Nine* had so successfully strayed from. Instead of updating *Star Trek* for the new century, both *Voyager* and prequel series *Enterprise* set about recreating the deep-space exploration tropes of *The Original Series* from the 1960s, and even tried to create new versions of the iconic 1960s characters through relatively colourless avatars like Captain Archer and Chief Engineer 'Trip' Tucker. Concurrently, *The Next Generation* movies had trouble defining themselves, failing to service the ensemble cast that had blossomed on television, yet succeeding when adopting the style and approach of the contemporary summer blockbuster in *First Contact*. Even here, though, the producers of *Nemesis* were looking backwards, attempting to model their new *Star Trek* movie for 2002 on the one that had succeeded twenty years earlier, 1982's *The Wrath of Khan*.

Alongside these series and movies, a different type of utopian experiment was going on as *Star Trek* fandom developed, grew and changed, aided and abetted by developments in modern technology (the Internet, cheap video). Starting out in the

1960s as isolated local clubs and mail-order fanzines (fan-produced magazines), *Star Trek* fandom grew during the 1970s thanks to mass conventions that brought like-minded people together to celebrate their obsession. The future depicted on *Star Trek* created a genuine new community here on Earth. *Star Trek* served to free fans' imaginations and to spark their creativity, allowing them to become creators (of, among other things, slash fiction). The fans themselves became *Star Trek* storytellers, bringing their short stories to each other through communities spawned on the internet and in the making of officially tolerated not-for-profit fan video films, such as the *New Voyages/Phase II* fan-made movie series.

All of this began with the vision of one man: Gene Roddenberry. His basic ideas were taken by others, shaped and reshaped, stories told and retold. Actively involved audiences took it upon themselves to create their own versions of *Star Trek*, keeping the concept alive during the ten-year gap between the end of *The Original Series* and the arrival of the much-compromised *The Motion Picture*. *Star Trek* endured for the simple reason that Gene Roddenberry's creation allowed all those involved to tell great, relatable stories.

## Note on Titles Usage

In this volume I've adopted the official Paramount/CBS designations for each of the *Star Trek* TV series and movies. Each TV show or film is usually prefaced with the label '*Star Trek*:', but I've sometimes dropped that in the interests of providing a smoother read. Below, 'TV' indicates a television series, while 'F' indicates a cinema release. The series and films will be referred to using the following notation (in strict chronological order):

*The Original Series* (TV, 1966–9)
*The Animated Series* (TV, 1973–4)
*The Motion Picture* (F, 1979)

*The Wrath of Khan* (F, 1982)
*The Search for Spock* (F, 1984)
*The Voyage Home* (F, 1986)
*The Final Frontier* (F, 1989)
*The Undiscovered Country* (F, 1991)
*The Next Generation* (TV, 1987–94)
*Deep Space Nine* (TV, 1993–9)
*Generations* (F, 1994)
*Voyager* (TV, 1995–2001)
*First Contact* (F, 1996)
*Insurrection* (F, 1999)
*Enterprise* (TV, 2001–5)
*Nemesis* (F, 2002)
*Star Trek* (F, 2009)
*Star Trek sequel* (F, 2012)

# Chapter 1

## Evolution: *Star Trek* Creator Gene Roddenberry

*'If you are cursed with a somewhat logical mind, you ask questions. I have many thoughts which, if I were to voice them, would turn many people against me.'* Gene Roddenberry

Science fiction has a long and proud history across all media, but it has perhaps had the most impact and success with mainstream audiences through the visual media of film and television.

Ancient literature is rife with tales of the fantastic, often used by developing cultures as ways of exploring and explaining the wider world they were beginning to discover beyond their immediate environment. Modern science fiction can generally be dated to the early-nineteenth-century works of Mary Shelley with *Frankenstein* and *The Last Man*, followed by the speculative novels of Jules Verne, such as *From the Earth to the Moon*. A series of turn-of-the-century novels by H. G. Wells developed many of the basic tropes of modern science fiction, primarily in *The Time Machine*, *The Invisible Man* and *The War of the Worlds*. Wells' work can even be seen directly in a *Star Trek* episode, with his 1901 short story *The New Accelerator* a clear inspiration for *The Original Series* episode 'Wink of an Eye', in which Kirk is physically speeded up so much he vanishes relative to those around him.

The 'scientific romances' of the late nineteenth century led to the science fiction magazine boom of the early twentieth century, with the genre becoming codified and popularised. Printed on cheap wood-pulp paper (leading to the usually derogative 'pulps' tag), these popular magazines featured fast-paced, adventure-driven tales and prospered from the mid-1890s (with Frank Munsey's *Argosy Magazine*) through to the mid-1950s, when cheap paperback novels largely replaced them. Titles such as editor Hugo Gernsback's *Amazing Stories* (from 1926 onwards) and John W. Campbell's *Astounding Science Fiction* (from 1929, later *Analog Magazine*) gave an outlet to the first wave of professional science fiction authors in the 1930s and 1940s. Emerging in this period were writers such as Isaac Asimov, Damon Knight, Fred Pohl, James Blish, E. E. 'Doc' Smith, Robert Heinlein, Arthur C. Clarke and A. E. van Vogt (and several of these 'first wave' science fiction storytellers would later have *Star Trek* connections).

The science fiction novel developed in the 1950s and 1960s and brought new, longer-form writers to the genre, including epic and influential works by Frank Herbert (*Dune*), Harlan Ellison (known for his short stories and essays) and Philip K. Dick (a major influence on film and television fantasy and SF from the 1980s through to the twenty-first century). With the longer form came a more in-depth exploration of ideas and a better focus on character, along with an improvement in the literary quality of the writing.

The same period saw a dramatic boom in science fiction on radio, film and television, much of which had a direct influence on those who'd later tell their stories through *Star Trek*. Radio is the perfect medium for science fiction drama. It is a truism that the locations are much better on radio, not requiring the extravagant budgets often needed for visualising science fiction settings in film and TV. On radio, ideas and settings could be explored in dramatic fashion, relying on the listener to fill in the blanks with their imagination. Shows from the 1950s – such as NBC's *Dimension X* and *X Minus One* – dramatised short stories from the pulps and the new paperbacks, as well as producing original scripts. Other shows included *2000 Plus* and

*Beyond Tomorrow,* although much of the material produced was simplistic and juvenile.

Several of these early science fiction radio shows were transferred to the new medium of television in the early 1950s, including *Tom Corbett – Space Cadet* and *Space Patrol.* Television was welcoming to science fiction from the earliest days, despite the difficulties of visually realising spaceships, alien worlds and new high-tech gadgets. Most of the early series were broadcast in short episodes (fifteen to twenty minutes, often transmitted live) and mostly aimed at the children's audience (shown in the early-evening 'kid-vid' time slots). *Captain Video and His Video Rangers* was one of the first, starting in 1949 and running until 1955. The show revolved around the adventures of Captain Video (Richard Coogan) and a space police squad who patrolled the solar system. It featured the first robot character as part of a regular television cast. Many well-known science fiction authors wrote some of the later *Captain Video* scripts, including Isaac Asimov, Cyril Kornbluth, Robert Sheckley, Damon Knight, James Blish, Jack Vance and Arthur C. Clarke. Similarly, *Tom Corbett – Space Cadet* starred Frankie Thomas, Jr. and included science fiction author Alfred Bester among the principal scriptwriters. The similar *Space Patrol* reached 210 half-hour shows and almost 900 fifteen-minute shows across that series' five-year run.

While these shows were largely primitive, regarded as disposable and aimed at children, they did pave the way for the more adult approach of *Star Trek* in the late 1960s. Youngsters who'd enjoyed the juvenile adventures of Captain Video, Tom Corbett and Space Patrol's Buzz Corry (Ed Kemmer) in the mid-1950s were teenagers in the mid-1960s and ready for something more substantial in their television science fiction.

There were some slightly more adult – or at least more pseudo-scientific – TV shows in the 1950s and 1960s that may have influenced *Star Trek*'s approach to the science of its fiction. Between 1955 and 1957, Ziv-TV produced seventy-seven episodes of an anthology show called *Science Fiction Theater.*

Introduced by respected former war correspondent Truman Bradley (often against a science laboratory background), the series told a different story every week with a different cast involved in a scientific dilemma, often based around new discoveries or the ways in which new technology might change society or humankind. The show purported to draw its stories from the headlines, and used realistic scientific approaches and data in formulating many of its tales. More cerebral than the likes of *Tom Corbett* or *Space Patrol*, *Science Fiction Theater* provided more thoughtful drama readily enjoyed by teenagers who'd outgrown the early kid-vid space operas.

By 1957, Russia had launched the Sputnik satellite into orbit and sparked the real-life space race between the Cold War superpowers. This gave rise to a new strain of more realistic science fiction shows based around the imagined realities of the exploration of near space. Ziv-TV's *Men into Space* ran for a year in 1959–60 and took a more grounded approach to space exploration, dealing with the scientific minutiae of space suits, re-entry trajectories and the challenge of sustaining human life on the moon. Among the writers on the show were Jerome Bixby (who'd go on to write four episodes of *Star Trek*) and B-movie specialist Ib Melchior.

*Men into Space* ran in parallel with *The Man and the Challenge*, produced by an ex-Ziv-TV creative, Ivan Tors (later responsible for Florida-based sea adventure series *Sea Hunt* and *Flipper*). That series took a similar tone, following a team of scientists as they tested human endurance on behalf of the US government in order to prepare astronauts for their travels into space.

Many early television science fiction dramas drew on the fantastic movie serials of the 1930s and 1940s for inspiration in their heavily serialised format and melodramatic approach to action. From the earliest days of film in the late 1890s, the medium was used to depict the fantastic. French surrealist Georges Méliès developed trick photographic effects, testing the limits of the new medium, and discovered that fantasy stories were most suitable to these explorations. From 1902's

*A Trip to the Moon* through 1912's *Conquest of the Pole*, Méliès' films were tales of the fantastic that also dramatically developed film techniques and technology. Fritz Lang's *Metropolis* (1927) and *Woman in the Moon* (1929) saw out the silent science fiction era.

Episodic serials dominated the 1930s through to the 1950s, spurred by comic strip-inspired characters like Buck Rogers and Flash Gordon, who also fuelled the early science fiction TV shows of the 1950s. Universal horror films of the 1930s, featuring supernatural creatures like Frankenstein's monster, Dracula, the Wolf Man and the Invisible Man, led to the 1950s' science fiction boom that was dominated by creature features in which post-war atomic fears inspired pulp thrills. Monster-dominated films included *Them!* (1954), *20 Million Miles to Earth* (1957) and *The Blob*. Aliens arrived on Earth – often set on domination of mankind – in *The Day the Earth Stood Still* (1951), *The Thing from Another World* (1951) and *The War of the Worlds* (1952). Another strand of science fiction film was based upon exploration of the unknown, whether it be *20,000 Leagues Under the Sea* (1954) or *Journey to the Centre of the Earth* (1959). Prime among the films that took the outward-looking exploration of deep space as their focus was *Forbidden Planet* (1956).

Easily the biggest influence on the development of the look and feel of *Star Trek*, *Forbidden Planet* featured many elements that would become standardised by the three-year run of the original *Star Trek* TV show. Creator Gene Roddenberry freely admitted to the influence of the film in an early memo to production executive Herb Solow in which he discussed the design of his proposed TV series' starship: 'You may recall we saw MGM's *Forbidden Planet* some weeks ago,' wrote Roddenberry on 10 August 1964. 'I think it would be interesting to take another very hard look at the spaceship, its configurations, controls, instrumentations, etc, while planning our own. We have no intention of copying that ship, but a detailed look at it again would do much to stimulate our own thinking.'

It wasn't only the ship from *Forbidden Planet* that would be echoed in *Star Trek*: much of the overall approach of the movie to its story, characters and setting would find a place on television in Roddenberry's space adventure series. Like *Forbidden Planet*, *Star Trek* would also be set around 200 years in the future; the ship would have an alpha-numeric designation (C57D in *Forbidden Planet*, NCC-1701 in *Star Trek*, both Navy-inspired); and *Star Trek*'s central trio of Kirk, Spock and McCoy would reflect the core triumvirate of the earlier film's crew: the captain, chief science officer and chief medical officer. These influences, while confessed to by Roddenberry in his memo, are more due to the creative people behind both *Forbidden Planet* and *Star Trek* looking to the American military, and in particular the Navy, for inspiration for their space exploration ships and crews. Even the uniforms, down to the departmental colour coding and insignia, on both the film and the later TV series, are uncannily similar. It should be noted, too, that as a space-set partial retelling of Shakespeare's *The Tempest*, *Forbidden Planet* was itself far from original.

Also of interest is a now little-remembered 1963 Czech movie *Ikarie XB-1* (released in an English-dubbed version as *Voyage to the End of the Universe*). The film follows the journey of the Ikarus XB-1 starship, whose multi-national crew must cope with the rigours of deep space travel. The episodic film has the crew encounter a derelict twentieth-century space vessel carrying still-deadly nuclear weapons, a radioactive 'dark star' that threatens the ship and the mental dissolution of a crewmember. Similar storylines would crop up in some very early *Star Trek* episodes.

All these preceding examples of science fiction, especially those in film and TV, undoubtedly had an influence on the development of Gene Roddenberry's *Star Trek*. Indeed, specific elements that made up *Star Trek* can be traced back to individual films and shows, mainly *Forbidden Planet*, as discussed, but also – for example – the 'United Federation of Planets' organisation featured in *Space Patrol*. However, the creation of *Star Trek* was not just a case of cherry-picking elements from the science fiction that came before it. Everything had to be filtered through one creative intelligence, a unique storyteller who was a TV writer and producer, and who'd paid his dues in detective and Western shows before winning the chance to explore the final frontier of unknown space: Gene Roddenberry.

Prior to creating *Star Trek*, Gene Roddenberry had filled many professional roles, including bomber pilot in the Second World War, commercial pilot for Pan-Am, police officer (following family tradition) and jobbing TV writer, who drew on his real-life experiences to create episodic television. However, when he died in October 1991 at the age of seventy, there was only one thing that obituary writers concentrated on: *Star Trek*.

Eugene Wesley Roddenberry was born in El Paso in Texas on 19 August 1921, the son of a police officer, who would eventually become a cop himself. Before he was two years old the Roddenberry family relocated to Southern California, where this born storyteller would find his natural environment.

Los Angeles in the mid-1920s had become the centre of the growing movie industry. The famous Hollywoodland (later just Hollywood) sign was erected in 1923. Both the city and the movies were growing and changing, and Roddenberry became ideally placed to take advantage of the opportunities offered. His father secured a job with the Los Angeles Police Department: they were desperate for beat cops and his Army service made the senior Roddenberry an ideal candidate.

Young Gene did well enough at school, attending to his studies as the lively 1920s gave way to the great depression of the 1930s. By then the Roddenberry family had grown, with Gene joined by a brother and a sister. Gene and his brother were encouraged by their father to take on odd jobs (delivering newspapers, working in a petrol station) in order to earn money and discover the meaning of independence. He took them both fishing and hunting – pastimes that Roddenberry senior enjoyed, but neither of his sons did.

Gene Roddenberry attended Los Angeles City College

(LACC) from early 1939, studying the police curriculum. Through the LACC Police Club he met several figures he'd later work with after the war. Various stints of further education followed, but Roddenberry never formally graduated.

Aged eighteen in 1940, Roddenberry signed up to the Civilian Pilot Training programme, a scheme designed to increase the number of trained American pilots in the run-up to the country's likely entry into the conflict in Europe. Having long been interested in flying and aeroplanes, he was awarded his pilot's licence and in 1941 joined the US Army Air Corps, just before it became the US Air Force. Combat missions followed in the wake of the attack on Pearl Harbor in December 1941, including action with the 394th Bomber Squadron. In August 1943 Roddenberry's B-17E Flying Fortress crashed on take-off due to a mechanical failure, with the loss of two lives. Despite that setback, Roddenberry claimed to have chalked up eighty-nine missions (his natural storytelling abilities would lead him to often embellish his personal achievements) and was awarded the Distinguished Flying Cross and Air Medal prior to leaving the Air Force in 1945.

Roddenberry married his college girlfriend Eileen Rexroat in 1942 and they had two daughters, Darlene and Dawn. Using the knowledge and skill accumulated during the war years, he became a commercial pilot for Pan American World Airways (Pan-Am). Following a June 1947 crash in the Syrian desert, the second of his flying career, Roddenberry was awarded a Civil Aeronautics commendation for his involvement in the rescue efforts (another account embellished in the telling). During his time as a commercial pilot, Roddenberry had become interested in the relatively new medium of television and was keen to develop a career as a TV writer. This was a new business, with opportunities for the right people – and the ambitious Roddenberry felt he could find a role.

In the meantime, to generate income, Roddenberry fell back on the family tradition and joined the LAPD at the start of 1949. He became an officer in 1951 and a sergeant in 1953, all the while optimistically submitting story outlines to various TV shows. After six weeks of perfunctory training, Roddenberry began his police life as a traffic cop.

In mid-1950 William H. Parker became the LAPD Chief with a mandate to clean up corruption in the force. By 1951 Roddenberry realised his ambition to begin writing professionally by securing a job in Parker's PR division, writing speeches for the Chief. Roddenberry delivered talks to schoolchildren on road safety, but it was as publicist to Parker that he became invaluable. Later in 1951 he sought permission to accept outside work, intending not to take the usual security job, but to explore whether he could make some headway as a writer for television.

For Roddenberry, television was the equivalent of the 'pulps' of the 1930s: a here-today, gone-tomorrow medium that provided a perfect training ground for would-be writers. He used his office at the LAPD to obtain old scripts from shows like *Dragnet* in order to learn the formal layout and techniques of teleplays, then by 1953 the hopeful TV writer began to send his own scripts to producers, believing his real-life police experience would give his writing authenticity.

Thus, Roddenberry's first television success came in selling storylines to cop shows, often based directly on his own experiences or tales he'd heard from other officers. He quickly discovered LA's TV writer hangouts – the bars, the restaurants – and began to spend time there off duty, making friends and building contacts. This paid off and he wrote episodes for various shows through the mid-1950s, including six instalments of *Mr. District Attorney* and five of *Highway Patrol*.

In April 1956 he sold a script to *The West Point Story*, a TV show about US Army cadets, produced with the cooperation of the military. Roddenberry had accosted E. Jack Neuman, the show's producer, on a cross-country flight. Over the next year he would write eight more episodes, and one other in collaboration with Neuman himself. Stories came easily to the *West Point* staff, drawn as they were from the actual files of the real-life New York US Military Academy. Actors who appeared on the show and later became big names included Clint Eastwood, Barbara Eden (*I Dream of Jeannie*), Larry Hagman (*Dallas*), and Leonard Nimoy. Over two seasons on air, *West Point* clocked up forty episodes, and Roddenberry had written, co-written or rewritten a quarter of them. It was a baptism by fire and one he was keen to learn from.

In 1956 Roddenberry quit the LAPD to become a full-time TV writer, continuing to draw on his police experience for his first commissions. One script Roddenberry rewrote for *West Point* was by Sam Rolfe (rewriting often involved taking a writer's original work and making it more suitable for the production realities of any given show: it's something Roddenberry would do a lot during the early days of *Star Trek*). Rolfe would soon go on to create *Have Gun, Will Travel*, and Roddenberry would quickly move on to that show, writing twenty-four of the half-hour Western adventure episodes. The light-hearted show ran from 1957 to 1963 and starred Richard Boone as 'gentleman gunslinger' Paladin, a champion-for-hire who liked to right wrongs without violence, but was an excellent shot when required. Paladin had been an Army officer and graduate of West Point and used a knight chess piece as his calling card. Among the episodic guest cast were DeForest Kelley (a veteran of many film and TV Westerns), Whit Bissell and William Schallert (all seen in later *Star Trek* episodes). Another significant writer who graduated from this series to run his own show was Bruce Geller (*Mission: Impossible*, *Star Trek*'s stablemate at Desilu Studios).

Having won a Writers Guild Award for an episode of *Have Gun, Will Travel* in 1957, the early 1960s saw Roddenberry develop a career as a jobbing TV writer, moving from show to show, building experience and contacts in the business. He was reliable, but he'd often write no more than one or two episodes for each series and never secured a staff-writing job. In 1962 he wrote instalments of some of American TV's top-rated shows, including *Dr Kildare*, *Naked City* and *The Virginian*.

Roddenberry tried several times to get his own programme

off the ground. He'd written a pilot script in 1959 called *Night Stick* about a Greenwich Village cop, while his 1960 episode of *Alcoa Goodyear Theatre* called '333 Montgomery Street', about a criminal defence attorney, was intended as a possible series pilot. It at least aired (unlike *Night Stick*), but didn't go to series. His third pilot script – *APO 923*, a drama about three Army servicemen stationed on an island – was made but not seen except by network executives and ad agencies. Finally, *Defiance County* was written but never made.

Now aged forty-two, Roddenberry was keen to make a break from run-of-the-mill episodic TV writing. Pitching a series to *Dr Kildare* producer Norman Felton, he fell back on his days in the service and came up with an idea about the work of a professional soldier during peacetime. Through Felton's industry connections Roddenberry secured a pilot deal with funding from MGM and a commitment that allowed him to produce the series, if it was commissioned. The writer believed that becoming a producer was the vital next step in his TV career: that was where the power lay in the business and to achieve that he had to secure a show he'd created. Realising this new project through Felton's independent Arena Productions meant that the resulting show could be pitched to all three broadcast networks. The downside of this freedom was that as none of the networks had a funding commitment to the pilot, it was much easier for them to reject the show.

*The Lieutenant* was built around the leading character of William Tiberius Rice, a second lieutenant in the US Marine Corps. In his mid-twenties and a recent graduate of the Annapolis Naval Academy, Rice is sent to investigate an alleged assault by a private against a corporal. Fearing he'll miss out on a plum posting in the meantime, Rice resists but falls in with an attractive young woman named Lane Bishop. Through her, Rice discovers the private had good reason for attacking the corporal – he was having an affair with the private's wife – but refuses, due to the potential embarrassment, to reveal these mitigating circumstances. The script, 'A Very Private Affair', was circulated within Arena Productions in January 1963 with a view to producing it that spring.

Roddenberry's troubled private life may have informed his teleplay. Although still married to Rexroat, Roddenberry had begun an affair with a young aspiring actress named Majel Barrett, only the latest in a long series of extra-marital affairs he'd pursued. As his twenty-year marriage slowly disintegrated, Roddenberry found himself out of his depth on the set of *The Lieutenant* pilot, contributing to delays on the already complicated location shoot at Camp Pendleton, where the military were lending their cooperation. The episode was finished just in time to be presented to the network executives who'd decide which new shows they'd commission for the fall TV season.

Despite the problems, which included tensions between Roddenberry and the episode's director, the very experienced Buzz Kulik, and between Roddenberry and executive producer Felton, the resulting show was good enough for NBC to commit to a full series. After almost a decade in the TV writing business, Gene Roddenberry had successfully made the switch from episodic writer to series producer.

His euphoria was short-lived, however. Almost immediately, *The Lieutenant* ran into trouble. In order to secure the continued involvement of the Marines and the Department of Defense – the show would not be half as effective without it – the producers had to abide by a lengthy list of prohibitions from the military. Given that the core of drama is conflict, the requirement that *The Lieutenant* should portray military life positively severely restricted the new series' storytelling possibilities – oddly, an approach Roddenberry himself would later take in his vision of the future on *Star Trek*. Roddenberry also ran up against his own creative limitations. As 'showrunner' it was down to him to determine the tone and direction of the series, but beyond making a version of *Dr Kildare* set in the Army, he was at a loss for a way to distinctively define his series. He only knew the show had to focus on Rice (Gary Lockwood), while each episode had to introduce one-off characters and situations for him to learn from.

Screenings of the pilot were arranged for LA's freelance TV writers in the hope they could generate fresh story ideas. Roddenberry picked pitches he liked and commissioned scripts, appointing Del Reisman (*The Twilight Zone*) as story editor. Unhappy with the quality of the scripts and story outlines coming in, but finding it difficult to articulate exactly what he wanted, Roddenberry began to rewrite each script until he was happy with it. Reisman found himself on the receiving end of many complaints from the nineteen different writers who contributed to the twenty-nine episodes of the series. Roddenberry only scripted the opening and closing episodes, but he rewrote just about every other instalment.

From September 1963 *The Lieutenant* began airing on NBC, opposite the ratings giant *The Jackie Gleason Hour* on CBS. The show was quick to catch on, proving to be a ratings record-breaker. However, the behind-the-scenes troubles continued. By early 1964 the Pentagon had complained about *The Lieutenant* directly to NBC, who in turn raised the issue with MGM. The final straw was a script called 'To Set It Right', dealing with racism in the service. Always aware of the big issues of the day, Roddenberry had decided to spice up his show by including some 'hot-button' topics. The episode saw a black Marine and his wife (*Star Trek*'s Uhura, Nichelle Nichols, with whom Roddenberry also later had an affair) attacked by a racist Marine (Dennis Hopper). Although Rice is able to overcome the issue and the men agree to work together for the good of the platoon, it was not enough to mollify the military: official cooperation was finally withdrawn.

Thanks to the use of the MGM back lot, as well as materials left over from assorted war movies and a lot of stock footage, *The Lieutenant* was able to struggle through to completion of its one and only series. As the US involvement in Vietnam escalated and looked ever more questionable, a series extolling the virtues of the armed forces looked decidedly out of date: NBC decided not to renew the show. Roddenberry wrote the final episode himself, sending Rice to an unnamed south-east Asian country where he has to cooperate with a representative of 'the enemy' in order for both to survive. The episode features a debate on the nature of war and warfare that prefigured several episodes of Gene Roddenberry's much more successful second TV series as producer: *Star Trek*.

Gene Roddenberry was desperate to get another TV series up and running to prove he was not a one-hit wonder. This time it had to be entirely his idea and a production wholly under his control. He'd realised control by the producer was necessary, but also that such control was often hard won in battles with networks and financiers. He was equally realistic that both the broadcast networks and the financiers were necessary evils he'd have to contend with. *The Lieutenant* was only the beginning: after all, as a natural storyteller he had so many other tales to tell.

One he'd outlined previously concerned a Zeppelin-style dirigible crewed by a team of multi-racial explorers that crisscrossed the United States at the end of the nineteenth century, discovering 'new civilizations'. The idea had not progressed far, until Roddenberry revived it after *The Lieutenant*. This time, it was to be set in the future, the hot air balloon replaced by a spaceship.

The suggestion to develop a science fiction series had come from Alden Schwimmer, Roddenberry's agent and the West Coast head of the Ashley-Famous agency. In 1963 the space race between Russia and the US was starting to heat up. Two years previously President John F. Kennedy had made his speech committing the country to 'landing a man on the Moon and returning him safely to Earth' before the 1960s came to an end. Russia had been active in space since the launch of Sputnik, with Yuri Gagarin the first man in space in April 1961. Astronaut Alan B. Shepard Jr had become the first American in space in May 1961, followed by John Glenn circling the Earth in 1962. A TV series that could capture the excitement and optimism of the space programme would surely attract a huge American television audience hungry for drama chronicling the conquest of this wild, new frontier.

The first few years of the 1960s had seen science fiction continue to feature in television and film. Movie audiences had visited *The Angry Red Planet* (1959), journeyed to the past and the future in *The Time Machine* (1960) and saw the world survive *The Day the Earth Caught Fire* (1961). Irwin Allen had begun his *Voyage to the Bottom of the Sea* (1961, developed into a TV series in 1964). Television had brought viewers such fantasy shows as *The Twilight Zone* (Rod Serling's weird tales had begun in 1959 and would run until 1964), and *One Step Beyond* (1959–61).

Schwimmer felt sure he could sell a Roddenberry-devised serious science fiction drama. Discussing the idea with others, including Schwimmer and Norman Felton (his executive producer on *The Lieutenant*), Roddenberry soon took to calling his space exploration series '*Wagon Train* to the stars' as a form of shorthand (after ABC's Sunday night hit Western series *Wagon Train*).

Roddenberry's March 1964 sixteen-page pitch outline summarised the show: '*Star Trek* is a "*Wagon Train*" concept – built around characters who travel to worlds "similar" to our own, and meet the action-adventure-drama which becomes our stories. Their transportation is the cruiser *USS Yorktown*, performing a well-defined and long-range Exploration-Science-Security mission which helps create our format. The time is "somewhere in the future". It could be 1995 or maybe even 2995. In other words, close enough to our time for our continuing characters to be fully identifiable as people like us, but far enough into the future for galaxy travel to be thoroughly established.'

However, Roddenberry's space-set *Wagon Train* looked to be an expensive proposition, requiring new planetary settings every episode: it was easy to create a new earthbound setting for each episode of *Wagon Train* (another town or desert oasis), but much harder to come up with convincing alien planets on a weekly television series budget and schedule.

Schwimmer had an ace up his sleeve. His company had become the agent for Desilu Studios, which had once produced the hit series *I Love Lucy* (1951–7) and now made *The Lucy Show* (1962–8). Star Lucille Ball had become the sole owner of the studio, following her divorce from husband Desi Arnaz. The extensive studio facilities (inherited from old Hollywood studio RKO, makers of *King Kong* and *Citizen Kane*) built up during the heyday of *I Love Lucy*, now stood largely empty, except for their once a week usage for *The Lucy Show* and occasional external space rentals. Desilu Studios were keen to find projects to utilise the studio space and their agent – Schwimmer – was keen for his client Roddenberry to launch a science fiction television series. It was a marriage of convenience from which all parties could benefit enormously.

As a result of her ongoing deal with CBS for *The Lucy Show*, Ball had access to a $600,000-per-year development fund. Schwimmer was tasked with finding new projects to spend the money on, in the hope that they'd develop into new hit shows. Pilots that eventually resulted from this development fund included *Mission: Impossible* (the series began in 1966, in the same season as *Star Trek*) and *Mannix* (which debuted the following year).

The Desilu development money allowed Roddenberry to further build on his ideas for '*Wagon Train* to the stars', which may not have happened otherwise without a firm series commission from a broadcaster. It was expected any resulting series would be produced by Desilu and would air on CBS, as they were providing the initial funding.

Roddenberry had a partner working with him on developing his new series proposal, Herb Solow – Desilu's in-house executive who would decide which projects would be pitched to the broadcasters. Solow saw Roddenberry's proposed series as another anthology show, like *The Lieutenant*, with new characters and settings every week, something he feared would be prohibitively expensive. Solow also worried that reintroducing the series concept each week would take up too much of the show's running time. His proposed solution was a voiceover from the spaceship's captain explaining the set-up, allowing the episode to get on with the drama. Later in life Roddenberry was reluctant to share the credit for the success of *Star Trek,* especially in the creation of the key elements that went into making up the series. In a memo from 1966 Roddenberry erroneously credited the captain's voiceover idea to 'my cousin in Ohio'. For him, it made for a better story.

There was another writer involved in developing ideas for *Star Trek* in addition to Roddenberry. Samuel A. Peeples, a prolific television screenwriter in the 1960s, had written for many Western series, including *Wanted: Dead or Alive, The Rifleman* and *Bonanza.* Roddenberry knew that Peeples had a significant collection of pulp magazines. Roddenberry had read some of the same story magazines — including *Amazing Stories* — as a teenager, but was not an expert or a particularly big fan of the genre. He remembered reading E. E. 'Doc' Smith's *Skylark* series and the Buck Rogers newspaper comic strip, as well as listening to the exciting radio serial. However, as a kid during the depression he'd been far more interested in the adventures of the Lone Ranger and the Shadow. He needed help putting his dramatic ideas into a plausible science fiction context.

Peeples recalled, '[Roddenberry] was trying to start a science fiction series and he knew that I had one of the largest science fiction collections in the world. He was researching his show and asked if he could go through my magazines and get some ideas for the *Enterprise.* Gene went through all the covers, and that's really how the *Enterprise* was born.'

Roddenberry felt he needed a crash course in science fiction and borrowed some books from Peeples — among them Olaf Stapleton's *First and Last Men* — to get a feel for what the genre encompassed. Peeples suggested other writers that Roddenberry should sample, including Theodore Sturgeon, Robert Bloch, Poul Anderson and Richard Matheson. From the beginning Roddenberry was keen to involve serious science fiction storytellers in his series to give the show authenticity.

One of the first television writers Roddenberry arranged to meet was Jerry Sohl, whose credits included *The Twilight Zone*, *Alfred Hitchcock Presents* and *The Outer Limits*, as well as several science fiction novels. He had the ideal combination of science fiction credentials and TV scriptwriting that Roddenberry would look for in the initial batch of *Star Trek* writers. Sohl clearly understood that the meeting was a fishing exercise on Roddenberry's part, with the putative showrunner asking for the names of other West Coast writers he could contact, as well as sounding out Sohl's opinion of his *Star Trek* idea. Among the names Sohl added to Roddenberry's growing list of writers to contact were William Nolan, George Clayton Johnson and Harlan Ellison.

Desilu's Herb Solow was charged with selling *Star Trek* to the studios. It was quickly rejected by CBS, despite them having initially funded development through the Desilu fund. Solow had more luck with NBC, who offered to finance the writing of a pilot script (subject to a choice from three outlines) that might result in the broadcaster funding the shooting of a pilot. Gene Roddenberry's *Star Trek* was about to blast off.

# Chapter 2

## First Flight: The Two
## *Star Trek* Pilots

'*I am Spock!*' Leonard Nimoy

Gene Roddenberry was first and foremost an accomplished storyteller, and *Star Trek* was the ideal vehicle for telling stories about the modern world that happened to be set in space, in a far-off future that seemed strangely to echo the present. He wasn't alone in creating *Star Trek* in its lasting incarnation: he drew on the talents of many other individuals who contributed key elements that went in to making the concept durable.

Unusually for television in the 1960s, *Star Trek* was allowed two pilot episodes to demonstrate to NBC that the show could work. The story of the two *Star Trek* pilots is the story of the two writers involved, Gene Roddenberry and Samuel A. Peeples. For the 1964 pilot, Roddenberry flew solo. In the script for 'The Cage' he brought to life the concepts that had featured in his March 1964 series outline in a dramatic form. For his critics, it was not dramatic enough and simply too thoughtful for American television in the mid-1960s.

For the show's second pilot in 1965, NBC chose Samuel A. Peeples' script, 'Where No Man Has Gone Before'. Peeples brought action and adventure to *Star Trek*, elements that Roddenberry later admitted had been missing from his effort. Between them, the two storytellers used their *Star Trek* pilots to lay down the template for a franchise that would 'live long and prosper' for the next forty-five years and beyond.

Gene Roddenberry had three alternatives to represent the potential of *Star Trek* through the initial pilot storylines requested by NBC in 1964. The first storyline was entitled 'Landru's Paradise' (and would later become the basis for the episode 'The Return of the Archons'). In the story, Captain Robert April (the name lifted from a character who'd appeared in the final episode of *The Lieutenant*) discovers a seemingly all-American town located on a distant planet. The contented inhabitants are reluctant to question their existence or challenge authority, apparently happy with their lot. Roddenberry's story outline reveals that this 'happiness' is imposed by a group called The Lawgivers, who issue severe punishments for even the mildest infractions of the rules (an idea later explored in more depth in the *Star Trek: The Next Generation* episode 'Justice'). The climax sees April confront the planet's ruling computer and proceed (as in several *Star Trek* episodes) to talk it to death, freeing the populace.

The second proposed storyline was 'The Women' (the basis for the later episode 'Mudd's Women'). The outline was clear about its inspiration: 'Duplicating a page from the "Old West"; hanky-panky aboard [the *Enterprise*] with a cargo of women destined for a far-off colony.' Essentially about prostitution, people trafficking and slavery, 'The Women' saw a space trader supply plain-looking women to lonely men on far-off mining planets, using a drug to create the illusion that the women are beautiful and happy to cater to the men's every need without question.

Finally there was 'The Cage', chronicling a battle between illusion and reality. Captured by powerful aliens, April is forced to live through memories and fantasies in the company of another human captive, the beautiful Vina. His captors feed off the emotions generated by his turmoil, and in the end April has to decide between the seductive illusions or harsh reality.

The three stories were surprisingly revealing and reflected Roddenberry's attitudes to life, especially as his marriage crumbled. In dealing with subjects such as God-like beings, judicial authority, and the role of women Roddenberry laid down a marker as to the ambitions of *Star Trek*: his science fiction TV show was going to be 'about' something, rather than just entertaining fluff filling the airwaves between advertisements.

There was no denying that living and working in the Hollywood milieu of 1960s television was having an effect on Roddenberry and his family life. He'd long had a roving eye and not thought twice about cheating on his wife, even during his police days. Now, in a position of relative power in the Los Angeles television business, it was easier than ever for Roddenberry to indulge his passions. His regular extra-marital relationship continued with actress Majel Barrett, but she wasn't alone. Roddenberry told friends he remained married for the sake of his children, but that did little to curb his wandering ways. One of the reasons for the growing distance between Roddenberry and his wife Eileen may have been the widening of his horizons compared to hers. While he grew and changed, perhaps not always for the better, she remained the policeman's wife and home-making mother, disapproving of the 'Hollywood' lifestyle. That they grew apart is not surprising.

As the distance between him and his wife grew larger, Roddenberry focused on his work. Although NBC had agreed to fund the writing of a pilot script for *Star Trek* in 1964, it would be a further two years before the regular series would reach American TV screens. The intermediate time was a frustrating one of repeated development and failure for Roddenberry, eventually followed by compromised success.

According to Desilu executive Herb Solow (in his personal memoir *Inside Star Trek*, co-authored with *Star Trek* producer Robert Justman), NBC continued to harbour doubts about whether Desilu could pull off a show as ambitious and complicated as the *Star Trek* pitch. Of the three storylines submitted, NBC finally chose 'The Cage'. The plot had been further refined in numerous pitching sessions with the NBC brass, so writing the script itself came fast and easy to Roddenberry. Dated 29 June 1964, his story outline featured a group of six-limbed, crab-like aliens who capture the *Enterprise*'s Captain April and subject him to a variety of tests. In captivity with him is another apparent human, a woman named Vina. Writing without much regard to budget – odd for someone who'd had a fair degree of practical television production experience – Roddenberry seemed more interested in concocting a dramatic introduction to his universe to sell the *Star Trek* concept to NBC than worrying about practical considerations that might face Desilu should the series enter production.

A bizarre menagerie of non-humanoid creatures featured in the draft script, including a six-legged 'Rigelian spider ape' and another character described as a cross between an angel and a snake. These visions would be easy to achieve on screen now with a decent budget and CGI technology. Back in the mid-1960s computers in special effects were non-existent and animation for television was prohibitively expensive. Nonetheless, Roddenberry stubbornly featured an intelligent lemur from Arcturus (the kind of truly alien character that would not be properly visually realised until *Star Trek: The Animated Series* in the early 1970s).

The final script delivered to NBC at the end of June 1964 featured Captain Pike (replacing April, but still not yet the familiar Kirk) commanding the USS *Enterprise*, en route to a Starbase for a spot of shore leave. Drawn by indications that a ship may have crashed on Talos IV, the *Enterprise* diverts to investigate. A landing party of Pike, Lieutenant Spock, Dr Phillip Boyce, navigator José Tyler and others is convened. The ship is left under the command of the cold, logic-driven female first officer, Number One.

A group of survivors is discovered, all that remain of the crew of the SS *Columbia*, a ship that crashed over a decade before. Vina – just a child when the ship crashed – forms a strong connection with Pike. Hidden alien intelligences observe them and use Vina to lure Pike into a trap. Captured by the Talosians (large-headed mute creatures, now humanoid in form), Pike is incarcerated with Vina, in fact the sole survivor of the *Columbia* crash. The remaining *Enterprise* landing crew see the encampment vanish, realising it to have been an illusion created by the aliens as a lure.

The Talosians (played in the episode by short actresses, but voiced by male actors for an 'alien' effect) want to breed a race of humanoids, and hope to mate Pike with Vina. Utilising a series of illusions, they try to force Pike to comply, but he resists. Number One and Yeoman Colt are kidnapped from the *Enterprise*, beamed by the Talosians directly to Pike's cage. If Vina is not to Pike's liking, think the Talosians, maybe they can tempt him with one of his own female crewmembers? Meanwhile, Spock and company have returned with a laser cannon and turn it on the hidden Talosians' lair. Although the weapon is effective, the Talosians maintain a psychic illusion so the *Enterprise* crew do not perceive the damage they have done.

Pike escapes and discovers the truth about the Talosians. Having wrecked their planet's ecology the race moved underground, developing their mental capacity but losing the ability to produce children (hence their interest in recreating their race via Pike and Vina). The truth is also revealed about Vina: she was disfigured in the crash of the *Columbia*, but the Talosians have psychically maintained her self-image as that of a beautiful young woman. Pike agrees to leave the Talosians alone, as long as they maintain Vina's illusion – in fact, they create an unreal Captain Pike who stays with her. The *Enterprise* crew resume their ongoing voyages . . .

Executives at NBC responded to Roddenberry's full pilot script with a series of 'notes' – comments on the settings, characters and structure of the drama. Roddenberry quickly took offence at this interference in 'his' project, thinking he knew best how to tell his story, but was persuaded by Solow that if he were to have any realistic hope at all of getting *Star Trek* on air, he'd have to work with NBC, not against them. Again, this was odd behaviour from a producer who'd already run his own TV show in *The Lieutenant* and had previously experienced the trials and tribulations of dealing with network executives. Roddenberry's strong personal investment in the *Star Trek* concept as a storyteller was beginning to get in the way of his duties as a practical producer.

Desilu had previously been known for comedy and variety shows, most of them simple vehicles for the star power of Lucille Ball. Now it was looking at a major, risky expansion into drama for network television with both *Star Trek* and spy thriller *Mission: Impossible* entering production simultaneously. Practical problems loomed, starting with assembling a production crew for the needs of an ambitious drama like *Star Trek*: the team who produced *The Lucy Show* would simply not be up to the task. Instead, Solow and Roddenberry were faced with the challenge of building a completely new production unit from scratch to film the revised *Star Trek* pilot script, in the hope that NBC would commit to a full series and so result in Desilu recovering its up-front investment. Although NBC would be paying for *Star Trek*, the fee Desilu would receive would regularly be less than the cost of making the show – the difference would have to be recouped through advertising and foreign sales.

The crew on *Star Trek* was made up of people selected by Roddenberry and Solow to realise the creator's storytelling ambitions. It was clear to the production team that for every episode of *Star Trek* as an ongoing series, everything would have to be re-invented, with the exception of the starship *Enterprise*, the 'police precinct' of this new show. Every new world, alien encountered and spaceship discovered had to be created from scratch, meaning a huge design workload and a thoroughly complex production process, much more so than any regular doctor, cop or lawyer show (the staples of American television in the 1960s, as today).

That burden would largely fall on set designer Walter 'Matt' Jefferies, an artist and designer who'd also been a pilot, so was aware of industrial and technical issues concerning aircraft that could be applied to the *Enterprise* and other starships. Roddenberry's only instruction to him was to avoid the Flash Gordon look that had previously defined movie spaceships. His task was to come up with something unknown to present-day science, and definitely not rocket powered. The result, based on images from the pulp magazine covers supplied by Samuel A. Peeples, was the saucer propelled by tubular engines, all tethered to a main body like a sailing ship. Star Trek's iconic *Enterprise* was born, and Peeples' first contribution to the *Star Trek* legend had been made . . .

Similarly, costume designer William Ware Theiss faced a series of unusual challenges. The crew of the *Enterprise* needed uniforms, and while there might be plenty of historical and contemporary earthbound military and civilian uniforms to draw on, Roddenberry wanted his crew clad in something viewers had never seen before. Like Jefferies, Theiss was also toiling under severe budget restrictions. Also like Jefferies, Theiss was given a clutch of Peeples' pulp magazine covers as reference, although instead of spaceships these largely featured scantily clad women being menaced by alien monsters, not really reflective of *Star Trek* at all. They were to function as inspiration for Theiss's costume choices.

Effects were a whole other problem. It was fine to build sets and create costumes, but it would be necessary to show the spaceships flying and the alien worlds hanging in space. Luckily the Desilu lot in Hollywood was home to the Howard Anderson Company, an experienced optical effects house. Roddenberry didn't have to go far to find the team who could put the 'special' into his effects requirements. Darrell Anderson, who ran the company, would be on set to ensure that any sequences needing added optical work were shot in such a way as to be suitable (and economic) for his team to apply their visual magic. Similarly, Anderson ran an off-stage model studio where the miniature spaceships designed by Jefferies could be shot separately. The model shooting stage was often entirely filled by the dominant, almost 14-foot-long model of the 'miniature' *Enterprise*.

The decision-making process involved in creating *Star Trek*'s first pilot meant that the many questions that came up during production came back to Roddenberry to be answered. It was undoubtedly a stressful time, but *Star Trek* was his vision and as the key storyteller behind the show, he was the only one who could clearly instruct the many practitioners hired to make it a reality. It was Roddenberry who dictated that everything aboard the *Enterprise*, from the uniforms through to how the crew conducted themselves, should have a US Navy feel. It was in the casting of the characters, however, that Roddenberry truly made his mark. Matching his draft descriptions in his series outline to suitable actors drew on all his television experience and resulted in characters that would go on to become international icons.

Key to Roddenberry's vision of the forward-looking, optimistic characters he wanted exploring deep space in his '*Wagon Train* to the stars' was the captain of the *Enterprise*. This character was a leader, a man's man, but one who had human weaknesses and frailties that he carried with him out to the final frontier of unknown space. Although the captain certainly had an eye for the ladies, his only true love would be his ship, the *Enterprise*.

The original 1964 pitch document defined Captain Robert K. April as 'the "skipper", about thirty-four, Academy graduate, rank of captain. Clearly the leading man and central character. This role is designed for an actor of top repute and ability. A shorthand sketch of Robert April might be "A space-age Captain Horatio Hornblower", lean and capable both mentally and physically. A colourfully complex personality, he is capable of action and decision which can verge on the heroic – and at the same time lives a continual battle with self-doubt and the loneliness of command.'

In 'The Cage', movie actor Jeffrey Hunter played Captain Christopher Pike (also named James Winter in early drafts). He was then best known for playing Jesus Christ in *King of Kings* (1961). Roddenberry was pleased to have secured the services of a well-known film actor for his potential TV series on the basis of his pilot script alone. Hunter had guest starred in various TV shows, but *Star Trek* was to be his first commitment to taking on a leading role in a series, following the failure of his 1963–4 Western/legal series *Temple Houston*. Other actors who'd been considered for the leading role included Peter Graves (soon to become the star of *Mission: Impossible*), *The Time Machine*'s Rod Taylor, Jack Lord (later famous for his long run on *Hawaii 5-0*), *Forbidden Planet*'s Leslie Nielsen (casting that would have done much to highlight the similarities between that movie and *Star Trek*), Ed Kemmer (Commander Corry in *Space Patrol*) and Canadian actor William Shatner.

With Hunter in place, attention turned to the other roles. Roddenberry and his casting team were looking at 'The Cage' not as a one-off TV movie but as the template for their ongoing series, so it was important to fill the key roles with the right actors: after all, they could be playing these parts for a good number of years if the show was a success.

The easiest part to fill – at least for Roddenberry – was the role of Number One, the emotionless female second-in-command on the *Enterprise*. The pitch document had billed this character as the Executive Officer, 'never referred to as anything but "Number One", this officer is female. Almost mysteriously female, in fact – slim and dark in a Nile Valley way, age uncertain, one of those women who will always look the same between years twenty to fifty. An extraordinarily efficient officer, "Number One" enjoys playing it expressionless, cool – [she] is probably April's superior in detailed knowledge of the multiple equipment systems, departments and crewmembers aboard the vessel.' The role was gifted to Majel Barrett without any serious consideration being given to any other actresses. Roddenberry's blatant favouritism (his weakness for women would be transferred to the character of the captain of the *Enterprise*) would be used against him by the network when it was time to cast important roles in *Star Trek*'s second pilot episode.

Perhaps the most important single decision made in the casting choices during pre-production in early November 1964 was the choice of Leonard Nimoy to portray the *Enterprise*'s alien science officer, Mr Spock. The pitch document focused on the First Lieutenant's alien appearance, but his later 'emotionless' character had already been given to Number One. Mr Spock is 'the captain's right hand man, the working level commander of all the ship's functions ... the first view of him can be almost frightening – a face so heavy-lidded and satanic, you might almost expect him to have a forked tail. Probably half-Martian, he has a slightly reddish complexion and semi-pointed ears. But strangely, Mr. Spock's quiet temperament is in dramatic contrast to his satanic look. His primary weakness is an almost cat-like curiosity over anything slightly "alien".' Other actors had been considered for the role, including Western actor DeForest Kelley, Rex Holman and dwarf actor Michael Dunn, best known for playing Miguelito Loveless, the recurring villain in *The Wild, Wild West* (1965–9). Their casting would have brought a very different interpretation to the character of Spock. It was, however, Majel Barrett who was instrumental in the selection of Nimoy, recalling him from a guest appearance in Roddenberry's *The Lieutenant* and bringing him to the producer's attention once again. His thin frame and angular features were ideal for the alien character Roddenberry had in mind.

While all the actors associated with *Star Trek* saw their professional lives changed by the series, this applied to no one more than Nimoy. Following his time in the US Army, Nimoy played a variety of guest roles in TV series, including episodes of *The Untouchables*, *The Outer Limits* and *Perry Mason*, but it was the character of Spock that would bring him public acclaim, private anguish and define him in the eyes of audiences right up to and beyond J. J. Abrams' 2009 movie reinvention of *Star Trek*. It is safe to say that *Star Trek* would not have been the same without Nimoy as Spock: within days of his casting Roddenberry had requested his props department cost up something simply described in a memo as 'ear appliances' ...

Rejected for the role of Spock, DeForest Kelley was up for the part of 'Doc', the ship's medical officer. The character was one of the more straightforward in Roddenberry's initial 1964 pitch document: 'Ship's Doctor – Philip Boyce, an unlikely space traveller. At the age of fifty-one, he's worldly, humorously cynical, makes it a point to thoroughly enjoy his own weaknesses. Captain April's only real confidant, "Bones" Boyce considers himself the only realist aboard, and measures each new landing in terms of relative annoyance, rather than excitement.' Kelley had played plenty of irascible country doctors in several Western movies and TV series, but he lost out on the role in 'The Cage' to B-movie actor John Hoyt. Neither the character of Dr Philip John Boyce nor the actor's participation in *Star Trek* would last beyond the filming of this pilot. After a fairly fruitless search for an actress to play Vina, Roddenberry eventually secured Susan Oliver for the guest starring role.

With the creative and casting work complete, shooting began on 'The Cage' on the day after Thanksgiving, 27 November 1964 on Desilu's Stage 16 in Culver City. Fittingly, the first scenes shot involved one of *Star Trek*'s iconic sets: the transporter room of the *Enterprise*. Roddenberry had dreamt up the 'transporter' as a method of getting characters to and from planets (and other locations) without a lot of messing about in space shuttles (or, indeed, having the *Enterprise* repeatedly land and take off from planets). It was an elegant solution to a practical problem (saving a fortune in regular effects work, although the transporter 'beaming' effect itself became a regular feature).

The two weeks' filming saw Roddenberry engaged in script rewrites as well as supervising the entire production process. Shooting wrapped on 11 December and a period of frantic post-production followed in which special effects and model shots were worked into the edited footage. Three days after Christmas 1964, Gene Roddenberry viewed a completed rough cut of his debut episode of *Star Trek* – but he was not a happy man.

According to a memo he prepared after viewing the episode, and other correspondence with friends, Roddenberry felt the action in 'The Cage' didn't start quickly enough, that the character of the captain was not defined clearly enough in the show's opening moments, and that the time constraints involved in filming the episode over just two weeks had damaged the final product. A revised edit was prepared for mid-January 1965, and then the show had to be screened for NBC executives, ready or not. Roddenberry admitted that if he'd had more time, he'd have continued to rework 'The Cage'.

Screenwriter William Goldman's famous maxim about Hollywood – 'Nobody knows anything' – applied equally to US television in the 1960s. Reluctant to make choices themselves about which programmes to back, NBC executives relied on flawed audience tests to tell them whether a show would be a hit or not. Such a different, unknown and untested quantity as *Star Trek* was always going to throw a regular test audience more used to generic Westerns, cop shows or sitcoms than challenging space adventures. So it proved.

With mixed results from the audience tests, NBC were still unsure about whether to back *Star Trek*. There was a lot about the show – as exhibited in 'The Cage' – that they liked, but there were other areas they were concerned about. Their primary worry was that if they failed to develop the show, they could be losing a potential hit series.

Roddenberry now felt he and the team had ironed out many of the problems they expected to encounter in creating and mounting a dramatically different TV series like *Star Trek*: he and the others involved wanted to capitalise on the lessons learned and get stuck in to producing the series proper. Throughout February 1965 Roddenberry felt trapped in a kind of limbo in which the fate of his show lay in the hands of a group of nervous NBC executives who, reluctant to make the wrong decision, were thus delaying making any decision at all. If an answer wasn't forthcoming very soon Roddenberry knew the series would not be able to enter production quickly enough to make the forthcoming fall 1965 NBC schedule. Just as it started to look like *Star Trek* would be an ignoble failure, Gene Roddenberry was given a unique second chance.

Against usual practice for the time, *Star Trek* was afforded the unexpected luxury of a second attempt at creating a viable pilot episode. NBC itself accepted some of the blame for the failings of 'The Cage', in that they had selected that storyline from the three on offer. Additionally, the network had already spent $630,000 making 'The Cage' (at that point, *Star Trek*'s initial pilot was the most expensive ever made) and while the expense of failed pilots was a recognised part of the television business, they saw enough potential in the *Star Trek* concept to let a frustrated Gene Roddenberry try again.

In *Inside Star Trek*, Desilu executive Herb Solow and associate producer Robert Justman offered their take on the reasons for NBC's rejection of 'The Cage': 'The NBC party line was that it was "too cerebral". The unspoken reason, however, dealt more with the manners and morals of mid-1960s America. NBC was very concerned with the "eroticism" of the pilot and the ensuing series. Their knowledge of Roddenberry's attitude toward [women] didn't help. NBC sales was equally concerned with the Spock character, [fearing he'd be] seen as demonic by Bible Belt affiliate-stations and advertisers. Their concern presented a serious stumbling block to the sale of the hoped-for series.'

Roddenberry discussed his view of the rejection of 'The Cage' at a *Star Trek* convention in 1986. 'The reasons [for NBC's rejection] were these: too cerebral, not enough action and adventure,' said Roddenberry, creating his legendary explanation for the first pilot's failure. '"The Cage" didn't end with a chase and a right cross to the jaw. Another thing they felt was wrong was that we had Majel [Barrett] as a female second-in-command. In the test reports, the women in the audience were saying, "Who does she think she is?" They hated her. It is hard to believe that in twenty years, we have gone from a totally sexist society to where we are today.

'We also had what they called a "childish concept" – an alien with pointy ears from another planet [Spock]. People in those days were not talking about life forms on other worlds. It was generally assumed that this [Earth] is the place where life occurred and probably nowhere else. It would have been all right if this alien with pointy ears, this "silly creature," had the biggest zap gun in existence, or the strength of 100 men, that could be exciting. His only difference from us was [that] he had an alien perspective.'

In a letter from February 1965 to his agent Alden Schwimmer, Roddenberry had defended 'The Cage' from the criticisms of NBC. 'Whether or not this was the right story for a sale [to the network], it was definitely [the] right one for ironing out success-fully a thousand how, when and whats of television science fiction. It did that job superbly and has us firmly in position to be the first who has ever successfully made TV series science fiction at a mass audience level and yet with a chance for quality and network prestige too. I have no respect or tolerance for those who say things like "If it were not so cerebral . . .", and such garbage. [I] am wide open to criticism and suggestions, but not from those who think answers lie in things like giving someone aboard a dog, or adding a cute eleven-year-old boy to the crew.' Later, *Star Trek: The Next Generation* would come close to the 'cute eleven-year-old boy' in Roddenberry's own creation of the youthful wunderkind character of Wesley Crusher, while *Star Trek: Enterprise* would include Porthos, the captain's dog, among the ship's crew.

Despite this combative attitude, Roddenberry did admit (quoted in *Captains' Logs: The Unauthorized Complete Trek Voyages*) that as a producer he'd perhaps failed to deliver what he'd promised. 'They probably felt that I had broken my word. In the series format I had promised a *Wagon Train* to the stars action/adventure, science-fiction style. But, instead, 'The Cage' was a beautiful story, but it wasn't action/adventure. It wasn't what I had promised. Clearly the problem with the first pilot was easily traced back to me. I got too close to it and lost perspective. I had known the only way to tell *Star Trek* was with an action/adventure plot. I forgot my plan and tried for something proud.'

With 'The Cage', Roddenberry's storytelling ambitions had trumped his years of practical production experience. According to him, it was only the prospect of the US landing a man on the moon before the end of the 1960s, as pledged by President Kennedy at the start of the decade, that made NBC pay con-tinued attention to *Star Trek* beyond 'The Cage'.

In approaching a potential second pilot episode, Roddenberry was willing to tone down the Spock character, a compromise as NBC has originally wanted him removed altogether. Ironically, the alien Spock would turn out to be the only character retained from 'The Cage' in the ongoing *Star Trek* series. Indeed, he would go on to become one of the most iconic characters in the history of television and one of the most loved of all the *Star Trek* characters.

'They rejected most of the cast [of "The Cage"] and asked that Spock be dropped too,' Roddenberry recalled. 'I said I would not do a second pilot without Spock because I felt we had to have him for many reasons. I felt we couldn't do a space show without at least one person on board who constantly reminded you that you were out in space and in a world of the future. NBC finally agreed to do the second pilot with Spock in it, saying, "Well, kind of keep him in the background."'

Once again, the network requested a trio of potential story outlines for the second pilot. Roddenberry himself had originally written two of them ('Mudd's Women' – heavily rewritten by Stephen Kandel – and 'The Omega Glory', a take on the politics of the Cold War), while the third was 'Star Prime' (later retitled 'Where No Man Has Gone Before'), written by Roddenberry's pulp fiction source, Samuel A. Peeples.

NBC thought Peeples' 'Where No Man Has Gone Before' offered a better showcase for the potential of *Star Trek* than any of the ideas put forward by the show's creator. Born in 1917, making him four years older than Roddenberry, Peeples would go on to write one other *Star Trek* episode (for *The Animated Series*), and he contributed to the storyline for the second *Star Trek* movie, *The Wrath of Khan*. However, having written hundreds of television episodes in his time, he knew how good drama worked, and he brought that to his script for *Star Trek*'s second pilot.

One aspect of 'The Cage' NBC had disliked was the casting of Jeffrey Hunter as Captain Pike. By 1965, the actor was also reluctant to commit to a potentially long-running TV series, so when his option was not picked up for the second pilot, it came as a relief. This move allowed Roddenberry and Peeples to develop a different kind of captain for their *Enterprise*, and to build the drama around a key relationship between the captain and his antagonist, Gary Mitchell (*2001: A Space Odyssey*'s Gary Lockwood).

Roddenberry modelled his new captain more closely on Horatio Hornblower: a flawed hero, or at least a hero who believed himself to be flawed. Given that, according to Robert Justman, NBC saw Hunter as 'wooden', Roddenberry sought out an actor with a more dynamic range and a more expressive approach to television acting.

Roddenberry first approached Lloyd Bridges (father of actors Jeff and Beau Bridges and star of *Sea Hunt*) for the new role of Captain James Kirk. He also once again approached Jack Lord, who had been sounded out about the role of Pike in the previous pilot. Neither actor secured the job, but it was third time lucky for Gene Roddenberry in his hunt for a new *Enterprise* captain.

Robert Justman had worked with William Shatner on anthology show *The Outer Limits*. '[Shatner] had a good reputation in the television and entertainment industries. He was someone to be reckoned with and we certainly understood that he was a more accomplished actor than Jeff Hunter . . . he gave us more dimension. Shatner was classically trained. He had enormous technical abilities to do different things and he gave the captain a terrific personality. He embodied what Gene had in mind.'

While the drama of 'Where No Man Has Gone Before' was built around the captain trying to rescue his friend Gary Mitchell from the consequences of his transformation into a God-like being, the recasting of the central role allowed for new relationships with the ship's other remaining crewmembers, especially Spock.

For the second pilot, the character of the strong female Number One was dropped (relegating Roddenberry's lover Majel Barrett to the smaller background role of Nurse Chapel in later episodes) and Spock promoted in her place. The emotional Spock of 'The Cage' was rethought and he acquired the coldly logical characteristics of Number One, his new nature playing nicely with his unearthly looks. Noted Nimoy, 'Bill Shatner's broader acting style created a new chemistry between the captain and Spock, and now it was quite different from that of the first pilot.' The central trio of *Star Trek* legend was not yet complete, however, as the second pilot did not feature the yet-to-be-developed character of Dr McCoy. Although Roddenberry had included a ship's doctor in the series outline, the role of captain's confidant was filled in the second pilot by the character of Gary Mitchell.

To ensure that such an effects-heavy, unconventional TV show could be made in a standard television time scale of around a week per episode, NBC insisted that *Star Trek*'s second pilot be shot in an eight-day period rather than the sixteen days taken to film 'The Cage' (each episode of the regular series would have to be shot in seven to eight days if it was to meet fall transmission dates). Director James Goldstone was hired to helm the show. '"Where No Man Has Gone Before" [went through] a great deal of polishing and rewriting on a conceptual and physical level, so that we could make it in eight days', he later said. '[It] seemed to have the potential to establish those characters on a human level. The only gimmick is the mutation, the silvering of Gary Mitchell's eyes, and it works because it's simple, as opposed to growing horns or something. Ours was a human science fiction concept, perhaps cerebral [but] certainly emotional.'

Production on 'Where No Man Has Gone Before' began on 15 July 1965, with shooting commencing on 19 July on Stage 15 at the Desilu Studio in Culver City. As the production was able to use many of the sets already constructed for 'The Cage', the budget for the new episode came in at just $300,000, around half of the first attempt. The second pilot featured all the elements that NBC had liked about the *Star Trek* concept, but thanks to Peeples' script, the action-adventure element that had been missing from 'The Cage' had been beefed up considerably. It didn't take NBC long, upon viewing the completed cut of 'Where No Man Has Gone Before', to greenlight *Star Trek* as an ongoing TV series for the fall 1966 schedule.

# Chapter 3

## Where No One Has Gone Before: *Star Trek*'s First Year

'*Although we were in the seemingly simplistic medium of television, this simplistic medium allowed us to really ask very deep
questions. And we didn't always give deep answers, because it
wasn't possible. That's why the audience, over the last twenty-five
years has stayed with* Star Trek.' Gene Roddenberry

*Star Trek* was all about its characters. That was as much a sensible
storytelling decision as anything else. Gene Roddenberry's
'*Wagon Train* to the stars' concept was sound enough, but someone – in this case the practical production team of Robert Justman
and Herb Solow – had to realise the planets, creatures, aliens and
future technology that was required every week. Hence, rather
than focus on the set dressing or the 'wow' factor of alien environments, *Star Trek*'s core – and the main reason it has endured for
over forty-five years – was to be in its unique characters.

It is the distinctive triumvirate of Kirk, Spock and McCoy
that has resulted in the *Star Trek* phenomenon living long and
prospering. Each of the characters in the original series of *Star
Trek* has become iconic, and that is because they are simply
defined (which is not the same as being simple). The central trio
are positioned at distinct points of an emotional continuum, at
least to begin with. Spock is the cold, logical alien who looks
quizzically upon humanity. Dr McCoy is essentially Spock's
opposite, driven by his emotions and his natural engagement

with humanity (that's why he's a doctor, dammit!). In between is Kirk, the leader who must strike a balance between the opposing viewpoints of Spock and McCoy, and take into account the wider welfare of his crew and the new life forms and new civilisations the *Enterprise* encounters through its explorations of the galaxy. Each is prone to extremes, and their actions are often modulated by one (or both) of the other two.

That each of *Star Trek*'s core characters is easily summed up in an instantly recognisable iconic catchphrase is a testament to the impact of these characters on viewers worldwide. They may not have actually used any of these specific phrases that often, but they became embedded in popular culture (along with the never-uttered 'Beam me up, Scotty') as central to viewers' experiences of *Star Trek*. When novelty group The Firm bizarrely reached number one in the UK music charts in 1987 (and became the ninth best-selling single that year) with 'Star Trekkin'', it was because the song was made up of nothing but phrases associated with each iconic *Star Trek* character. They were instantly recognised by British viewers who'd grown up watching the show in endless reruns throughout the 1970s. Rather than the oft-uttered 'Hailing frequencies open, Captain', Communications Officer Uhura gets "There's Klingons on the starboard bow', while Spock is represented by the classic 'It's life, Jim, but not as we know it'. McCoy gets a variation of a phrase he did often say on TV, 'It's worse than that – he's dead, Jim', while Chief Engineer Scotty is represented by the famous 'Ye cannae change the laws of physics'. Kirk himself gets 'We come in peace; shoot to kill', a phrase that never appeared on the show, but summed up a popular impression of the trigger-happy captain's approach to alien encounters (when he was not bedding alien women, of course). This approach would not necessarily work as well with the characters from *Star Trek: The Next Generation*, who were harder to sum up in such simple, iconic and memorable lines.

That these characters could be invoked in a novelty song made up of simple catchphrases twenty years after *Star Trek:*

*The Original Series* was in production is astonishing and stands as a testament to the storytelling of Gene Roddenberry, the writers and producers and William Shatner, Leonard Nimoy, DeForest Kelley and the rest of *The Original Series* cast. It is this trio of characters that explains the lasting impact of *Star Trek* on pop culture worldwide.

With an order for an initial sixteen episodes of *Star Trek* delivered by NBC in February 1966, it was down to Gene Roddenberry to draw together the stories and scripts needed to feed Robert Justman's weekly production machine if air dates were to be maintained. The two pilots had shown just what an uphill task it would be to bring the diverse and exotic worlds of *Star Trek* to the TV screen on a weekly basis. Jefferies and Theiss were central to the task, as was Fred Phillips, who would have to handle the make-up requirements of Spock and any visiting guest star aliens-of-the-week.

Roddenberry's biggest and most immediate requirement by early March 1966 was for writers for the new series, with shooting due to begin at the start of June. The executive producer himself would function as an ideas and rewrite man, not an original writer, but he needed scripts he could rewrite to make them uniquely *Star Trek*. The TV writers who were to be involved in the creation of the show had to be comfortable with the fact that their work would always be subject to Roddenberry's revisions – but not all were.

Talent agencies, independent agents and professional colleagues all got the call: *Star Trek* needed writers! Groups of aspiring episodic contributors were invited to a Desilu screening room, there to be shown the second pilot episode and to hear Roddenberry outline the premise of the series and the requirements the show had for scripts. The process was enough to turn off many established TV writers who just didn't get the concept, didn't think the show would last, or simply knew that 'sci-fi' was not for them. It was a disappointing process for Roddenberry, who realised he was going to have to put in much more one-on-one time with individually selected writers if he was going to succeed in generating the story ideas and finished scripts he urgently needed.

Roddenberry drafted a memo (largely based on his original 1964 series proposal) for aspiring *Star Trek* writers that outlined the series and included a collection of 'springboard' storylines as examples of the kind of thing the series required. The new 'writer's guide' outlined the main characters, the series situation, the world of the future the characters inhabited and the science and sociology of the show. It was hoped this document would provide enough information for writers more comfortable with Western towns, courtrooms or hospital emergency rooms to write for a space-traversing ship and her diverse crew.

Roddenberry, however, had ambitions to reach beyond just TV writers: he wanted to appeal to successful science fiction novelists and short story writers. His thinking was that such people, even if they had no experience of writing for television, would be familiar with the ideas behind the futuristic drama of *Star Trek* and so would be able to contribute in a unique way to the development of this most singular of television series. While his instinct was right in reaching out to other accomplished science fiction storytellers, it was to be an approach that produced very mixed results.

Of those consulted, the one who most readily grasped the concepts and characters of *Star Trek* was Richard Matheson. He had contributed episodes to Rod Serling's groundbreaking SF, horror and fantasy anthology *The Twilight Zone* (which, like *Star Trek*, had initially begun life as a pilot at Desilu), and had written a series of fantasy novels, several of which would later become films (among them *What Dreams May Come*, *Somewhere in Time* and *I Am Legend*). He would contribute 'The Enemy Within', the fifth episode of the first season, that saw a transporter accident split Captain Kirk into his 'good' and 'evil' personalities.

Others, such as novelist A. E. van Vogt, could not come to terms with the economic limitations of weekly television compared to the limitless canvas of the blank page. The ideas and characters he submitted to Roddenberry were either not well developed enough for television or unsuitable for the medium, being better suited to a 200-page novel than a one-hour TV episode.

Throughout the original three-year run of *Star Trek*, several well-known science fiction writers did get episodes on air, not all of them without incident. Among those who succeeded were Ted Sturgeon (who did much to develop Spock and Vulcan culture in the second season opener 'Amok Time'), Jerry Sohl, Robert Bloch, Harlan Ellison (the most problematic), Jerome Bixby, George Clayton Johnson (another *Twilight Zone* veteran) and Norman Spinrad.

Roddenberry welcomed their inventiveness and ideas, but he had to put huge amounts of work into translating their concepts into shootable scripts for Justman to get on the stages at Desilu. Not all the authors understood or were comfortable with the process of weekly television, but most were content to bow to Roddenberry's reworking of their originals (Harlan Ellison being the notable exception). After all, most reckoned, who knew *Star Trek* better than Gene Roddenberry?

Many of the initial basics of the show were driven by the realities of television production. As well as the time-saving transporter that 'beamed' the crew up and down from planets, it was deemed that the crew should predominantly visit Earth-like worlds (labelled Class-M planets) as then the production could avoid the need to put the show's stars into bulky space suits every week. Additionally, although the opening mantra of the show promised voyages 'where no man has gone before', in the old *Star Trek* joke there always had to be someone there when they arrived (alien or human) otherwise there was no drama . . . The civilisations discovered far out in space would also often reflect those on Earth (whether it be Romans, Greeks, Chicago gangsters or Nazis) in order that viewers could relate. In his original 1964 pitch document, Roddenberry had called this the 'parallel worlds concept. It means simply that our stories deal with planets and animal life, plus people, quite similar to that on Earth. Social evolution will also have interesting points of similarity with ours. There will be differences, of course, ranging from the subtle to the boldly dramatic, out of which comes much of our colour and excitement. The "parallel worlds" concept makes production practical by permitting action-adventure science fiction at a practical budget figure via the use of available "Earth" casting, sets, locations, costuming, and so on . . . The "parallel worlds" concept tends to keep even the most imaginative stories within the general audience's frame of reference.'The truly alien would have a hard time holding the attention of a mid-1960s TV audience, or so executives and creatives alike believed. Roddenberry also had an ulterior motive for this propensity for Earth-like planets . . .

From the very beginning *Star Trek* was about exploring 'strange new worlds', but as it turned out, the strangest world the series would explore was 1960s America. As with Rod Serling before him, Gene Roddenberry wanted his stories to mean something, to contain some kind of social or political commentary, but to evade the attentions of nervous commercial sponsors and network censors he found a way to disguise his social commentary in science fiction stories of far future worlds.

Second only to Roddenberry in controlling the creative story-telling side of *Star Trek* was writer and story editor D. C. Fontana. She had briefly been Roddenberry's secretary, but quickly became a writer on the new show, starting with the seventh episode of the first series, 'Charlie X'. This was based on one of Roddenberry's 'springboard' storylines titled 'The Day Charlie Became God'. As with the second pilot, it was another story about a crewman attaining God-like powers. Fontana would go on to write several notable episodes of the series, but more importantly she quickly replaced the show's initial story editor Steven W. Carabatsos in early 1967. She would go on to story-edit *The Animated Series* of 1973, contribute scripts to *The Next Generation* and *Deep Space Nine*, as well as various *Star Trek* spin-off projects, and co-write the post-*Star Trek* TV pilot *The Questor Tapes* (1974) with Roddenberry.

Supporting Fontana on the creative story side was John D. F. Black. He was the executive story consultant on the series, hired by Roddenberry after he won a Writers Guild Award for an episode of the series *Mr. Novak*. His role was to supervise the various freelance writers, monitor their work and get their scripts in on time and in suitable shape for Roddenberry's review. Although Black didn't write much for the series itself (in fact he contributed only a single episode, 'The Naked Time' – and its follow-up on *The Next Generation*, 'The Naked Now'), he was crucial in shaping other writers' work.

There was another Gene, writer–producer Gene L. Coon, who was a key authorial voice alongside Gene Roddenberry in the early codification of the *Star Trek* universe. Following the departure of John D. F. Black, who had difficulty dealing with Roddenberry's constant rewriting, Coon became the key creative force behind the development of *Star Trek* beyond Roddenberry's original series concept, joining the series as producer after the initial thirteen episodes.

Like Roddenberry, Coon was an accomplished TV writer mainly on episodic Western series like *Have Gun, Will Travel*, *Wagon Train* and *Rawhide*. Also like Roddenberry he'd served in the military during the war, although his experience came from the Pacific theatre. From the middle of the first season to the middle of the second, Coon brought a strong streak of moral thought to the drama, something that defined many of the best and best-remembered *Star Trek* episodes. Coon directly scripted twelve episodes in all, more than any other writer, and he closely influenced many more.

During this period it was Coon, not Roddenberry, who created several key concepts, including many that survived well beyond *The Original Series* to inform the movies and successor TV shows. Among them were the Klingons (in 'Errand of Mercy'), genetic Übermensch Khan Noonien Singh (in 'Space Seed'), warp speed developer Zefram Cochrane (in 'Metamorphosis') and the concept of the Prime Directive (which proposed non-interference in undeveloped indigenous planetary cultures). Coon's supervision also resulted in the naming of the United Federation of Planets, while Starfleet Command was established as the body that directed the voyages of the *Enterprise*.

Coon's work, alongside that of Roddenberry, Fontana, Black and the individual episodic writers served to create a coherent, seemingly consistent universe within which the *Star Trek* TV adventures could take place. There is a sense of completeness and consistency to the environment in which the characters exist, even if individual early episodes feature glaring continuity errors or shifts in the naming of parts of the ship or peoples (is it deflector screens or deflector shields? Vulcanians or Vulcans?). These details would be more clearly defined over time, but the bigger picture made the future world of *Star Trek* feel like a real, coherent place.

These details accumulated, episode by episode, and were shaped by Roddenberry's rewriting into a gradually more cohesive universe. As well as Coon's major contributions, other elements that make up the recognisable *Star Trek* universe came from a variety of people. D. C. Fontana gave Spock his parents – a Vulcan father and human mother (he'd previously only admitted to 'human ancestors' in 'Where No Man Has Gone Before') – as well as the two-handed Vulcan 'death grip' (a bluff used by Spock to fake Kirk's death in 'The *Enterprise* Incident'). It was from her episodes that two alien races emerged, the blue antenna-sporting Andorians and the Tellarites, one of the founding races of the United Federation of Planets – both would survive right through to *Enterprise*. Leonard Nimoy came up with the more benign Vulcan nerve pinch for Spock, based on Richard Matheson's script 'The Enemy Within', which contained the idea that Spock could disable enemies in a non-violent, non-fatal way. Nimoy also contributed the Vulcan salute, a peaceful, welcoming hand gesture (with the raised palm held outwards and fingers parted in the middle in a V-shape), apparently basing it on a half-remembered Jewish blessing and the Hebrew letter Shin (meaning 'God'). The Romulans, a long-running *Star Trek* antagonist race based on the Romans, pre-dated the more well-known Klingons, first appearing in Paul Schneider's script 'Balance of Terror' (which also introduced actor Mark Lenard, later to play Spock's father, Sarek). Writer Schimon Wincelberg (under his pen name S. Bar-David) introduced the Vulcan mind-meld in 'Dagger of the Mind', allowing Spock to read the thoughts of other beings through physical contact. The background of Spock's Vulcan race was further developed by Theodore Sturgeon in 'Amok Time', which, as well as introducing the Vulcan salute, also saw the debut of the phrase 'Live long and prosper' as a Vulcan greeting.

While Roddenberry came to be affectionately fêted by *Star Trek* fans as 'the Great Bird of the Galaxy' and sole creator of *Star Trek*, it is clear that (as with all television productions) many creative hands were involved, even if one person provided the initial guiding force for all the others to follow. In a later speech, Roddenberry noted: 'When they say on a show "Created by" anyone, like "Created by Gene Roddenberry", that is not true. I laid out a pathway, and then the only thing I will take credit for is [that] I surrounded myself by very bright people who came up with all those wonderful things.'

Writing about the creation of *Star Trek*, D. C. Fontana noted: 'It was not one mind, but many – a creation by people who lived and loved the show. More than forty years later audiences still watch and enjoy *Star Trek*, quite an accomplishment for a show that almost didn't make it.'

By early 1966 Gene Roddenberry had secured his long-held dream: an order for sixteen episodes of his own space show on network television. *Star Trek*'s production was in full swing by summer 1966, with the lessons learnt on the two pilots applied to the shooting of individual episodes in the space of six to eight days. The scripts were flowing in and Roddenberry's rewrites were flowing out, via line producer Robert Justman, to the creative departments who had to supply the costumes, the props and the planetary locations used to tell *Star Trek* stories.

Roddenberry had determined that by including 'Where No

Man Has Gone Before' and by using 'The Cage' footage as the basis for a later two-part episode, he could reduce the required number of new episodes by three. For those first thirteen new instalments, storyteller Gene Roddenberry owned *Star Trek* – others may have contributed to the series' core concepts and ideals through their scripts (as noted), but every one of those initial thirteen episodic scripts went through the ruthless Roddenberry rewrite machine. He was the final arbiter as to what was or was not part of his *Star Trek*. Working late nights and weekends on others' scripts, Roddenberry was determined that his universe would make sense and be attractive to viewers. That was one reason he insisted on his show depicting an optimistic future. 'I believe in humanity', noted Roddenberry during a speech marking his acceptance of a star on Hollywood Boulevard in 1985. 'We are an incredible species. We're still just a child-creature, we're still being nasty to each other. And all children go through those phases. We're growing up, we're moving into adolescence now. When we grow up – man, we're going to be something.'

Shooting on the first of the new episodes ('The Corbomite Maneuver') began on 24 May 1966, with script revisions continuing right up until the days that various scenes were shot, common practice in television. By now the *Star Trek* production unit was firmly established within Desilu. The budget per episode was set at around $193,000, at the top end of the scale for one-hour drama in the late 1960s, but this was due to *Star Trek*'s many unique production and post-production requirements in sets, props and costumes, as well as special visual and sound effects. One way to keep down costs was in establishing an effects library. Fly-by shots of the *Enterprise* were regularly reused as the ship came into orbit around another planet (usually the same stock planet, recoloured), while regular bits of tech like the medical tricorder, the phaser or the communicator were given their own signature sounds. The background noise for the bridge of the *Enterprise* similarly worked its way into the consciousness of a generation through constant repetition.

The pulsing sound effect itself was not created especially for *Star Trek*, but instead came from the Paramount sound library. It can even be disconcertingly heard in earlier episodes of *The Outer Limits* and *The Twilight Zone*, pre-dating *Star Trek*. The consistent use of these sounds establishes time and place in *Star Trek*: they're different from the sounds surrounding the 1960s viewer at home or at work, yet through reuse and repetition they provide a consistent sense of place in a far out (in time and space, as well as in concept) drama.

Only William Shatner and Leonard Nimoy were contracted to appear in all thirteen of the first batch of episodes. DeForest Kelley – one of the original actors under consideration for the role of Dr Boyce on 'Where No Man Has Gone Before' – filled the role of the irascible Doctor McCoy, but was only signed up for seven of the first thirteen episodes. Canadian actor James Doohan was cast as Scottish engineer Scotty and guaranteed five shows. George Takei was cast as Sulu, fulfilling Roddenberry's hopes for a multi-ethnic range of characters on the *Enterprise*, and signed up for seven shows. Nichelle Nichols won the role of Communications Officer Uhura, but no minimum number of episodes was guaranteed. Actress Grace Lee Whitney was guaranteed four days' work across seven episodes, as her character of Yeoman Janice Rand was then considered part of the core group indicated by her inclusion in many of the pre-publicity photos. Rand was, however, quietly dropped while Uhura went on to become one of the characters instantly connected with *Star Trek*. These contractual arrangements go some way to explaining why across the early *Star Trek* episodes, characters appear to come and go and some don't feature in certain episodes at all, even McCoy, who was nonetheless quickly established as one of the core trio. This flexibility, however, allowed the production team to respond to audience reaction to characters and make changes and substitutions in the hope of firming up that audience appeal. This was quite far-sighted and fortuitous, especially as one *Star Trek* character proved to be more popular with 1960s viewers than any other: the 'satanic-looking' Mr Spock.

Prior to *Star Trek*'s September 1966 debut, a few pivotal details had to be locked down. The opening of the show would be important in highlighting the setting of *Star Trek* in the viewers' minds every week. This had to be done in a succinct manner, quickly and easily over the show's opening credits. Alexander Courage had been commissioned to produce the theme tune for the first pilot and that would be retained, but Gene Roddenberry wanted a voiceover explaining what the series was about (following Herb Solow's early suggestion). As the episodes featured regular 'Captain's Log' story updates, it seemed sensible to have the 'saga sell' (as the dramatic statement of the concept of a show is called today) narrated in character by William Shatner as Captain Kirk. The only debate was around the exact detail of what he would say.

In August 1966, just five weeks before the first episode aired, associate producer Robert Justman sent an urgent memo to Roddenberry pointing out: 'It is important that you compose, without delay, our standard opening narration for Bill Shatner to record. It should run about fifteen seconds in length.' That opened the floodgates for various *Star Trek* creatives to try their hands at crafting a suitable opening narration, something that encapsulated the story of this new show. Roddenberry's first attempt was rather long-winded: 'This is the story of the United Space Ship *Enterprise*. Assigned a five-year patrol of our galaxy, the giant starship visits Earth colonies, regulates commerce, and explores strange new worlds and civilizations. These are its voyages . . . and its adventures.'

Although that contained some of the now classic *Star Trek* opening narration, it wasn't quite snappy enough. Justman's turn at honing Roddenberry's words got closer to what was needed: 'This is the story of the starship *Enterprise*. Its mission: to advance knowledge, contact alien life and enforce intergalactic law . . . to explore strange new worlds, where no man has gone before.'

Although Justman developed the distinctive rhythm that would be used in the final narration, it still needed editing and revising. Producer John D. F. Black took a pass at crafting suitable opening words. 'The USS *Enterprise* . . . starship . . . Its mission, a five-year patrol to seek out and contact alien life . . . to explore the infinite frontier of space . . . Where no man has gone before . . . A Star Trek!'

His second attempt introduced more pivotal elements that would influence the final, now classic, narration: 'Space, the final frontier . . . Endless, silent, waiting . . . This is the story of the United Space Ship *Enterprise*. Its mission, a five-year patrol of the galaxy – to seek out and contact all alien life, to explore, to travel the vast galaxy where no man has gone before . . . A Star Trek!'

After over a week of this, Gene Roddenberry pulled together the various drafts on 10 August 1966 and crafted this final (and now famous) version for Shatner to record: 'Space, the final frontier. These are the voyages of the starship *Enterprise* . . . Its five-year mission to explore strange new worlds, seek out new life and new civilizations, to boldly go where no man has gone before . . .'

Roddenberry had successfully fused the best elements of all the drafts by himself, Justman and Black to craft a new, snappier and more rhythmic narration, while also introducing, in 'to boldly go', the infamous split infinitive that would haunt him. The narration's indication of a five-year mission for the *Enterprise* was also a statement of intent on behalf of the show's producers, who hoped to secure a lengthy and profitable run for *Star Trek*, as after five years there'd be enough episodes to put the show into syndication.

Prior to the launch of *Star Trek*, Gene Roddenberry had the good sense to court the growing body of science fiction fans that gathered regularly at conventions. He felt they could act as ambassadors for his show, spreading awareness to their friends and family via word of mouth. Roddenberry felt that such fans (often more wedded to literary science fiction than the 'lighter' film and TV variety) were so starved of decent television fantasy that they'd support *Star Trek* regardless of whether they personally liked the show or not.

Some television producers may have seen Roddenberry's attendance at the 24th Annual World Science Fiction Convention in Cleveland – just five days before his new show premiered on NBC – as foolhardy. They'd no doubt be keener on him touring the TV talk shows and news studios to promote their new show. Roddenberry, however, felt it important to cultivate fan support – you never knew when it might come in useful . . .

Roddenberry screened 'Where No Man Has Gone Before' to a 500-strong fan audience, who welcomed the new show with a standing ovation. This was just the prelude to Thursday, 8 September 1966 when NBC aired 'The Man Trap' as the first episode of *Star Trek*. Most critical reaction was lukewarm, seemingly preferring to postpone judgement until the series had run a little longer. Only the *Hollywood Reporter* wholeheartedly endorsed the new series as a 'winner'. One appreciative viewer, though, was Lucille Ball, who sent a note to the production team's Desilu offices congratulating them all on having 'a hit on your hands' and expressing how 'proud and happy I am'.

Never one to waste anything, Roddenberry had come up with an idea on how to use the material shot for 'The Cage' pilot episode – and keep the production on schedule at the same time. That pilot could not now be screened as so much had changed in terms of cast, approach and even the look of the show. However, by concocting a 'wraparound' story featuring the current *Enterprise* crew, Roddenberry figured he could use the material from 'The Cage' as a flashback, with the common link being Spock. The result was the two-part tale 'The Menagerie'. Spock hijacks the *Enterprise*, along with the now-crippled Captain Pike (Sean Kenney standing in for the non-returning Jeffrey Hunter), and returns to Talos IV. Trapped aboard the *Enterprise*, Kirk and Starbase Commodore Mendez stage an investigation into Spock's actions – aided by a visual record of his previous visit to Talos IV, transmitted from the now forbidden planet itself. The new material was shot in just five days at a lesser cost than a regular episode, while the participants in 'The Cage' were paid additional fees for the reuse of their material. The result was a cheaper-than-usual two-part *Star Trek* story (the only one in *The Original Series*) that made the universe of the show appear just that little bit larger – and helped the production make up for time lost when it slipped behind schedule.

Leonard Nimoy's Spock rapidly proved to be the break-out character in *Star Trek*. NBC had initially objected to his look and depiction in 'The Cage' and 'Where No Man Has Gone Before' – even going to the lengths of 'doctoring' publicity material to tone down his Vulcan ears. Executives had urged Roddenberry to drop the 'satanic-looking' character, but the series' creator was not to be dissuaded. He knew that *Star Trek* needed a regular alien character as part of the *Enterprise* crew, alongside his diverse selection of humans. Just as the Lone Ranger needed his Tonto, the Green Hornet his Kato, so Captain Kirk needed Spock by his side.

Roddenberry knew that the character opened up a whole universe of story possibilities that would otherwise be difficult to reach. His half-Vulcan, half-human heritage meant that Spock was a conflicted character from the beginning, striving to live up to the Vulcan ideals of non-emotionalism, yet torn by his genetic human leanings. In early episodes this would be explored through Nurse Christine Chapel's crush on Spock and how he dealt with the very human feelings she brought out in him.

It was under the influence of a mood-altering drug that Chapel admitted her feelings for Spock (in 'The Naked Time'), while Spock's experience of Pon farr (the Vulcan mating ritual) would bring out Chapel's maternal instincts (in 'Amok Time'). Their relationship developed in odd ways through *The Original Series*, with Chapel housing Spock's consciousness within her own mind in order to save him from Henoch, an evil disembodied energy being (in 'Return to Tomorrow', an inspiration for the Spock-centric trilogy of *Star Trek* movies, II–IV), while the pair 'enjoyed' a forced kiss while controlled by bored telepaths (in 'Plato's Stepchildren'). Much later, Spock himself expresses his infatuation with Chapel while under the effect of Harry Mudd's love potion (in the episode 'Mudd's Passion', from the mid-1970s animated *Star Trek* series).

In the first J. J. Abrams' *Star Trek* movie, Uhura controversially filled the Chapel position in connection with the new Spock. In 'The Man Trap', the original Uhura had shown similar interest in romancing Spock, even though he seemed unable to comprehend the nature of her advances or her desire to take a stroll in the moonlight. 'This Side of Paradise' sees Spock infected by Omnicron spores, allowing him once again to drop his Vulcan inhibitions and express his human emotions, in this case falling in love with botanist Leila Kalomi on Omnicron Ceti III and ignoring Kirk's orders. Kirk's destruction of the spores causes Spock's submerged anger to surface, while later – once recovered – he confesses that his time with Kalomi, although his brain chemistry was 'altered', had been the first time he'd truly felt happy . . .

Spock provided the outsider's view of humanity. While his human side gave him some kinship with Captain Kirk, Doctor McCoy and the crew of the *Enterprise*, his Vulcan heritage meant that he could look upon humanity in a colder, more detached way. Certainly, in early episodes of the series it is Spock who is quick to jump to the logical, sometimes violently destructive solution to a problem. Spock calculates the odds and weighs up the options coldly. He is the first to suggest killing Gary Mitchell in 'Where No Man Has Gone Before' as Mitchell poses a clear danger to the *Enterprise* and her crew (and beyond). In 'Balance of Terror' Spock wants to destroy the Romulan ship, believing that its return, unharmed, to its own space would signal Federation weakness and lead to eventual invasion. In 'The City on the Edge of Forever' it is Spock who convinces Kirk that 'Edith Keeler must die' in order to protect the timeline, regardless of the captain's feelings for her (a viewpoint Kirk comes to reluctantly recognise). Although Spock, along with many of the characters in *Star Trek*, mellows as the series progresses, he never loses this outsider perspective. It was the ideal viewpoint to make the character a counter-culture icon in the late 1960s. His character was, as Spock himself might say, 'fascinating'.

Nimoy had come to *Star Trek* a hungry, young, but serious-minded actor. He welcomed a regular role on a prime-time TV series, but for most of the rest of his life he would have very mixed feelings about playing Spock. More specifically, he (like NBC initially) was worried about the physical appearance of the character and the need to wear false ear appliances for that all-important alien look. Roddenberry had promised the actor that if they remained a problem he could come up with a story reason for their removal later in the series, but it never came to that. The character quickly became the most popular on the show – further adding to Nimoy's mixed feelings.

Nimoy had been engaged to play a supporting role to the leading character of the captain – ironic considering how popular his character was to become – and so was being paid $1,250 per episode compared to Shatner's leading man remuneration of $5,000. After just a handful of episodes had been filmed, and even before the show had aired, it had become clear to Nimoy's agent that the character of Spock was taking on a role that went way beyond that of a mere supporting character. Meetings were held, but a request for increased pay was refused, with an offer to revisit the issue if the show was renewed for a second season. Nimoy, not happy with this outcome, was to hold a minor grudge against both the production's executives and the show's leading man for the run of the series as he felt he was being undervalued and underpaid.

Despite the success of Spock, by November 1966 Gene Roddenberry was a nervous man. *Star Trek* was doing all right, ratings-wise, but it was by no means a hit show and so was not guaranteed a continued life beyond the initial sixteen episodes NBC had committed to. Almost as soon as the show was born, the 'Save *Star Trek*' campaigns began.

*Star Trek* had started well with the debut episode ('The Man Trap') airing during an NBC 'sneak preview' special presentation opposite repeat programming. It won the time slot with a 40.6 per cent share (meaning the percentage of all television sets in actual use during the broadcast that were tuned to that programme). The second show ('Charlie X') dropped dramatically as it was broadcast opposite new programming on rival channels, scoring a 29.4 per cent share, putting NBC in second place behind CBS. For the next two episodes (second pilot 'Where No Man Has Gone Before' was aired third, followed by 'The Naked Time'), *Star Trek* ranked 33rd out of the top 100 US TV shows. The next two episodes ('The Enemy Within' and 'Mudd's Women') saw viewership collapse and the show languish at 51st place. After just six weeks on air, the first season of *Star Trek* was heading towards an average 52nd place in the top 100, a position that would not lead to automatic renewal for a second season.

Roddenberry turned to the science fiction fan community for support. He had already built a relationship with fans Bjo (a shortened version of Betty Joanne) and John Trimble at the 24th World Science Fiction Convention in Cleveland, and they volunteered to spearhead a fan letter-writing campaign. However, worried that NBC might respond to *Star Trek*'s falling ratings by pulling the show off air before completion of the first season, Roddenberry set about coordinating a 'Save *Star Trek*' campaign directly from within the show's production office. Roddenberry himself drafted a series of letters making key points about the show, which were then offered to leading authors to use as the basis of their own campaigning efforts in support of the programme.

In November 1966 Roddenberry co-opted fantasy author Harlan Ellison to spearhead the campaign. Aimed at recruiting more science fiction professionals, the Roddenberry-drafted letter highlighted the positive effect the existence of 'adult' science fiction television could have on the field as a whole. Encouraging authors and fans to write letters to their local TV stations and newspapers in support of *Star Trek*, Roddenberry's campaign was a dry run for those that would come at the end of each of the show's three troubled seasons on air. Among those writers who signed up to the campaign alongside Ellison were Theodore Sturgeon, Richard Matheson, A. E. van Vogt, Robert Bloch, Lester del Ray, Philip José Farmer, Frank Herbert and Poul Anderson.

Despite the low ratings, and almost in spite of the limited letter-writing campaign of 1966, NBC decided it would extend *Star Trek*'s first season by another thirteen episodes for 1966–7 and then pick up the show for a second season of episodes for 1967–8. Recognising the series' appeal among younger viewers, especially teenagers who were otherwise hard to reach through television drama, NBC announced *Star Trek* would return in the 7.30 p.m. slot on Tuesdays, before changing its mind and moving the show to the difficult 8.30 p.m. Friday night slot – a time when the target audience of teenagers and college students would most likely not be bothering to watch broadcast television.

It was the beginning of the long, slow death of *Star Trek*.

# Chapter 4

## Too Short a Season:
## Consolidating *Star Trek*

'Star Trek – *despite the wild enthusiasm of science fiction aficio-nados – had a rough go its first year, due mainly to that purblind arrogance of the nameless decision-makers on their skyscraper mountaintops.*' Harlan Ellison

Series creator Gene Roddenberry took a step back from the day-to-day running of *Star Trek* halfway through its first season on air. His credit changed from producer on those first sixteen episodes to executive producer for the remainder of the series. Into the second season, he continued to rewrite scripts to ensure they fitted with the *Star Trek* universe he'd created, but producer Gene Coon took a stronger hand on the script-editing front, with associate producer Robert Justman continuing to handle the physical production process. This team, along with screen-writer Harlan Ellison, were to be behind the creation of the episode cited as *Star Trek*'s all-time best instalment.

Despite his wholehearted involvement in the campaign to raise the profile of *Star Trek* with science fiction fans and profes-sionals, Ellison would prove to be a thorn in Gene Roddenberry's side when he came to script an episode for the series. The making of 'The City on the Edge of Forever' – an episode from towards the end of *Star Trek*'s debut season – was extremely troubled from the beginning.

Ellison was primarily a short story writer, essayist and

columnist who'd scripted various TV shows including two
acclaimed episodes of *The Outer Limits* ('Soldier' and 'Demon
With A Glass Hand') and instalments of *The Man From
U.N.C.L.E.* He would go on to become a creative consultant and
writer on the 1985 revival of *The Twilight Zone* and J. Michael
Straczynski's groundbreaking 1990s TV space opera *Babylon 5*
(a rival to the same era's *Deep Space Nine*). Getting a *Star Trek*
script from Ellison was a priority for Justman. 'We wanted a teleplay from Harlan as soon as possible, but despite a lot of badgering
Harlan was behind schedule right from the start, taking two
months to write his final revised story outline. The usual time
allocated for a story was more like two or three weeks.'

In a memo Justman described the long-awaited story outline
as 'beautifully written', but he recognised that Ellison's proposed
story contained huge challenges for practical television production. Several of Ellison's scenes featured locations and effects
that would simply be beyond *Star Trek*'s budget and may even
have been challenging for a major movie production to realise.

A shimmering time vortex, an angry woolly mammoth, too
many locations and too many speaking parts all caused
Roddenberry to request a revision of the story. Additionally,
concerned by how long it had taken Ellison to draft just the
outline, he suggested the writer should be based in the studio
offices for the writing of the first draft teleplay. That way,
Roddenberry, Coon and Justman could keep a close eye on the
maverick writer. 'Harlan arrived with his own typewriter, his
own portable radio, and his own original approach to creativity',
recalled Justman in *Inside Star Trek*.

Located in the studio's wardrobe storage room, Ellison felt
the need to escape his limited confines at regular intervals and
was often to be seen wandering the back lot checking out whatever happened to be shooting. Even when he was locked in the
'office', he'd escape out through the window. He complained of
being forced to work under 'inhuman and inhumane conditions', with constant interruptions from people using the
wardrobe store forcing him to work at night. In response,

Justman moved Ellison into his own office and supervised him directly as he finished the teleplay (the pair had previously worked together on *The Outer Limits*). Important meetings conducted with Justman would continue around Ellison as he pecked away at his typewriter over a three-week period and gradually completed a first draft of what became 'The City on the Edge of Forever'.

Justman described the finished script as 'without a doubt . . . the best and most beautifully written screenplay we've gotten to date'. However, he also knew 'we cannot afford to make this show as it presently stands [due to] set construction costs, location shooting, crowds of extras, crowds of stunts, special effects onstage, special photographic effects, wardrobe costs, period props and set dressing rentals, and other costs too numerous to mention . . . We have to find a way to retain all the basic qualities contained within this screenplay and make it economically feasible to photograph it.'

What Ellison's script revealed about *Star Trek* was that it was a strictly budgeted production – that's why so many of the planets visited resembled Earth-type settings (allowing easy use of the back-lot standing sets), why alien races often consisted of a handful of representatives, and why special effects shots (such as the *Enterprise* orbiting a planet) were repeatedly reused.

The decision to redraft the screenplay to make it producible within a television budget saw the beginning of a long-running feud between Ellison and Roddenberry that was to run for decades, even beyond the latter's death. Roddenberry faced rewriting what Justman had estimated to be an eight-day shooting schedule for the episode down to *Star Trek*'s standard seven days per episode, over Ellison's loud objections. Roddenberry also felt that some of the 'guest characters' featured in the episode did not represent the 'best of humanity' that he saw in Starfleet's officers. The blame, or credit, for the rewrite was spread around, however. Gene Coon had the first try at rewriting the show, following Ellison's own changes under Justman's direction. Then story editor D. C. Fontana found the script on

her desk for another redrafting, which although now shootable
resulted in Justman expressing his view that the revised teleplay
lacked 'the beauty and mystery that was inherent in this screenplay as Harlan originally wrote it. It is very good *Star Trek*
material, but has none of Harlan's special magic.' In response,
Roddenberry had no choice but to take on the task himself,
attempting to fuse the drafts from his staff with the original
from Ellison, picking out the best from each while still resulting
in a practical screenplay that the production could shoot.

'It budgeted out at nearly $100,000 over what we had to
spend on an episode', wrote Roddenberry of Ellison's first draft.
'His use of our characters was not according to format. When
he couldn't do an acceptable rewrite job, I rewrote the script to
bring it within budget and within line of our *Star Trek* format.'

Even during filming of the episode in February 1967,
Roddenberry continued to revise pages of the script. Ellison
complained to the production, on the day shooting began, that
he was not happy about the rewriting process. He requested
that his traditional alias of dissatisfaction, 'Cordwainer Bird', be
credited on screen. Roddenberry, however, saw great value in
the Ellison name and fought to keep him attached. According to
Justman, 'After a lot of fussing and, according to Harlan, an
"absolute threat" from Gene to keep him from ever working in
Hollywood again, Cordwainer Bird was convinced to revert to
being Harlan Ellison again, and his screen credit reflected the
fact. Nevertheless, the uneasy truce that ensued between Harlan
and Gene was never again remotely approaching comfortable.'

The resulting episode saw Kirk and Spock pursue a drug-
crazed McCoy through a newly discovered time portal known as
The Guardian of Forever, to 1930s Earth. There Kirk falls in love
with social campaigner Edith Keeler (Joan Collins), only for
Spock to reveal that she must die to protect the timeline . . .
Fantastic ideas, a great emotional dilemma and high stakes, as
well as superb production design, all combined to make this one
of *Star Trek*'s best-loved episodes. The original script (before the
*Star Trek* staff rewrote it) went on to win Ellison the Writers Guild

Award for most outstanding script for a dramatic television series, and he took the opportunity of his acceptance speech to berate studio 'suits' for 'interfering with the writing process'. Ellison would go on to chronicle his side of the creation of the episode in a book-length study that included a lengthy essay and reprinted his original, award-winning screenplay.

Towards the end of the episode, the dialogue from Edith Keeler does much to highlight the then-growing iconic status of the characters of Kirk and Spock. Noting how out of place Kirk and Spock are in 1930s America, Spock asks her where she thinks they belong. 'You?' she says to Spock. 'At his side, as if you've always been there and always will.' To Kirk, she says, 'And you? You belong in another place, I don't know where or how, but I'll figure it out eventually.' She notes Spock's relationship with Kirk by completing his statement with the word 'Captain. Even when he doesn't say it, he does.' With these few lines, this episode encapsulated the relationship between Spock and Kirk and did much to define their iconic natures.

The first season of *Star Trek* ended on a creative high in April 1967 – 'The City on the Edge of Forever' was followed by the final episode, 'Operation: Annihilate!' The show had come a long way from the two pilots, but Roddenberry and his team knew there were even more new worlds and new civilisations to be encountered.

Season two of *Star Trek* was all about honing Gene Roddenberry's vision, as well as providing enough action-adventure content to please the network (and younger viewers) and so hopefully win the series another year on air.

The second year saw the introduction of a new character to the regular *Enterprise* crew. While Roddenberry had tried to balance ethnic and gender representations on the *Enterprise*, he'd given little thought to other nations. This was redressed with the addition of Russian Pavel Chekov (Walter Koenig), a mop-topped youth designed to appeal to young fans of The Monkees and The Beatles. The inclusion of a Russian character was meant to indicate that sources of then-current tension, such as the Cold War of the 1960s, would be long resolved by the time of *Star Trek*'s utopian future.

Continuing mediocre ratings meant that *Star Trek* scraped through to a third year on air, but only after another vociferous fan campaign which this time included student demonstrations outside NBC's headquarters in Los Angeles. A letter-writing campaign resulted in a steady flow of *Star Trek* mail to NBC. According to Roddenberry his show had actually been cancelled by the end of its second season in 1967, only for it to be renewed thanks to the volume of mail the broadcaster received.

Like the previous campaign, Roddenberry himself had been heavily involved in coordinating things from behind the scenes, but NBC were never to know that. They actually investigated the legitimacy of the letter-writing campaign and established to their satisfaction that the more than one million letters that arrived at NBC were representative of a genuine outpouring from real *Star Trek* fans.

By the end of the second season *Star Trek* had produced fifty-five episodes, not enough for NBC to run the show in syndication and thus maximise its returns on the series through daily reruns. With a third season of episodes, the series total would rise to enough for a decent syndication package (even though the usually preferred number of episodes was around 100) and a chance at generating a profit. The decision to renew may have been more of a sensible business move on the part of NBC than a response to any fan campaign (and in later years NBC claimed the number of letters received was actually less than 150,000). The decision to grant the series a third year would give *Star Trek* the chance to achieve serious longevity.

The show was back on, but despite his role in rescuing *Star Trek* from oblivion after its second year, Gene Roddenberry was to be even less involved in the production than ever before. Writing to author Isaac Asimov, Roddenberry addressed the changes behind the scenes of the third season and his hopes for *Star Trek*'s future. 'This year I am pulling back from . . . the show and will try to operate now as a real executive producer. I had offered to NBC to line produce it myself if they gave us a good hour on a good weeknight, but you know what happened there. I decided it was simply not worth the crippling expenditure of time and energy if I could not have a night and an hour which gave us at least a fair chance of reaching a mass audience and staying on the air. It is always at least possible that Friday night at 10 p.m. may work, or we might get a mid-season shift to a good time slot. I hope it works. I hope I can supervise the new team in keeping the quality of the show up, I hope *Star Trek* stays on for five or ten years. I've done my damnedest for the show.'

Like any successful TV producer, Roddenberry was always on the lookout for a way to advance to the next project, to a higher earning bracket or even into motion pictures. A third year of *Star Trek* was just another way for him to further that goal of advancing his own career. The new time slot helped Roddenberry to step back from the show he'd created: he'd promised hands-on involvement if NBC would return *Star Trek* to its previous successful early-evening slot early in the week, when younger viewers and students could watch. The Friday late-night slot was a blow, but it did help Roddenberry detach himself from his creation more easily. As far as he was concerned, cancellation after the third year was all but inevitable now, fan campaign or no fan campaign.

For its third year, producing duties on *Star Trek* fell to Fred Freiberger, an experienced TV producer hired by Roddenberry (he'd written for many of the same shows as Roddenberry, including *Highway Patrol* and *West Point*). In fact, Freiberger had initially been interviewed in 1966 for the producer role taken by Gene Coon. However, in the eyes of *Star Trek*'s fans, he would carry the responsibility for the reduction in quality of the episodes in the series' third season. This had as much to do with a huge reduction in budget as it had with a lack of creative ideas. Even so, a number of the later episodes of the third year continued to prove that when *Star Trek*'s producers applied their minds, their stories could still challenge audiences.

Halfway through transmission of the third season in January 1969, Roddenberry confided in a letter to a friend his fears about cancellation. 'I have grave doubts that we will be picked up for a fourth season. The Friday night at 10 p.m. slot is an almost impossible one for a show like this and it hurts us badly.'

Around the same time, Roddenberry outlined his frustrations with the final year of *Star Trek* in a letter to his mentor and inspiration John W. Campbell. '[*Star Trek*] is being made by someone else [Freiberger] and comes out quite different in important ways from the way I envisioned the show. The kind of creativity and imagination you saw in the first year of *Star Trek* is hard to find. Time, I think, to wash *Star Trek* out of my hair.'

January 1969 saw the shooting of 'Turnabout Intruder' – the final episode of the initial run of *Star Trek*, and the last live-action *Star Trek* adventure for a decade. The series had begun airing the previous September with 'Spock's Brain'. Those two bookend episodes are widely regarded by fans as two of the worst *Star Trek* instalments ever made. Ratings continued to be low and NBC did not help the situation by 'pre-empting' (replacing scheduled episodes with other programmes) the show three times and leaving a three-month gap between the airing of 'All Our Yesterdays' in March 1969 and burying the final new episode at the start of reruns in June 1969. NBC had issued a press release that February listing the shows that would be picked up for the following year – *Star Trek* was not among them. The network pulled the plug on the show before the final few episodes of the third series could even be shot.

Not only was *Star Trek* over but the show had been branded a failure by both its network, NBC, and its producer, Paramount (who had bought Desilu). NBC had cancelled the show – as they stated in a form letter sent to complaining fans – because it had failed to achieve the 30 per cent audience share the network required, even though the network's poor scheduling of the series had contributed heavily to this failure. It was also true that the show had never cracked the Nielsen Top 20 listing of TV shows for any of its three difficult years on air.

In financing the show Paramount had sold *Star Trek* episodes to NBC at two-thirds of their actual cost to make (known as deficit funding), so when production wrapped on the series, *Star Trek* showed as a $4.7-million debt on the Paramount balance sheet. With no more episodes forthcoming and ancillary income streams (merchandise such as model kits) unlikely to develop any further, Paramount saw little chance that the show would recover that expenditure. The only hope was that some of that money might be recovered by selling the series into syndication, which consisted of cheap reruns on affiliated local TV stations – not seen as an important outlet or revenue stream until after *Star Trek* proved a success through this very outlet in the 1970s.

One of the main reasons that Roddenberry claimed he had developed *Star Trek* was so he could deal with then-contemporary issues (race, war, social conditions) in the guise of far-future science fiction. The 1960s was a revolutionary period for representations of ethnicity, gender and sexuality, as well as being the height of the Cold War and a period of social turmoil – all of which was reflected (often in disguise) in various *Star Trek* episodes. Learning from his struggles on *The Lieutenant*, Roddenberry dramatised his social comment within a fantasy context, much as Serling had done on *The Twilight Zone*. 'The first pilot really began with the fact that TV in the days when I began was so severely censored', said Roddenberry at a TV industry event in 1988. 'I thought maybe if I did what [English satirist Jonathan] Swift did, and used far-off polka-dot people on far-off planets, I could get away with it.'

*Star Trek* reflected contemporary 1960s social and cultural issues in its storytelling. As the series progressed Roddenberry smuggled social issue dramas onto television disguised as science fiction action-adventure. On the TV show *Livewire* Roddenberry admitted: 'I saw an opportunity to use the series, to really use it, to say the things I believe, like to be different is not necessarily to be ugly. I wanted to make some comments. In television in those days you couldn't talk about sex, unions, politics – anything of any meaning – I thought if I have it happen "way out there" maybe I can get it past the censors. And I did: every fourteen-year-old knew what I was talking about, but it went right over the censor's head.'

Of the seventy-nine episodes that make up *The Original Series*, twelve of them deal with computers or artificial intelligences that set out to dominate organic life. Among those in the first season are 'The Return of the Archons', which sees the descendants of Starfleet officers freed from the control of a supercomputer, and 'A Taste of Armageddon', in which two warring cultures abide by a computer's assessment of virtual casualties and then calmly kill their own people. In both, Kirk destroys the computer at the heart of the respective cultures, and in the process tries to teach the now freed peoples to think for themselves. It was a clear reflection of thinking promoting individuality in the 1960s, while 'A Taste of Armageddon' also functioned as an allegory for the futile nature of war, particularly the ongoing controversial conflict in Vietnam at that time.

In 'The Changeling', early in the second season, the *Enterprise* encounters an artificial intelligence known as Nomad, a long-lost Earth probe, damaged during its long voyage and reconstituted by superior machine intelligences. Its altered programming now has Nomad seeking out life in order to exterminate it, a mission only put on hold as the machine believes Kirk to be its creator. Kirk demolishes the machine's claim to infallibility by adopting the risky strategy of revealing he is not Jackson Roykirk, creator of the Earth Nomad probe, and so the machine is wrong. Naturally, this breakdown in logic causes Nomad to self-destruct.

Other episodes from *The Original Series* dealing with the theme include 'The Doomsday Machine', about a relentless weapon that destroys all before it (a space-based variation of *Moby Dick*, essentially), while 'The Apple' features yet another world run by a computer intelligence that is eventually destroyed by Kirk. 'The Ultimate Computer' sees an artificial intelligence installed on the *Enterprise* to demonstrate that a computer can run the ship better than its human crew. In the course of the episode, Kirk begins to despair that he is no longer needed, until the computer (which is augmented by creator Daystrom's disturbed mental patterns) acts illogically and begins destroying other starships. It's another opportunity for Kirk to talk a computer to death – in Roddenberry's *Star Trek*, the organic always overcomes the artificial and mechanical.

The appearance of malevolent computers or artificial intelligence in *Star Trek* episodes are often used to highlight the character of Spock: while his logic often causes him to agree with a computer's processing, he's always on the side of Kirk in prioritising organic life and intelligence over the artificial. In 'The Ultimate Computer', Spock goes so far as to say, 'Computers make excellent and efficient servants, but I have no wish to serve under them.' In 'The Apple', he can see the virtue in the computer-controlled primitive (and stagnant) society, much to Dr McCoy's disgust.

Another favourite topic of many episodes in *The Original Series* was superpowered or God-like beings. While Gene Roddenberry professed humanist beliefs and was disdainful of organised religion, he seemed fascinated by the concept of God and this often arose in *Star Trek* stories. In a letter to a cousin in 1984, Roddenberry wrote: 'The real villain is religion – at least, religion as generally practised by people who somehow become sure that they and only they know the "real" answer. How few humans there are that seem to realise that killing, much less hating, their fellow humans in the name of their "god" is the ultimate kind of perversion.'

From the second pilot, 'Where No Man Has Gone Before', through a handful of first season episodes – 'Charlie X', 'The Squire of Gothos', 'The Return of the Archons' and 'Space Seed' prime among them – the theme occurs repeatedly. Often, the powers that these beings demonstrate come with a degree of immaturity. The Squire of Gothos himself is a child, and Balok in 'The Corbomite Maneuver' is child-like' (a concept well spoofed in the *Futurama* episode 'Where No Fan Has Gone Before'). Even the Greek 'god' Apollo in 'Who Mourns for Adonais?' seems out of his depth when he attempts to make the *Enterprise* crew worship him, just as the humans of old did. He has to be persuaded by Kirk that his time has passed and he must move on to the spiritual plane, like his contemporaries did before him.

'Space Seed' presents the most obvious example of a super-human in the genetically engineered Khan. His biological superiority, a legacy of the Eugenics War of the 1990s, allows him to feel it is his right to dominate those around him. Khan uses crewmember Marla McGivers to facilitate his takeover of the *Enterprise*, and she eventually joins him in his exile to Ceti Alpha V after Kirk regains his ship. The story provided the springboard for Nicholas Meyer's *The Wrath of Khan*.

The many other episodes featuring superior or God-like beings include 'Catspaw', a Hallowe'en trifle that puts the *Enterprise* crew at the mercy of Korob and Sylvia, powerful aliens exploring human emotions, and 'Obsession' (yet another *Moby Dick* variant) in which Kirk faces off against a truly alien gas cloud responsible for the deaths of fellow crewmembers earlier in his career. Most of *Star Trek*'s superior beings, however, are humanoid, like those in 'The Gamesters of Triskelion'. They force the *Enterprise* crew to take part in gladiatorial contests for their amusement, an idea echoed in 'Plato's Stepchildren' that again sees the crew acting against their natures at the behest of superior powers. In 'By Any Other Name', the *Enterprise* is hijacked (again) by powerful beings from Andromeda (although, as in 'Catspaw', we only ever see two of them due to the limited budget). They intend to use the ship to invade another galaxy, but Kirk is able to use extreme human emotional states against them, thus recapturing his beloved vessel.

The 1960s was a peak period of the Cold War stand-off between the United States and the Soviet Union, culminating in the October 1962 Cuban missile crisis. The Vietnam War had escalated throughout the decade, and by the late 1960s, when *Star Trek* was on air, public opinion was increasingly turning against it. War, conflict, political matters and diplomacy became a central part of Gene Roddenberry's plan to use 'far-off polka-dot people on far-off planets' to make his political comments through drama.

A variety of episodes depict straightforward conflicts that allow Kirk to become a mouthpiece for a variety of views, mainly from Roddenberry and Coon. Sometimes, the use of force is justified whereas at other times the need to battle an enemy is a cause for lament. Early in the first season, 'The Corbomite Maneuver' sees the human race branded as aggressive savages by Balok, who threatens to destroy the *Enterprise*. Only the bluff of the title, that the *Enterprise* has a weapon that deflects energy back upon the aggressor, allows Kirk to stop Balok. 'Balance of Terror' shows the battle of wits between Kirk and a nameless Romulan Commander (Mark Lenard) where the technology of destruction available to each is almost equally balanced. 'A Taste of Armageddon' takes this idea one step further, pitching two equally matched war-like cultures against each other. The war between Eminiar VII and Vendikar has lasted for 500 years, but there is no destruction of property – each planet abides by casualty figures produced by computer and a docile populace meekly turns up at the disintegration booths in the required numbers. Clearly a comment on Vietnam, the satirical intent was buried beneath a great science fiction concept. The Vietnam issue was even plainer in 'A Private Little War', a story that sees the Klingons and the Federation arming opposite forces in a conflict on a developing world. The only way to 'preserve both sides', according to Kirk, is to create a balance of power by arming both forces equally, driving Kirk to match the Klingons move by move. Interviewed on *Good Morning America* in 1986, Roddenberry made the claim that *Star Trek* was 'the only dramatic show that ever talked against Vietnam. We set it on another planet. Kirk essentially played the role of our presidents in those years, where he'd gotten into it and was having trouble getting out of it. It's a pity: Vietnam would have ended many years sooner if it had been on dramatic shows on television because of the impact of these dramatic shows. If Dr Marcus Welby had come out and said something against Vietnam, my maiden aunts would have carried placards!'

A later episode, 'Day of the Dove', reversed this plot by having an alien entity arm both the Klingons and the *Enterprise* crew with swords, setting them against each other. Kirk and his Klingon opponent Kang have to stop fighting each other and cooperate if they are to understand what's happening. Like the majority of *Star Trek* episodes, it's entertaining even if the moral of the story (peace is better than war) is simplistic and obvious.

*Star Trek* was often less than subtle in its political analogies: such was the case with the 'Nazi planet' in 'Patterns of Force'. In an effort to depict the rise of a totalitarian state, this episode comes close to using Nazi iconography carelessly in a simple entertainment, while trying to convey a history lesson to the show's young viewers about events then a mere twenty-five years in the past. A Federation historian has employed Nazi methods to run a planet, hoping that Nazism-with-a-conscience might have a different outcome – the conclusion of the story is that it doesn't. 'The *Enterprise* Incident' – apart from giving William Shatner a taste of wearing Spock-style pointed ears – was a Cold War espionage tale in which Kirk and Spock go undercover as Romulans to steal their technology.

Perhaps the most interesting of all the Cold War-themed episodes of *Star Trek* is 'Mirror, Mirror'. This well-remembered episode sees Kirk, Spock, McCoy and Uhura attempt to beam aboard the *Enterprise*, only to find themselves transported to an alternative universe version of the ship. Here they find a ruthless Terran Empire wreaking havoc throughout the galaxy, and a ship where promotion is obtained through assassination. In this universe, Mr Spock – sporting a goatee beard – is a ruthless enforcer, although he doesn't want command of the ship. Chekov attempts to assassinate Kirk, while Sulu runs a sinister surveillance operation. The crewmembers from 'our' universe must strive to fit in while trying to find a way back home – but Kirk can't resist going one step further in trying to persuade the mirror Spock that there is a different way of running things. The episode gave rise to a series of follow-ups, in *Deep Space Nine* and *Enterprise*, as well as in a series of spin-off novels. 'Mirror, Mirror' offers a vision of how the Federation might have turned out if the positive future for humanity as depicted by Gene Roddenberry had not come to pass.

Diplomacy was explored in a variety of episodes, as the *Enterprise* crew played the role of diplomatic ambassador to new and developing civilisations or functioned as an intermediary between disputing cultures. 'Errand of Mercy' sees the Klingons and the *Enterprise* personnel battle for influence over the strategically important planet of Organia. The seemingly unconcerned Organians refuse to resist either side, frustrating Kirk and encouraging Klingon Commander Kor in his desire to dominate the planet. As the conflict escalates, the Organians reveal themselves as dominant energy beings that use their powers to prevent the battle. Kirk finds himself arguing against the Organians for his right to wage a war that he initially came to the planet to prevent. It was a rare moment of self-awareness for the *Enterprise* captain that plainly stated the case for and against the kind of conflict then raging in Vietnam.

More traditional is the second season episode 'Journey to Babel', which sees various alien races transported aboard the *Enterprise* to a diplomatic meeting on the planet Babel. A murder mystery is the backdrop for the introduction of Spock's parents, the Vulcan Sarek and the human Amanda. The diplomacy-as-drama storytelling approach would be hugely expanded by *The Next Generation*, reflecting the era in which the show was made.

The *Enterprise* crew intervened in events more proactively in 'Friday's Child', an episode that saw the Klingons involved with the political development of a primitive culture. The battle for control of the planet is made personal, with Kirk, Spock and McCoy protecting the dead leader's pregnant widow from aggression until she can give birth to a rightful heir. Kirk's action results in the Klingons being driven out and the *Enterprise* winning the valuable mining rights on the planet, an analogy for US foreign adventures.

There's more Federation-driven diplomacy in 'Elaan of Troyius', in which Kirk ferries Elaan to her arranged marriage to the leader of an antagonistic planet in order to avert a war. The involvement of the Klingons – again – highlights the role of diplomacy in finding solutions to conflict.

Another 1960s hot-button topic regularly revisited by *Star Trek* was prejudice and racism. At a time when the civil rights movement was progressing in America, Roddenberry felt it was important to tell stories in *Star Trek* that showed in the future such issues had been resolved within humanity, even if sometimes Kirk had to show the various peoples of other races a more enlightened way of relating to each other.

The most blatant example was 'Let That Be Your Last Battlefield', a third season episode that sees the *Enterprise* involved with the last two representatives of a warring race. Lokai of Cheron is half black on one side of his face, half white on the other. Bele of Cheron is his mirror image, and his pursuer. Originally conceived by Gene Coon as a story about two beings – one angelic, one satanic – in conflict, the story was revised to be not just a comment on surface appearances being deceiving, but the futility of hatred motivated purely by physical (or social, religious or ethnic) difference.

*Star Trek*'s belief in 'infinite diversity in infinite combinations' – the Vulcan philosophy of tolerance outlined by Spock in the episode 'Is There in Truth No Beauty' – extended to non-humanoid life forms. In 'The Devil in the Dark', the *Enterprise* comes to the aid of a mining colony planet where miners are being killed off by a mysterious beast. Kirk and Spock discover the 'beast' is a sentient, silicon-based life form called a Horta. Spock mind-melds with the rock-like creature, discovering its intelligence. Communicating with the pair, the Horta carves the words 'No Kill I' into the rock, either as a plea for mercy or a statement of intent. The *Enterprise* pair learns that the creature is a mother, who has been attacking the miners in order to defend its eggs (not recognised by the miners as such). In a neat solution, the natural rock-carving ability of the Horta is harnessed to aid the mining activities of the colonists while the creature and its progeny are protected. The point expressed by the episode is that life can come in the most unexpected forms, and limited perceptions can blind people (like the miners) from recognising it. It's quintessential *Star Trek*, and one of the series' best episodes.

Patrick Stewart, captain of the *Enterprise* on *The Next Generation*, was one of the speakers at Gene Roddenberry's memorial service in 1991. Despite the solemnity of the occasion, he addressed an issue that continued into the spin-off *Star Trek* TV series: the show's sometimes controversial depiction of women. '[*Star Trek*] wasn't always consistent, especially where it concerned women', noted Stewart. 'Infuriatingly, *Star Trek* remains simultaneously liberated and sexist. Maybe even in that, Gene remains, sadly, a visionary.'

Stewart's phrase 'liberated and sexist' is the perfect, seemingly contradictory way to describe *Star Trek*'s attitude to and depiction of women. Much of it seems to be rooted in Roddenberry's own private life and his womanising ways: he idolised and loved women, believing them capable of as much, if not more, than men. This resulted in a series of strong, independent, clever female characters throughout *Star Trek*, but also the infamous short skirts and revealing outfits of the series that replaced the more sensible trouser suits seen in the original pilot. While Kirk may be seen as a stand-in for Roddenberry, seemingly with a woman on every planet, those women themselves are often depicted as irresistibly alluring (even if such allure is sometimes chemically assisted). Both Kirk and Spock have sacrificed the possibility of relationships to their careers: Kirk in his obsessive connection with his ship (best displayed in the early episode 'The Naked Time') and Spock in his devotion to logic and duty (he gives up his long-promised Vulcan bride in 'Amok Time').

Women in *The Original Series* often find themselves in thrall to powerful men, whether it be Marla McGivers with Khan ('Space Seed') or Carolyn Palamas and faux-god Apollo ('Who Mourns for Adonais?'). The spectre of rape, or at least forced physical contact, seems to haunt some of these relationships. In 'Shore Leave', the men's fantasies revolve around whimsy (McCoy sees Alice and the White Rabbit, Kirk encounters Finnegan, a joker from his past, and old flame Ruth), while Tonia Barrows' fantasy involves a violent seduction at the hands of Don Juan. Similarly, Carolyn Palamas is ravaged by a violent storm of Apollo's making when she rejects his advances. Both encounters leave the women traumatised and in torn clothing, yet both events are depicted as being a result of their own wishes or desires.

Through the years *Star Trek* has often shown women as the equal of men, from the quickly axed Number One of 'The Cage' to Captain Janeway in *Voyager*. In *The Original Series* even the strongest female characters were often reduced to mere romantic interests to service the story of the week: Nurse Chapel would occasionally be seen to moon over the unobtainable Mr Spock, while Yeoman Janice Rand seemed to have a thing for the heroic captain. Even Edith Keeler, a woman who gives Kirk more than a run for his money in 'The City on the Edge of Forever', must perform the role of a tragic, lost love interest. Kirk has a string of ex-lovers littered around the galaxy (including Areel Shaw in 'Court Martial', Ruth in 'Shore Leave', Janice Lester in 'Turnabout Intruder' and Dr Carol Marcus in *The Wrath of Khan*), but he always puts his career in space ahead of any lasting relationships. The temptation of casual liaisons was seemingly ever-present for the captain of the *Enterprise*, as evidenced by the number of women Kirk would seduce – and be seduced by – during the three years the show aired.

Sex between aliens and humans was never explicitly tackled by the show, although it was implied in many of Kirk's relationships. Perhaps the most explicit case was that of Zefram Cochrane and the amorphous, alien companion who loved him (in 'Metamorphosis'): he rejects the creature, until it adopts the form of a shapely female. While science was shown to have made great steps forward on *Star Trek*, the role of women still more often fell into stereotype occupations, especially among the regular characters such as Nurse Chapel and Communications Officer Uhura – a failing highlighted in the *Star Trek* movie satire *Galaxy Quest*.

Seth McFarlane, inducting Roddenberry into the TV Hall of Fame in 2010, summed up much of Roddenberry's success in making *Star Trek*'s stories mean something: '[*Star Trek*] made you think. Roddenberry was the closest thing you could get in television to an actual philosopher. He had a point-of-view and he was not afraid to express it. He believed that making a statement with regard to political or social issues in the form of televised narrative was not being "preachy" but rather the responsibility of a thoughtful writer. Gene did not offer us the murder of the week or the disease of the week, he offered us the idea of the week. The messages Roddenberry was sending were timely and important.'

However, these added layers of social and political comment were not enough to save *Star Trek*. Within weeks of the series concluding on television, a real-life space opera reached its climax in July 1969 as Neil Armstrong walked on the moon. It appeared that real-life space adventure had finally outstripped television science fiction.

# Chapter 5

## Timeless: The Birth of a Franchise and Fandom

*'It turns out that the Trekkies have been right all along, on nearly everything they have tried to tell us.'* Gene Roddenberry

By the middle of 1969 *Star Trek* was dead. Yet the show that had battled for survival for each of its three years on air was about to sow the seeds that would allow it to, in the immortal words of Mr Spock, 'live long and prosper'. The show's fans were about to become *Star Trek*'s newest storytellers.

After the cancellation of his TV show, Gene Roddenberry finally achieved what he'd hoped for all along: a transition into motion pictures. While *Star Trek* continued for its final year without his regular input, he'd been scripting a film version of Edgar Rice Burroughs' *Tarzan*. In keeping with the ethos of the 1960s (and his personal interests), Roddenberry had created a more sexualised Tarzan than had been seen before, while attempting to stay true to Burroughs' original. However, the budget was slashed, the theatrical film downgraded to a TV movie, and Roddenberry's script rejected, as its sexual content was now unsuitable for TV.

Roddenberry's first completed post-*Star Trek* project was the script for an adaptation of Francis Pollini's novel *Pretty Maids All in a Row*, about the dalliances of a schoolteacher with his female students. The film was produced by Roger Vadim (*Barbarella*) and Roddenberry, but was not considered to be a success upon its release in 1971. The job had been a favour to Roddenberry from *Star Trek* producer Herb Solow, now also working success- fully in movies. Roddenberry then scripted the fifth episode of Glen A. Larson's comedy Western series *Alias Smith and Jones*, 'The Girl in Boxcar #3', which aired in February 1971. Professionally, things were rather quiet for the *Star Trek* creator in the immediate aftermath of the show's cancellation.

During this period there was a dramatic change in Rod- denberry's personal life: he divorced his wife Eileen in 1968 and married Majel Barrett in a Shinto-Buddhist ceremony in Japan in 1969. The marriage had to be legalised later in the US in December once Roddenberry's divorce was finalised.

At the dawning of the new decade, Paramount seemed keen to divest itself of *Star Trek*. As the show's creator and executive producer, Roddenberry was apparently offered the opportunity to purchase all rights to the show for a figure in the region of $150,000. This was, however, beyond Roddenberry's means, both personally and in terms of commercial fundraising or bank loans. There was little sign that *Star Trek* would ever recover its original investment, so Roddenberry didn't feel he was missing out on a potential future windfall. Others, however, such as *Star Wars* creator George Lucas, would later learn from Roddenberry's mistake. Roddenberry would continue to bene- fit from the show to the tune of one-third of any future profits, but without any guaranteed creative input into the show's future direction (if, indeed, it were to have any).

Certainly, *Star Trek* did not seem to have an immediate future, consigned to the television graveyard of off-network syndica- tion where old series went to die. This meant entire seasons of shows being sold to many individual local TV stations, often at knockdown prices. It was seen as a way of generating additional revenue, especially for shows such as *Star Trek* that had not made a profit during their first-run network screenings. Over 100 was the ideal number of shows required for successful syndication in the 1960s and 70s because that allowed daily 'stripping' of the show five days a week with the same episodes only coming around twice a year or so. *Star Trek* had fallen short of the 100-episode target, but at seventy-nine episodes, the package of three years worth of shows was considered just about worthwhile for syndication. By January 1972 *Variety* reported that *Star Trek* was airing in over 100 local markets in the US and another seventy overseas.

This move into syndication would not only prove to be the saviour of the original show, but also the jumping-off point for the revival of *Star Trek* as a fully-fledged franchise of several more spin-off TV series and a hugely successful run of movies. *Star Trek* found new life and new viewers in syndication. Airing every day, often in an after-school slot, the show attracted school kids in their millions, as well as teenagers and students who had missed the first run of the series on NBC (especially in its third series' 10 p.m. Friday graveyard slot). *Star Trek* slowly but surely began to embed itself in American and then worldwide popular culture. Although the show had enjoyed a burst of popularity when it first aired, that had quickly faded during the lacklustre third series and *Star Trek* was on its way to being forgotten. Characters and phrases (including the iconic 'Beam me up, Scotty') became commonplace thanks to syndication, while the show was increasingly referenced in other TV programmes, newspapers and magazines. *Star Trek* fandom was building, and this would be instrumental in Paramount eventually reviving the concept.

The evidence for the growth of *Star Trek* fandom came in January 1972 with the first ever *Star Trek* fan convention in New York. There had been many science fiction conventions since the 1930s, such as the ones Roddenberry had attended to drum up interest in his new series. However, there had never before been a science fiction convention solely dedicated to a single TV show.

The organisers expected somewhere in the region of 500–600 attendees and had arranged to borrow twenty episodes of the show from Paramount to screen at the event. For three days, like-minded *Star Trek* fans could meet, discuss and view the show and start to build a community. Some, like the convention organisers, had previously come together as part of the various 'Save *Star Trek*' campaigns that had kept the show on air for three years. Others were isolated, mostly teenage viewers, who were happy to discover that there were other fans out there who felt the same passion for the show that they did.

*Star Trek* had already taken off on college campuses, and Roddenberry had begun lecturing at campus events to large numbers of interested students, passing on his unique vision of the future. Coming up to fifty and essentially out of work, Roddenberry welcomed this extra income. The organisers of the New York convention knew they had a success on their hands when registered attendees reached 300 by November 1971 and requests began to come in from fans across the country (and Canada) for group discounts as they planned to attend in large numbers. Two days before the event the front page of *Variety* trumpeted the unexpected success to come under the headline '*Star Trek* Conclave in N.Y. Looms as Mix of Campy Sct and Sci-Fi Buffs'. The organisers were overwhelmed when in excess of 3,000 fans turned up and spent the weekend in a convention space intended to hold no more than 1,200 people.

Roddenberry threw himself into the event, happy to talk to fans about his experiences of producing the series (for an appearance fee, of course). Beyond the formal events, Roddenberry stayed around the convention in the evening, holding court with fans in various bars telling tall tales of his exploits in the military and the world of television production, especially his *Star Trek* battle stories. Alongside Roddenberry was his wife Majel Barrett, the sole on-screen representative of *Star Trek*. She was surprised to find herself mobbed by enthusiastic fans seeking autographs.

Gene Roddenberry's Great Bird of the Galaxy moniker, accorded him in recognition of his role as creator of *Star Trek*, referred to a mythological creature mentioned by Sulu in an early episode, 'The Man Trap'. The original line was intended as a light-hearted invocation of good luck: 'May the Great Bird

of the Galaxy roost on your planet'. According to Stephen
Whitfield's *The Making of Star Trek*, written during the show's
second year, it was Herb Solow who first applied the name to
Roddenberry, but associate producer Robert Justman began
using it in memos, such as in this one from July 1966: 'If I don't
get those preliminary set sketches for "Mudd's Women", the
Great Bird of the Galaxy is going to do something nasty to you.'

As the Great Bird, Roddenberry, saw things, the New York
convention was an opportunity to reap some of the approbation
due to him that had been lacking from within the television
industry, where *Star Trek* was largely seen as a failure. He took
the chance to paint himself in as favourable a light as possible
and to claim primacy of creation when it came to *Star Trek*,
effectively sidelining all those many others who had contributed
to the effective realisation of his vision on screen. It was a process that early *Star Trek* fandom would happily collude with.
The New York event did much to create and fuel the myth of
Roddenberry as the sole creative intelligence behind *Star Trek*.

The possible return of *Star Trek* became a central discussion
point at the convention, something that Roddenberry himself –
ever the canny television producer – was keen to talk up. 'I didn't
think it was possible six months ago', said Roddenberry to *TV
Guide* about a revival of his show, 'but after seeing the enthusiasm
here [at the convention] I'm beginning to change my mind. It is
possible to do it from my standpoint.' In a prescient statement,
the *Los Angeles Times* agreed with Roddenberry's view, saying of
*Star Trek* in June 1972 that it was 'the show that won't die'.

Fan-produced *Star Trek* newsletters and fanzines had appeared
as early as 1967, with *Spockanalia* put together by fans Sherna
Comerford and Devra Langsam. As the title suggests, the first
*Star Trek* fanzine was inspired by the show's enigmatic Vulcan
character and the debut issue contained a letter from Leonard
Nimoy. The fanzine ran for five issues, through to 1970.

Many others followed into the 1970s, resulting in some
significant fan publications, notably *TREK: The Magazine for
Star Trek Fans* and *The Star Trek Concordance*. Such fan

magazines would contain non-fiction articles about the show, but would just as often publish fans' artwork, short stories or poetry, as well as often vibrant letters columns. With no new *Star Trek* on television, the fans themselves took control of the show, telling each other new adventures through fanzine short stories, many of which worked within Roddenberry's restrictions, while others set out to expand *Star Trek* beyond what was possible on 1960s television. The growing fan base for *Star Trek* demonstrated there was so much more to be explored in the concept Gene Roddenberry had brought to the screen for three short years. They took on the task of producing new stories in lieu of any new 'official' *Star Trek*, and would continue to do so even when the show returned in a series of movies and on TV. Many of those involved in fandom, fanzines and the various 'Save *Star Trek*' campaigns would go on to enjoy professional media careers, some closely connected with *Star Trek* itself.

The success of the original episodes in syndication and the visible growth of *Star Trek* fandom convinced Paramount to look once again at a property they still considered to have been something of a failure at the end of the 1960s.

An approach had been made early in 1973 by Lou Scheimer, president of the animation studio Filmation, to adapt *Star Trek* into a Saturday morning TV cartoon show. This may not have been how Gene Roddenberry had imagined *Star Trek* being resurrected, but as far as Paramount was concerned it was the only game in town: they could make some money for no outlay, while continuing to raise the profile of *Star Trek* among audiences.

Scheimer, who'd produced animated superhero shows such as *Superman*, *Batman* and *Teen Titans*, was a fan of the original *Star Trek*. However, he wasn't the only animation professional interested in the potential of an animated *Star Trek* series. Hanna Barbera – home of *The Flintstones*, the most successful TV cartoon before *The Simpsons* – had also entered talks with Paramount about bringing the show back as a cartoon.

This wasn't the first time Scheimer had pursued *Star Trek*. Back in 1969, just as the series was going off air, he'd contacted Paramount with a plan for a series of animated adventures set aboard Starfleet's training ship *Excalibur*, featuring some of the original *Enterprise* crew alongside new teenage recruits. Involved in the talks then was broadcaster NBC, who expressed concern that any planned series should be educational as well as entertaining. That project had not advanced beyond initial discussions, but in 1973 Scheimer found himself pursuing animated *Star Trek* once again.

Paramount would not sanction such a show without Roddenberry's creative involvement, while Roddenberry would not get involved in the project unless he had complete creative freedom. 'I got in touch with Roddenberry', Scheimer told Andy Mangels for *Star Trek Magazine*, 'and we hit it off very nicely. It re-established his relationship with Paramount. It literally brought them back together again. Paramount was happy because they had shows to distribute and we guaranteed the cost. Roddenberry was happy because he got to do exactly what he wanted to do. He was the one who asked me to hire D. C. Fontana. It was one of the easiest relationships I ever had with anybody.' Scheimer's willingness to accommodate all parties seems to have allowed his bid to win out over that of the bigger and more experienced Hanna Barbera.

With D. C. Fontana aboard as story editor, Roddenberry took up the role of executive consultant, guiding the series and ensuring it held true to *Star Trek* as he conceived it. Here was a chance to tell new *Star Trek* stories in a visual form, but one not limited by traditional physical television production. Writers of previous *Star Trek* live-action episodes, such as David Gerrold, Samuel A. Peeples and Steven Kandel were hired to add to the new show's authenticity. A series of seventeen (later extended to twenty-two) thirty-minute shows was commissioned by NBC Daytime, with a budget of $75,000 per episode. A total of seventy-five artists would produce between 5,000 and 7,000 drawings for each episode. The first eight hours of animation had to be created in just five months so the series could meet its September 1973 transmission date. 'Limited animation' was employed, which meant that instead of twenty-four drawings per second – as in an animated feature film – the new *Star Trek* episodes would only feature on average six drawings per second.

'We made a deal with the network [NBC] that we would do it, but we had total story control', Scheimer said. 'They had no input. They didn't want any because they were happy with what they were getting. They could talk about how much action was in there, not about any content.'

Scheimer's partner in Filmation, Hal Sutherland, directed the episodes, while Don Christensen and Bob Kline designed the animated characters. Norm Prescott handled the voice recording, and most of the original cast reunited to voice their characters. The only character missing was Walter Koenig's Ensign Chekov, supposedly due to budgetary restrictions – however, Koenig was hired to script an episode. James Doohan, a practised voice artist, would supply the voice not just for Scotty but also for new, semi-regular alien character Lieutenant Arex, as well as many other incidental voices. Majel Barrett returned to the series to voice Nurse Chapel, alien Lieutenant M'Ress and the *Enterprise* computer, beginning an association with *Star Trek* spin-offs that would continue up to her death (and even beyond, with 2009's *Star Trek* movie). Only the first three episodes saw the core trio of Shatner, Nimoy and Kelley reunite as a group to record their dialogue: subsequent episodes would be constructed from individual recordings made at times that suited the artists' availability. Nimoy had also made a successful argument for the continued involvement of George Takei and Nichelle Nichols when Filmation initially proposed using Doohan and Barrett to play their roles. Nimoy recognised the growing iconic nature of the characters and the fact that the original actors should continue to play the roles, effectively laying the ground for the later *Star Trek* movies.

Scheimer set out to make his animated *Star Trek* a match with the original series. Unlike most animated shows, it would not be aimed at children, with comedy characters and simple storylines. He wanted Roddenberry's *Star Trek* to essentially carry on where it left off, but in animated form, even though it would be appearing alongside the rest of the cheap and cheerful, child-focused animated fare on Saturday mornings. Speaking to *Show* magazine in the early 1970s, Roddenberry said: 'That was one of the reasons I wanted creative control. There are enough limitations just being on Saturday morning. We have to limit some of the violence we might have had on the evening shows. There will probably be no sex element to talk of either. But it will be *Star Trek* and not a stereotype kids' cartoon show.'

Several of the episodes were sequels or follow-ups to episodes of *The Original Series*, including David Gerrold's 'More Tribbles, More Troubles', 'Once Upon a Planet' (a follow-up to 'Shore Leave') and the Harry Mudd-featuring 'Mudd's Passion'. Koenig's episode, 'The Infinite Vulcan', had ties to the original series' 'Space Seed' (itself inspiration for the movie *The Wrath of Khan*). D. C. Fontana scripted 'Yesteryear' (a source heavily tapped for the young Spock sequences in 2009's *Star Trek* movie), which went on to win an Emmy Award for Excellence in Children's Programming. Great efforts were made to ensure that the animated series looked, felt and sounded like original *Star Trek*. The bridge of the *Enterprise* looked similar in drawn form (with the addition of an extra turbolift), as did the major characters, while the episodes used the same distinctive sound effects as the original series. Although the animation was limited and shots were often repeated within episodes, the series succeeded because of the serious stories it was telling. Fans who had come to *Star Trek* through the syndication reruns now had brand new episodes to call their own, and new sources to fuel their own fan fiction that was continuing to expand the storytelling of the *Star Trek* universe.

*The Animated Series* had several advantages over the previous live-action series. It was easier for writers to be sure that their outlandish notions could be realised in the medium of animation in a way that simply couldn't be achieved in live-action photography with 1960s resources. If it could be drawn, it could now be shown. Locations, aliens, monsters and starships were only limited by the writers' and artists' imaginations, the strictures of the *Star Trek* universe – and, of course, deadlines. It undoubtedly gave a new lease of life to *Star Trek* in a most unexpected way.

The animated show also managed several *Star Trek* firsts that would recur in later TV series or movies. The holodeck, so much a part of *The Next Generation* and subsequent series, was first portrayed in 'The Practical Joker', while 'How Sharper Than a Serpent's Tooth' featured the first Native American character in *Star Trek* (long before *Voyager*'s Chatokay). Even Captain Kirk's middle name (the initial 'T' was for Tiberius) was revealed in the animated episode 'Bem', and it became part of the official canon thereafter (no matter what the gravestone in 'Where No Man Has Gone Before' might read!). The series also introduced Commodore Robert April, a previous captain of the USS *Enterprise* (using the name for the original *Enterprise* captain from Roddenberry's series proposal).

The *Los Angeles Times* commented favourably on the new animated *Star Trek* in September 1973, noting its maturity for a Saturday morning cartoon show. 'NBC's new animated *Star Trek* is as out of place in the Saturday morning kiddie ghetto as a Mercedes in a soapbox derby. Don't be put off by the fact it's now a cartoon . . . It is fascinating fare, written, produced and executed with all the imaginative skill, the intellectual flair and the literary level that made Gene Roddenberry's famous old science fiction epic the most avidly followed programme in TV history, particularly in high IQ circles. NBC might do well to consider moving it into prime time at mid-series'.

A move to prime time never happened, but the animated *Star Trek* did prime the pumps for an audience now more hungry than ever for new *Star Trek* adventures. It would only be a matter of time, surely, until *Star Trek* returned as a full live-action TV series for the 1970s. '[*Animated*] *Star Trek* was not a children's show', Scheimer said. 'It was the same show that they would have done at night time. We did the same stories, [with] the same writers. The fans loved it, but it was not a kid's show.'

Gene Roddenberry was hoping for a positive outcome from *The Animated Series* – and that didn't necessarily include a full revival of *Star Trek*. For a few years after *Star Trek* ended, and with the failure of his attempts to break into Hollywood movies, Roddenberry was living off his not inconsiderable savings rather than generating any new income through writing.

He wasn't short of ideas for projects, and the success of *The Animated Series* made it possible for Roddenberry to get some of these long-gestating shows into production. He already had a new TV series pilot made and ready to air on CBS: *Genesis II*, a riff on *Buck Rogers* that sees a twentieth-century man thrown forward in time to the post-apocalyptic twenty-second century. Alex Cord starred as Dylan Hunt, a name reused by Majel Barrett, now Majel Roddenberry (who co-starred in the pilot) for the later Gene Roddenberry-inspired series *Andromeda*.

*Genesis II* was notable for its anti-*Star Trek* pessimistic view of the future in which the Earth has been ravaged by nuclear war and civilisation struggles to survive: all very far removed from the utopia of the Federation. Aired on 23 March 1973, the show did well enough for CBS to commission a further six scripts, including one by D. C. Fontana. When CBS eventually passed on the series, Roddenberry interested ABC, who backed a second, reworked pilot – in a situation very reminiscent of *Star Trek*'s origins. Roddenberry rewrote his material under the new title *Planet Earth*, with John Saxon replacing Cord as Hunt (mirroring Shatner replacing Jeffrey Hunter). Poor reviews for *Planet Earth* killed off any prospect of an ongoing series, and the name Dylan Hunt would be forgotten, until the debut of *Andromeda*, starring Kevin Sorbo, in 2000.

Also in development was *Questor*, a ninety-minute pilot co-written with *Star Trek*'s Gene Coon for NBC, and *Spectre*, another pilot script that Roddenberry worked on with Samuel A. Peeples. The pair also collaborated on *The Tribunes*, another

Timeless 85

script about futuristic law enforcement that did not sell. *Questor* was intended to be a series about a humanoid robot making his way in the modern world. Featuring some of the characteristics that would later be seen in the character of Data on *The Next Generation*, Questor was hunting for his creator while enjoying a buddy relationship with human engineer Jerry Robinson. Although written as a starring vehicle for Leonard Nimoy, the TV movie featured Robert Foxworth – a *Star Trek* guest star who was a studio-imposed choice that Roddenberry could not reject. Retitled *The Questor Tapes* – in anticipation of a weekly series – an additional six scripts had been ordered in case the series was commissioned. However, the proposed show was thought to clash too strongly with another Universal project that was due to air on ABC: *The Six Million Dollar Man*, a series eventually produced by future *Star Trek* movie producer Harve Bennett.

In spring 1975 Gene Roddenberry found himself moving back into his old *Star Trek* office on the Paramount lot. Although he'd made several attempts to move on from *Star Trek*, Roddenberry had bowed to the inevitable and was back working with Paramount to develop a potential $5-million *Star Trek* movie. *The Animated Series* – concluded just seven months before – had shown there was still life in the concept, as had the unexpected success of *The Original Series* in syndication and the exponential growth of *Star Trek*'s creative fandom.

Roddenberry started work on a movie script called *The God Thing*. The story reunited the crew of the starship *Enterprise*, with Kirk now an admiral and Spock having returned to Vulcan to explore his heritage. They set out to confront an unknown force threatening Earth – which may be God, the Devil or something else altogether. These basics would survive through to the eventual *Star Trek: The Motion Picture* in 1979. However, Paramount studio executives Barry Diller and Michael Eisner rejected Roddenberry's script treatment – an outline of the proposed screen story – in the summer of 1975. This was followed by the cancellation of the scheduled start of shooting, originally planned for July 1976.

Roddenberry then turned to recent film school graduate and writer Jon Povill (who'd co-drafted a screenplay for the Philip K. Dick short story 'We Can Remember it for You Wholesale' under the title *Total Recall*, finally filmed in 1990). Povill came up with a *Star Trek* time travel story in which Scotty was transported to Earth in 1937 and changed history by introducing advanced Starfleet technology. As a result, humanity found itself enslaved by an all-powerful computer and the future was changed. Travelling back in time, the *Enterprise* crew had to find Scotty and correct the altered timeline. Roddenberry judged Povill's work to be great for an episode of an ongoing TV series, but not suitable for a would-be blockbuster motion picture. The pair then set to work together on a new approach to *Star Trek* that would please Paramount's executives, who were seeking an epic story suitable for the big screen. In an echo of the early days of *The Original Series*, other writers were also asked to pitch ideas for the proposed movie, among them *Star Trek* veteran John D. F. Black and science fiction author Robert Silverberg. Black's story, which saw the *Enterprise* save the entire universe from an all-consuming black hole, was deemed by Paramount to be 'not big enough' for a movie, while Silverberg's plan to have the *Enterprise* crew battle aliens for possession of the artefacts of a long-dead advanced civilisation was similarly rejected.

Things became so desperate at Paramount that even Harlan Ellison – still sore at Roddenberry for comprehensively rewriting his series episode – was called in to pitch a *Star Trek* movie idea. 'Between 1975 and 1979 there was a parade of writers through Paramount's gates whose abilities were sought for a *Star Trek* film', wrote Ellison in *Starlog* in 1980. 'I know because I was one of them.' Ellison's story saw a race of intelligent reptiles travel back in time to wipe out mankind and allow lizards to evolve as the dominant species on Earth. Distortions of the timeline result, causing the *Enterprise* crew to travel back to the dawn of time to confront the reptile aliens, only to be faced with the moral question of whether they have the right to eliminate an intelligent species simply to ensure their own survival. 'The story spanned all of time and all of space, with a moral and ethical problem', noted Ellison, suggesting it might be 'big' enough for Paramount. At a meeting of movie executives and Roddenberry, Ellison was asked if he could work in the ancient Mayan civilisation (then a hot topic in books such as Erich von Däniken's *Chariots of the Gods?*). When Ellison pointed out that there were no Mayans at the dawn of time, the Paramount executive claimed no one would know the difference. Ellison said he'd know the difference. 'I got up and walked out', Ellison told Stephen King for *Danse Macabre*, King's book on the craft of writing, 'and that was the end of my association with the *Star Trek* movie.'

By July 1976, Chris Bryant and Allan Scott – a British writing team – had been recruited for the stalled *Star Trek* movie. They had written the Nicolas Roeg-directed thriller *Don't Look Now*, drawn from a Daphne du Maurier short story. Paramount studio executives approved their new *Star Trek* treatment, entitled *Planet of the Titans*, in October 1976 and they set about writing the full screenplay. This *Star Trek* film even had a budget and a director attached: $7.5 million and Philip Kaufman (later to write and direct *The Right Stuff*, an adaptation of Tom Wolfe's novel). Ken Adam – who'd worked on the James Bond movies *Dr. No*, *Goldfinger* and *Thunderball* – was hired as production designer. Ralph McQuarrie, fresh from working on the yet to be released *Star Wars*, was working on a new look for the big screen *Enterprise*.

Initially the movie was written without the character of Captain Kirk, after Paramount failed to agree terms with William Shatner to reprise the role. However, with the film now a 'go' project, Shatner soon changed his position, signing on to the project.

In the script, Starfleet and the Klingons are brought into conflict by the discovery of the apparent home planet of a long-extinct, but legendary, race known as the Titans. The technological secrets of this ancient race could be valuable to whoever controls them. Two new threats emerge – a black hole about to consume the planet, and the Cygnans, the ancient enemies of the Titans. Attempting to escape both threats, the *Enterprise* plunges into the black hole. The ship arrives in the distant past, apparently orbiting Earth. Kirk and the crew encounter primitive man, shows them the benefits of fire, and in the process themselves become the Titans of galactic legend.

Despite all the positive moves surrounding the pre-production of *Planet of the Titans*, Paramount rejected the completed screenplay. Kaufman undertook a drastic rewrite, trying to match the screenplay to Paramount's notion of what *Star Trek* on the big screen should be, but all he had to go on was that they wanted more than an expanded TV episode. Kaufman set out to explore the dual nature of Spock in some detail, teaming him up with a Klingon to be played by Japanese actor Toshiro Mifune. 'My idea was more of an adult movie dealing with sexuality and wonders [with] Spock and Mifune's characters tripping in outer space', claimed Kaufman. 'I'm sure the fans would have been upset.' By May 1977 – after two years of development work on a *Star Trek* movie – *Planet of the Titans* was as dead as Roddenberry's *The God Thing*, and Kaufman moved on to remake *Invasion of the Body Snatchers* instead. That same month saw the release and phenomenal success of *Star Wars*. Paramount was worried that the appetite for a blockbuster science fiction film had been sated by George Lucas' super-successful space opera, so felt no one would now want to see a *Star Trek* movie, not realising that *Star Wars* was about to kick-start a whole new era in science fiction filmmaking. It was only the success of Steven Spielberg's *Close Encounters of the Third Kind*, later that same year, that prompted Paramount executives to think again about *Star Trek*. They had one of the most widely recognised science fiction concepts of all time, and now they were about to bring it back where they felt it belonged: on television!

In the middle of 1977, *Star Trek* was promoted as the flagship show to lead a proposed fourth US television network (alongside CBS, NBC and ABC) backed by Paramount Studios. The network would be launched with an all-new two-hour *Star Trek* TV movie in February 1978, followed by an ongoing series of one-hour episodes. As well as a series of original TV movies, the network would also carry mini-series based on successful epic novels such as *The Winds of War* and *Shogun*.

Gene Roddenberry had been on the Paramount lot for almost two years, working on the various aborted *Star Trek* movie ideas. Now he was back in comfortable territory: in charge of a *Star Trek* television show. Dubbed *Star Trek: Phase II*, the new series would take advantage of technological advancements in television production, while recapturing *The Original Series'* sense of optimism and wonder about the future in space. Unlike in the late 1960s, both Paramount and Roddenberry were now confident that new *Star Trek* episodes on TV would be met by a welcoming and growing audience: the fans were out there, and they were hungry for new stories. It was time to make the most of this previously neglected studio asset.

Roddenberry recruited two key staff members: production executive Robert H. Goodwin (filling the practical producer role previously held by Robert Justman) and creative producer Harold Livingston, who would be responsible for developing the scripts. Roddenberry attempted to poach designer Matt Jefferies, who had worked on the original *Star Trek* series and had originated the look of the *Enterprise*, from his job on *Little House on the Prairie*. Jefferies managed to briefly work on both projects, before recommending his old Desilu assistant Joe Jennings for the art director role. Jefferies rapidly updated the old *Enterprise* design for the new series, while retaining many of its distinctive features.

While scripts were being devised and a series 'bible' created,

Paramount had to negotiate once more with *Star Trek*'s main cast members. Most had been signed up, paid and released in relation to *Planet of the Titans*, so the hope was that an offer of a pilot TV movie plus an initial thirteen-episode television series would be attractive to actors whose careers had not exactly blossomed since *Star Trek*. The sticking point this time was Leonard Nimoy. Fearing that the actor – who had perhaps been the most successful of the *Enterprise* crew post-*Star Trek* – would not want to commit to a full-time series, Roddenberry offered him the pilot and guest appearances in two episodes. It was hardly surprising he turned that offer down. It looked like *Star Trek: Phase II* would launch without Spock, so Roddenberry devised a new Spock-like replacement. A Vulcan named Xon with many of the characteristics later echoed in *The Next Generation*'s android Data would feature instead.

Similarly, although William Shatner was happy to sign up for the new show, Paramount feared they would not be able to retain the expensive actor for subsequent years if the series was to take off. As a form of insurance, Roddenberry devised a second-in-command character who could become a replacement captain if need be. Commander Will Decker was put in place as the *Enterprise*'s number two (anticipating the creation of Commander Will Riker for *The Next Generation* in the 1980s). Meanwhile, Shatner reportedly feared that his role of Captain Kirk would either be reduced to cameo guest appearances in a handful of episodes or dispensed with altogether through the dramatic move of killing off Kirk.

While a new six-foot fibreglass *Enterprise* model was being constructed, *The Original Series* costume designer William Ware Theiss was back on *Star Trek*, developing new uniforms for the crew of the revamped 1970s *Enterprise*. Roddenberry, Livingston and Povill had all contributed to the new series bible and writers' guide. 'The challenge was coming up with things that weren't repeats of ideas already explored [in *The Original Series*]', said Povill. 'We were definitely striving for things that were different, fresh and also *Star Trek*.' *Phase II* was now ready to recruit a new team of storytellers to add to Roddenberry's growing universe.

Among the writers signed up for the new show was USC screenwriting tutor Alan Dean Foster. He'd adapted the animated *Star Trek* series episodes into short stories for the *Star Trek Logs* paperbacks (just as James Blish had adapted the majority of the live-action *Star Trek* episodes into short story form). Foster was hired to adapt an old story idea from Roddenberry into a *Star Trek* outline. Entitled 'Robot's Return', the story was originally planned for the aborted *Genesis II* series. Alan Dean Foster adapted it into a script entitled 'In Thy Image'.

Originally intended as the first of the regular one-hour episodes of *Phase II*, 'In Thy Image' brought the action back home to twenty-third-century Earth, a place never visited by the original *Star Trek* series. The action of *Phase II* was to take place in a period after the conclusion of the original 'five-year mission', prompting a visit by the *Enterprise* to Earth for a complete overhaul. In developing the project, it was felt that Foster's story should become the basis of the two-hour pilot movie, which would begin with the *Enterprise* refit just being completed in Earth orbit. The crew reunion aspects of the original planned pilot (drawn from Roddenberry's *The God Thing* movie idea) would be merged with Foster's version.

There was an important *Phase II* creative meeting in early August 1977, attended by Paramount executives Jeffrey Katzenberg and Michael Eisner. Alan Dean Foster pitched his 'In Thy Image' story in some detail, at the end of which Eisner (seemingly without any irony, given this was a *Star Trek* TV series meeting) declared: 'We've been looking for a [*Star Trek*] feature [film] for years, and this is it!' Those attending the crucial meeting, including Goodwin, Livingston and Roddenberry, were stunned. For the past month Paramount executives had been struggling in their attempt to secure advertiser support for their fourth television network concept, which was itself to have been built around the *Phase II* series. By the end of July 1977 it was clear that the time was not right for Paramount to proceed. That decision also meant the end of *Star Trek: Phase II* as a television series. The project had already incurred $500,000 in development costs and there were several significant future commitments (to potential cast and crew) that would have to be honoured, whether the project progressed or not. Whatever the fate of the proposed Paramount TV network, something would have to be salvaged from the wreckage of *Phase II* so the studio could recover the substantial investment already made.

The initial plan was to continue with production on the two-hour pilot movie and see if that could be sold to one of the existing networks as a broadcast event. If that succeeded, then perhaps a full television series could follow. However, at the conclusion of the August meeting, Eisner decided that *Star Trek* would instead become a movie – as had originally been intended when Roddenberry had returned to Paramount almost three years earlier.

However, until the administrative requirements of switching the *Phase II* project to a feature film could be completed, production would have to continue as if *Star Trek* was still returning as the already-announced TV series. Having cancelled *Planet of the Titans* and announced *Phase II* in quick succession in recent months, Paramount did not want to suffer the embarrassment of a third disappointing *Star Trek* announcement. Nothing could be said publicly until the studio was ready to fully announce the new *Star Trek* feature film.

By the middle of 1977, *Star Trek: Phase II* was essentially a zombie project – it was still walking around as if it were alive, but the top creatives involved knew their new TV show was dead on its feet. The intended fate of the project would be kept secret from those working on it – only those who were in attendance at the August meeting knew the truth. There was still a possibility that a new *Star Trek* TV series might follow the film, so any script, production art and other material produced for *Phase II* might then prove to be useful (much of the development work would actually prove to have a direct influence on

*The Next Generation* in the late 1980s). For the next five months (essentially the rest of 1977), development work on *Phase II* would continue.

Gene Roddenberry's immediate task was to adapt the 'In Thy Image' story to a movie screenplay while keeping the pre-production work on *Phase II* ticking over, without giving anything away to the team putting in the creative work on the officially abandoned show. The basic story of an unknown, artificial object heading for Earth – clearly a potential threat – and the entanglement with it of the *Enterprise* crew was retained. However, the big problem Roddenberry had to solve was the nature of this unknown object: what is it and what does it want? The breakthrough came when Roddenberry moved on from the object being 'God' to it being something in search of 'God' (or, at the very least, its creator). He also noted that the creative team had discussed making the object 'Pioneer 10 [or] a later NASA probe'.

Meanwhile, Harold Livingston was commissioning writing assignments for *Phase II*, canvassing likely new *Star Trek* episodic storylines from writers such as Ted Sturgeon ('Shore Leave', 'Amok Time'), Walter Koenig (who'd scripted an episode of *The Animated Series*), and David Gerrold ('The Trouble With Tribbles'). By the end of the month, building had begun on the brand new, revamped *Enterprise* bridge set – with few of those involved aware that it would not be used for *Phase II* but would instead feature as the central set for *Star Trek: The Motion Picture*.

In September William Shatner was contracted to once again play the role of Captain James T. Kirk, presumably contracted to a feature film rather than a TV series. The search was ongoing for actors to portray Commander Decker and Spock replacement Lieutenant Xon, as well as the new female character of Ilia (a forerunner of *The Next Generation*'s Counsellor Troi).

The drive to commission thirteen individual episode scripts proceeded alongside the building of the *Enterprise* sets, even though Livingston knew the writers' work would be unlikely to be used. Following 'In Thy Image' would be Norman Spinrad's

'To Attain the All', concerning an artificial planet that is revealed to be a 'living' computer that enhances the crew's intellectual abilities. Other planned episodes included 'The Prisoner' by James Menzies, which had the *Enterprise* crew lured to a planet by visions of twentieth-century icons including Einstein and Buster Keaton. Logos, an alien, is behind the deception: he's so obsessed with mankind that he plans to absorb the entire species, beginning with the *Enterprise* crew. Scriptwriter Schimon Wincelberg would have returned to *Star Trek* with 'Lord Bobby' (AKA 'Lord Bobby's Obsession'), an episode that dealt with honour and sacrifice while featuring a character recalling Trelane in 'The Squire of Gothos' and anticipating *The Next Generation*'s Q, alongside the return of the Romulans. William Lansford's 'Devil's Due' drew heavily on one of *Star Trek*'s predecessors, *Forbidden Planet*, and was later adapted for *The Next Generation*'s fourth season.

Richard Bach, writer of *Jonathan Livingston Seagull*, had two scripts in development for *Phase II*. 'Practice in Waking' was an alternate reality story that put the *Enterprise* crew in artificial environments created through directed dreaming. 'Bach is a *Star Trek* fan', wrote Harold Livingston in a 1977 memo, '[and] has submitted two stories'. The second was 'A War to End Wars' that saw a repressed society annually release its emotions through starship combat (somewhat echoing *The Original Series* instalments 'The Return of the Archons' and 'A Taste of Armageddon'). A rewrite by Arthur Bernard Lewis replaced the starships with combat by android and saw Kirk get romantically involved with a female android.

'The Savage Syndrome' seemed to combine the titles (if not the plots) of 'The Savage Curtain' and 'The Immunity Syndrome' from *The Original Series*. This storyline, by Margaret Armen and Alf Harris, was a ship-set story designed to be a cheaper to make episode (often called 'bottle shows' and made using only regular standing sets). Alien technology would have unleashed the *Enterprise* crew's primal urges and seen them split into warring factions (one led, of course, by Kirk). It was an exploration of the inherent savagery lying just beneath the surface of mankind's civilisation, and in theme and character exploration, ideally suited to the new *Star Trek*.

Alongside the revised 'Devil's Due', another storyline originally intended for *Phase II* was later revived for *The Next Generation* due to the 1988 Writers Guild of America strike. Jon Povill's 'The Child' (initially co-written with Jason Summers) saw Lt Ilia give birth to a Deltan child that attracts the interest of a curious alien life form that wishes to study the *Enterprise* crew. The episode was eventually rewritten, replacing Ilia with ship's counsellor Troi.

Old *Star Trek* episodes were often the inspiration for ideas developed for *Phase II*. 'Tomorrow and the Stars', by Larry Alexander, was a virtual retelling of Harlan Ellison's 'The City on the Edge of Forever'. Thrust back in time due to a transporter malfunction, Kirk falls in love with a married woman on the eve of the Japanese raid on Pearl Harbor. As before, Kirk has to resist the temptation to put a woman he loves – and the lives of hundreds of others – above ensuring history unfolds as it should. The story originated in an abandoned outline for Roddenberry's planned *Genesis II* series and had been allocated to Alexander. 'Pearl Harbor is good because it is visual' said the writer.

David Ambrose, author of the British 1970s conspiracy-based TV hoax *Alternative 3*, wrote a teleplay entitled 'Deadlock', dealing with mind control. A subversive paramilitary organisation within Starfleet plots to overthrow the Federation by seeding mind-controlled 'fanatics' in key positions. It's a very 1970s conspiracy-minded idea, like *All the President's Men* or *The Parallax View*. Some of these concepts resurfaced in *The Next Generation* episode 'Conspiracy', originally planned as the basis for an abandoned ongoing story arc.

Other *Phase II* storylines that were ultimately dropped included 'Are Unheard Melodies Sweet?', an episode that saw an alien try to capture the crew using illusions and fantasy, an idea dating back to 'The Cage'. Worley Thorne's story was distinguished by its inclusion of nudity and suggestive situations that would never have made it to air. Theodore Sturgeon proposed a comedy episode called 'Cassandra', about a young, clumsy yeoman and a tiny, Tribble-like creature that causes havoc aboard the *Enterprise*.

Perhaps the most promising of all the storylines was John Meredyth Lucas' planned two-part episode 'Kitumba'. The story would have seen the return of the infamous Klingons, but would have explored their culture in a more serious way than ever happened on *The Original Series*, and was only achieved to a greater extent on *The Next Generation*. Kirk is sent on a secret mission, accompanying a Klingon defector to the Klingon home world. Their plan is to locate the 'Kitumba', the rightful ruler of the planet, in order to avoid a war between the Klingons and the Federation. 'I wanted something we'd never seen on the series before', said Lucas, who'd been a producer in *The Original Series*' second year and had written 'The Changeling', 'Patterns of Force' and 'That Which Survives', and directed 'The Ultimate Computer' and 'The *Enterprise* Incident'. He'd also both written and directed the episode 'Elaan of Troyius'. '[I wanted] penetration deep into enemy space – then I began to think about how they lived. I tried to think what Klingon society would be like and the Japanese came to mind'.

While Roddenberry believed writers would have no trouble getting to grips with the new *Star Trek*, he failed to understand that television and its audiences had moved on in the decade since the original show was on air and so would be expecting a different kind of storytelling. There were also three new characters (Decker, Xon and Ilia) for scriptwriters to contend with, and one major character (Spock) missing altogether. There was also the question of making a new show that appealed to the original *Star Trek* fans (who were desperate for their favourite show to return) and a potentially wider audience turned on to space opera science fiction by *Star Wars*.

With Shatner on board, the new character roles were quickly filled. David Gautreaux won the role of Xon, while model–actress – and former Miss India – Persis Khambata was signed up to play the sensitive Ilia. Despite this sign of progress, those working on *Phase II* began to notice that deadlines were being ignored, shooting dates were looming and the studio executives appeared unconcerned. This was extremely unusual in television production, and it soon began to become apparent to all that the show they were working on was destined never to appear on a television screen. The shooting date was looming for the two-hour pilot episode, and the pivotal role of Commander Decker had still not been cast. There was even some question about whether the character (originally a possible Kirk replacement) was needed for what was now intended to be a movie rather than a TV series. The real priority was the feature film script for 'In Thy Image' that Harold Livingston and Gene Roddenberry were rapidly – but secretly – redrafting.

Roddenberry's November 1977 rewrite of Livingston's script was the first step in a process that would cause him to once again lose control of *Star Trek*. The others involved in the movie and *Phase II* project considered Roddenberry's rewrite to be too intellectual (a criticism similar to those aimed at the original *Star Trek* pilot 'The Cage') and – more damningly – dull. It fell to Paramount executive Michael Eisner to decide between the scripts. He dubbed Roddenberry's version to be 'television' and Livingston's to be 'a movie' and 'a lot better'. Roddenberry's take was not without merit, so a decision was taken to create a third draft combining the best elements from both the competing versions, leaning heavily on the Livingston draft.

The biggest problem came at the climax. The alien threat was now identified as the long-lost Earth space probe *Voyager* (dubbed *V'ger*), searching for its creator. Unconvinced that mankind, as represented by the *Enterprise* crew, would be capable of creating an entity such as *V'ger*, the wayward probe threatens to destroy the planet. The solution was to see the largely redundant Will Decker merge with *V'ger*, thus informing the intelligent probe of mankind's achievements and saving Earth. Many of these core elements would be maintained through to the eventual production of *Star Trek: The Motion Picture*.

By December 1977, Hollywood gossip columnist Rona Barrett had gone public with information well known within the upper echelons of Paramount: *Star Trek: Phase II* was a dummy project and the space-faring franchise was now set to be revived as a movie. Her report was business based, focusing on Paramount's abandonment of the planned fourth TV network. The studio continued to deny anything had changed, except for a delay in the launch of the Paramount network to fall 1978. Among those still in the dark about the project's change in nature were the series' episodic writers, who continued to work on scripts for a show that the studio knew was never going to happen. Povill, Livingston and Roddenberry participated in the charade, taking the time to read all the story outlines and offer notes as if the series were going ahead. No one involved creatively at the lower levels of the production of *Star Trek: Phase II* had any real reason to suspect otherwise. But after a decade of struggle and false starts, by 1979 *Star Trek* on television was finally pronounced dead. Now, *Star Trek* was going to the movies.

# Chapter 6

## Persistence of Vision:
## The Original Cast Movies

*'The question was not whether we killed Spock, but whether we killed him well.'* Nicholas Meyer

The story of the most successful *Star Trek* movies is primarily the story of three creative individuals: Harve Bennett, Leonard Nimoy and Nicholas Meyer. They would be the driving forces – in various capacities – behind the movies from *Star Trek II* to *Star Trek VI*, with William Shatner carrying the can for the poorly performing *Star Trek V*. However, to begin with it was down to one man to launch *Star Trek* on the big screen: the series' creator, Gene Roddenberry.

All the work done on the TV series was now repurposed for the movie, which was not as easy as it might sound. For example, the quality of finish required for sets (such as the new *Enterprise* bridge) on television was much lower than that required for a film image that would be projected onto the big screen. Everything – sets, costumes, props and special effects – now had to be brought up to movie quality.

The biggest problem of all was still the script, which had gone through many drafts with several writers alternately tackling the story ideas in the form of a TV pilot or a would-be blockbuster movie. It's little wonder that the attempted November 1977 combination of all previous scripts into one satisfied no one. There were questions of approach and tone: was this to be like an expanded episode of the original series? Would broad comedy be suitable for *Star Trek*? Should it be heroic space adventure, like *Star Wars*, or a more contemplative, thoughtful film, like *Close Encounters of the Third Kind* or some of the better episodes of the original *Star Trek* series? The questions were endless, and few people – even Gene Roddenberry – had answers that everyone involved could get behind and support. The only thing that seemed to be agreed on was that the *Star Trek* movie should be full of 'startling special effects', a 'light show' that would 'dazzle the senses', according to a script memo from Jon Povill.

What had been proposed originally as a $3-million TV movie in the mid-1970s quickly ballooned to an $8-million feature film, then a $15-million blockbuster (in comparison, 1977's *Star Wars* had cost in the region of $9 million in direct production costs). The final tally (including all the amounts spent in development on *Phase II*) would eventually be a whopping $44 million.

Although Paramount had tried to maintain the fiction that *Phase II* was an active project, by March 1978 they had to come clean. The appointment of director Robert Wise to helm what was now being dubbed *Star Trek: The Motion Picture* gave the game away. Wise was an old Hollywood hand who'd directed many classics, including *West Side Story* (1961) and *The Sound of Music* (1965). More relevant to Paramount were his science fiction and fantasy credentials on *The Day the Earth Stood Still* (1951), *The Haunting* (1963) and *The Andromeda Strain* (1971). Wise had started out as a film editor working with Orson Welles on *Citizen Kane* (1941), before moving on to directing for producer Val Lewton with *Curse of the Cat People* (1944). He was regarded as a safe pair of hands to helm Paramount's biggest movie project in years.

As the creative point man on any film project, the director is generally regarded as the authority figure on set (sometimes for specific projects producers or writers can hold that position, but for the majority of films the director is the driving force). A single voice in the form of an authoritative director was exactly what *Star Trek: The Motion Picture* needed to break the logjam that was crippling the production. The problem was that this was not any run-of-the-mill movie but *Star Trek*, and the series' creative godfather Gene Roddenberry was still very much involved. While Robert Wise was able to take command of the creative departments (sets, costumes, props, make-up, special effects) and get them all pulling in the same direction to realise the film, he still had to deal with the politics of Paramount, the involvement of Roddenberry and a far from finished script.

The first action Wise took was to resolve any outstanding issues with Spock actor Leonard Nimoy, bringing him back on board the project (and in the process dropping new Vulcan character Xon), as he knew it would be impossible to have *Star Trek* without Spock. Secondly, Wise recalled writer Harold Livingston to rework the 'In Thy Image' script from the ground up, removing all the rewriting done by Roddenberry, Povill and others through countless confused drafts. Wise wanted a script that contained the same ideas and action, but was written for the big screen rather than cobbled together from failed TV pilot drafts.

From the first musings about a possible *Star Trek* film, by D. C. Fontana in a fanzine called *Star-Borne* in 1972, through Gene Roddenberry's 1975 script 'The God Thing' to Harold Livingston's 1977 script 'In Thy Image', the voyage of *Star Trek: The Motion Picture* to its first day of principal photography on 7 August 1978 had been a long and complicated one.

Robert Wise started shooting barely eighteen months before the planned December 1979 release date, with an unfinished script and no idea if the studio could handle the special effects required by the story (which had remained true to the basics of *Phase II*'s 'In Thy Image'). With new script pages arriving on set daily, the film was still without an agreed ending well into shooting (script revisions were so numerous that some were noted not just by the day they were made, but by the hour).

With scenes on the redesigned *Enterprise* bridge and transporter platform completed in the studio, the production relocated for three days to Yellowstone National Park to shoot the scenes on Vulcan featuring Nimoy. The film's realisation of

Vulcan (easily outstripping anything seen on the original TV show) would be augmented with the use of visual effects and matte paintings for a convincing otherworldly feel. However, by the end of August the production was around two weeks behind the planned shooting schedule. It would be 26 January 1979 before shooting wrapped on the film after 125 days, with a huge amount of post-production work still to be done.

The creation of the special effects for *Star Trek: The Motion Picture* proved to be the biggest headache for the production. Robert Abel and Associates were appointed to realise the *Enterprise*'s encounter with *V'ger*, but found the work and the tight schedule daunting. Paramount brought in effects specialist Douglas Trumbull (*2001: A Space Odyssey*, *Close Encounters of the Third Kind*) to rescue the project and ensure it met the release date. Despite all the time and money available, the film was barely completed in time for release, with Wise always considering it to have been a 'rough cut': an unfinished project released due to commercial deadlines. *Star Trek: The Motion Picture* was not audience tested due to lack of time (something Wise regretted) and the film's just-completed print was delivered to the premiere in Washington DC by the director himself. 'I saw the completed film for the first time on December 1, just three days before our premiere. I cut about ten minutes and had a new master printed. The film that was ultimately shown was a rough cut, the kind of film you show at your first sneak preview. You really never know what you have until you get your film in front of an audience.'

The reviews of *Star Trek: The Motion Picture* were definitely mixed, with *Variety* taking a positive view: '[The film] includes all of the ingredients the TV show's fans thrive on: the philosophical dilemma wrapped in a scenario of mind control, troubles with the spaceship, the dependable and understanding Kirk, the ever-logical Spock, and [a] suspenseful twist ending.' Roger Ebert, of the *Chicago Sun-Times* called the film 'about as good as we could have expected' but lacking the 'dazzling brilliance and originality of *2001*'. The film's lengthy running time – much of it taken up with special effects sequences – was heavily criticised, resulting in the movie becoming widely known as *Star Trek: The Motionless Picture* or *Star Trek: The Slow Motion Picture*. David Denby, of *New York Magazine*, noted how much of the film consisted of characters reacting to things on view screens, making the experience 'like watching someone else watch television', perhaps intended as a veiled criticism of the movie's television origins.

Opening in 859 cinemas, the movie grossed $11.8 million across the opening weekend, beating the record previously set by *Superman* (1978) for the same time of year. Within a week the box office had risen to $17 million, eventually reaching a final US total of $82.25 million. The film eventually grossed $139 million worldwide and scored three Oscar nominations (for Art Direction, Visual Effects and Original Score by Jerry Goldsmith). Despite this, within Paramount the long-gestating film was considered a disappointment. The costs of the abandoned *Star Trek: Phase II* project were attached to the movie. Blame was attached to Gene Roddenberry, and while the studio decided they would like to produce a quicker and cheaper sequel film, the creator of *Star Trek* would not be involved.

For his part, Leonard Nimoy was glad he'd returned to *Star Trek* but was equally glad that the process had come to an end with the release of *The Motion Picture*. 'I felt liberated', he wrote in his autobiography, *I Am Spock*. 'No longer would I have to deal with questions like "Why won't you do *Star Trek* again? Are you sick of Spock?" The hype and expectation brought out a large audience for a short period of time – and then it was over. I felt I'd taken off the Spock ears for the last time. That, I thought, is the end of that.'

For William Shatner, writing in his book, Star Trek *Movie Memories*, he came from playing Captain Kirk again to attending the premiere believing the film 'was gonna be nothing short of terrific. Later, watching the film with a perspective that was a bit more honest I thought to myself, "Well, that's it. We gave it our best shot, it wasn't good, and that'll never happen again." Shows you what I know.'

Director Robert Wise would get the chance to revisit *Star Trek: The Motion Picture* and finish it to his satisfaction in 2001, just four years before he died. An extended TV cut of the movie had debuted in 1983 on ABC, with twelve minutes of restored footage, but Wise had not been involved. The arrival of DVD allowed him to return to the 'unfinished' movie and advances in computer special effects allowed him to not only re-edit the movie but also revise and complete some of the special effects. Using the script, storyboards, studio memos and the director's recollections, an attempt was made in this special edition to bring the film closer to the original intentions. The re-released film was 136 minutes, four minutes longer than the original 1979 release. The re-edited Director's Cut of *Star Trek: The Motion Picture* was better paced, featuring a better balance between special effects and character drama, and was better reviewed than the original.

For all its faults, *Star Trek: The Motion Picture* succeeded in a most spectacular way. It not only brought *Star Trek* back from oblivion (thus setting the scene for all the spin-off TV shows that followed), but it also launched a new series of big screen adventures for the original *Star Trek* TV crew that would run throughout the 1980s.


After the overblown *Star Trek: The Motion Picture*, the executives at Paramount knew a very different approach had to be taken for the sequel. It had to be produced quicker, cheaper and better, yet still serve what they now had box office proof for: an audience that was hungry for more *Star Trek*. The second movie would be a chance for those now creatively in control to get it right.

Paramount's President of Production Jeffrey Katzenberg had been concerned about the race to have the first movie ready in time for its locked-in release date. He was not about to allow the same thing to happen again, so he sought out a safe pair of hands to look after the *Star Trek* movie franchise. Paramount's Barry Diller, Michael Eisner and Katzenberg collectively decided that Roddenberry would carry the can for the near-fiasco of *Star Trek: The Motion Picture*.

Reluctant to alienate Roddenberry completely, and worried what he might tell the *Star Trek* fan base if he was cut loose from the studio, Paramount offered the series' creator the role of 'executive consultant' on the planned second movie. It was a meaningless title with next to no creative involvement, but it came with a fee attached (and a share of the box office). More importantly for Roddenberry's not inconsiderable ego, it avoided the ignominy of him being thrown off his own creation entirely. It was not an ideal situation, but it was one Gene Roddenberry could live with if it meant the continuation of his *Star Trek*-related income.

Producer Harve Bennett was handed the *Star Trek* movie franchise, with a tight brief to bring the second film in on time, on budget and to quality. Bennett had come to Paramount from TV and had been on the lot less than a week when he was interviewed in connection with the *Star Trek* job. On graduating from film school, Bennett had been an executive at CBS and ABC before moving into television production in the late 1960s with *The Mod Squad*. Throughout the 1970s he'd produced several television series and mini-series, including *The Six Million Dollar Man* and spin-off *The Bionic Woman*; *Rich Man, Poor Man*; *The Invisible Man* and *The Gemini Man*.

Called to a meeting with Diller and Eisner, Bennett was surprised to also meet Charles Bluhdorn, head of Paramount's owner Gulf + Western. Bluhdorn had been very unhappy with *Star Trek: The Motion Picture*, but recognised that the company had a great asset in *Star Trek*, if used well. He quizzed Bennett about his opinion of the film. Deciding to be truthful, Bennett told the assembled executives that he'd found the movie 'boring'. Could he do better with less than the $45 million the first film had cost? Bluhdorn asked him. Without thinking, Bennett automatically responded with: 'Yes. In fact, I could make five or six movies for that!' He was tasked on the spot to produce the next *Star Trek* film.

One of Bennett's first questions was about Roddenberry's role in the new project. The new producer was told that Roddenberry was a consultant only, someone who'd pass comment on the script and creative elements of the film, but not someone to whom Bennett would have to report. In fact, across the next decade and four movies the bulk of their creative contact would be in the form of memos rather than in person. That was enough for Bennett, who saw an opportunity to escape his television background and make the break into feature film production. There was one problem: Bennett had never seen the *Star Trek* TV show.

The producer screened all seventy-nine episodes of the original series, both to familiarise himself with the show and to get a feel for the series – he was also on the lookout for suitable story ideas for the second film. One episode stood out for Bennett. 'Space Seed' starred Ricardo Montalban as a genetically enhanced villain named Khan Noonien Singh. Khan and his followers had been exiled upon a barren planet at the end of the instalment, with Kirk and Spock speculating about what might become of them. An answer to that question, and the return of the charismatic Khan, would form the basis for Bennett's *Star Trek II*.

Bennett worked out a sequel story that brought Kirk and Spock into conflict with Khan once again – and would result in the death of the Vulcan science officer. 'I wanted to do it suddenly', said Bennett of the death of Spock, originally planned for an end-of-act-one surprise, like the death of Janet Leigh in Alfred Hitchcock's *Psycho* (1960). He brought TV screenwriter Jack B. Sowards onto the project to draft an initial screenplay from his story, while he dealt with strong objections to the storyline from Gene Roddenberry.

Bennett was obliged to treat Roddenberry's input in good faith. 'I would estimate that about 20 per cent of the points that he made were included in some form in the next script draft', recalled Bennett, although the central storyline and approach formulated by the new producer changed little. Bennett believed that the death of Spock would up the ante for the *Star Trek* film series and prove to be an irresistible draw to fans and a wider audience.

Another reason for including that story development was to

secure the participation of Leonard Nimoy one more time. The actor had made it clear that following *Star Trek: The Motion Picture* he was once more done with the series. He refused to come back for the sequel, until Bennett said to him: 'How would you like a great death scene?' The promised death of Spock was enough to make the actor reconsider his position and sign on to star in the new film.

The surprise plot development was leaked to wider *Star Trek* fandom (almost certainly by a disgruntled Roddenberry) and was quickly distributed through a network of fan groups and fanzines (this was, of course, long before the days of the internet when such information is communicated so much more easily and widely). As a result, Paramount faced a 'Don't Kill Spock' letter-writing campaign run by *Star Trek* fans. Roddenberry seized on the outcry he had more likely than not created (after all, the producer did have form) to back up his argument that killing off such a pivotal character would be a mistake. Bennett continued to resist, arguing in favour of the drama of the scene and its consequences for the *Star Trek* universe, and concluding that he would not allow fans to dictate the dramatic development of *Star Trek*. The one concession he did make – now that the 'secret' plot point had leaked – was to move Spock's death to the climax of the film.

Hired to direct was Nicholas Meyer, whose only previous directorial credit was *Time After Time* (1979), which saw H. G. Wells (Malcolm McDowell) travel to modern San Francisco in pursuit of Jack the Ripper (David Warner). He would later direct the controversial nuclear holocaust TV movie *The Day After* (1983). Meyer was initially brought onto the project to write a further draft of the Bennett–Sowards screenplay (he'd started his career as a novelist, and had written a screenplay based on his own Sherlock Holmes novel, *The Seven Per Cent Solution*, made into a movie by Herbert Ross in 1977). Within twelve days Meyer delivered a reworked screenplay that was better organised dramatically and seemed to meet the needs of all the interested parties at Paramount. He was then confirmed as the director of the second *Star Trek* film.

Meyer recalled the writing process in his memoir, *The View From the Bridge*. 'I worked, juggling the plots, subplots and characters we had all agreed on – materials first imagined in bits and pieces by five disparate authors – trying to weave them into a cohesive whole. I was not burdened by reverence for the series. I was of the opinion that *Star Trek* could stand some fixing. I made up the rules as I needed them and wrote my own dialogue. I was writing the movie I wanted to see.'

Meyer combined the action-adventure requirements of a populist *Star Trek* movie with some thoughtful themes about ageing and death. 'This was going to be a story in which Spock died, so it was going to be a story about death, and it was only a short hop, skip, and a jump to realize that it was going to be about old age and friendship', noted Meyer.

He confronted head-on something that those involved in *Star Trek* could all see, but were reluctant to acknowledge – the 1960s cast was beginning to visibly age, despite their various Hollywood attempts to appear timeless and unchanging. By the early 1980s, none of the original *Star Trek* cast looked the same as they had in the 1960s, and Meyer felt it important to acknowledge what would be staring movie audiences clearly in the face on giant cinema screens. He opted to make that part of the theme of the film, a driving force for various characters' motivations and decision points. Meyer noted: 'The second *Star Trek* movie revolves around a training cruise aboard the *Enterprise*, supervised by a reluctant Kirk, who, promoted to Admiral, is now a depressed desk jockey, brooding about his age. Thirsting for vengeance, Khan and his band (marooned by Kirk) hijack the *Reliant* and lay a trap for Kirk. The climax of the film is a 'submarine' battle between Kirk and his nemesis in a lightning-splattered nebula, in which Spock sacrifices his life to save his captain and the crew of the *Enterprise*.'

Complicating the thematic content of the film and heightening the dramatic stakes, Meyer gave Kirk a long-lost old flame in the form of research scientist Carol Marcus and a son – David – whose life he'd not been involved in. Both are caught up in the machinations of Khan, and serve to remind Kirk of the kind of life he has missed through his commitment to Starfleet. These were issues that *The Original Series* had only occasionally been able to touch upon. Given the prominence of death in the movie, Meyer turned to Shakespeare for a quote to use as a title, settling on 'The Undiscovered Country', Hamlet's phrase for the world beyond death.

Leonard Nimoy had been tempted back aboard the *Enterprise* by the promise of a dramatic death scene, but the ship was still without a captain, the now Admiral Kirk. William Shatner reportedly hated the screenplay, probably because a lot of the dramatic focus fell on the character he'd always seen as his side-kick, Spock (although *Star Trek* fans had long ago decided on the importance of Spock's role to the franchise). While the screenplay contained many solid, dramatic scenes for Shatner to play, the actor was predictably uncomfortable with confronting the theme of ageing that was central to the drama.

The sticking point seemed to be the fact that the screenplay specified an age for Kirk, and it was this that was upsetting Shatner. 'The revisions proved remarkably simple', admitted Meyer in his memoir, 'and in the end Shatner's needs were easily fulfilled.' Shatner described the resulting revised screenplay as 'terrific', although all Meyer had done was to delete any specific numerical references to Kirk's age. The rest was the same script that Shatner had previously professed to 'hate'.

Meyer brought in George Lucas' special effects house Industrial Light and Magic (ILM) to provide many of the special effects for *Star Trek II*. While the majority of the work was traditional film models, especially for the climactic confrontation of the two starships (the *Enterprise* and the hijacked *Reliant*), ILM also pioneered the use of computer-generated imagery or computer graphics in the Genesis Project sequence. Intended to depict the terraforming of a planet – renewing a barren landscape to make it suitable for human habitation – in the past the sequence would have been traditionally animated. Using computers to create special effects would gradually become the norm in filmmaking, but *Star Trek II* was one of the first to use the technique in a commercial film.

The shooting of the pivotal death of Spock scene was saved until the end of the production process. 'It was my job to make Spock's death plausible, meaningful and moving', wrote Meyer in his memoir. 'If we botched the job, people would throw things at the screen. If we did it correctly and the death proceeded organically from the material, no one would ever question it.' After fifteen years of living with Spock, Leonard Nimoy was nervous on the day the scene was to be filmed – after all, he was saying goodbye to an alter-ego that had meant a lot to him, even if the relationship had been a troubling one. During the shooting of *Star Trek II* there was talk of making a third film in the series, and Nimoy's more commercial instincts may have been telling him he'd be silly to distance himself from *Star Trek* just as it was on the verge of ever-greater success. As it was, the atmosphere on stage during the shooting of the dramatic sacrifice scene anticipated that which would pervade cinemas where the movie screened: several of the production crew were observed to have tears in their eyes as *Star Trek*'s Vulcan hero breathed his last. 'It took about a day to film the death of Spock', relates Meyer. 'Some of us understood the significance of that eternal moment while it was unfolding.'

Released in the US on 4 June 1982, *Star Trek II: The Wrath of Khan* enjoyed considerable success, garnering $97 million worldwide on a budget of around $11 million. The film's opening weekend – at the time the largest opening weekend gross in movie history – brought in $14.3 million, reaching a total of $78.9 million in the US, and becoming the sixth highest grossing film of the year. The final total may have been less than that of *The Motion Picture*, but the substantially lower production cost meant the *Star Trek* sequel was much more profitable.

Critical reaction was more uniform than that in response to the first film, with many welcoming the dramatic nature of the easy to follow storyline. The improved pacing in comparison to its predecessor was much commented upon, with the *Washington*

*Post* and the *New York Times* feeling the movie was much closer in spirit to the original TV series. The stronger storyline was welcomed by the *New York Times*, while *Variety* praised the new movie's stronger character interaction. Spock's death was deemed to have been dramatic and well handled by the *Chicago Sun-Times'* critic Roger Ebert, although he feared the film sometimes verged on melodrama and he saw the climactic battle sequences as tepid.

For *Star Trek* fans (and many critics) *The Wrath of Khan* would be regarded as the film that saved the *Star Trek* movie franchise. It had shown that *Star Trek* could fill the big screen in a dynamic and exciting way that faithfully recalled the TV series but also pushed on to new frontiers – and was unafraid of taking risks, such as killing off Spock.

Recognising a successful production when they saw one, the executive team at Paramount kept Harve Bennett on board for the next *Star Trek* movie. Although there were plenty of sequel movies through the 1980s, few were as heavily serialised as Bennett would make the second, third and fourth *Star Trek* movies. *Star Trek III* would pick up directly from the end of the second film and take the characters and drama forward into a new adventure. There would also be a moment of high drama to match the death of Spock in *Star Trek II*: the destruction of the starship *Enterprise*. As with Spock's death, Gene Roddenberry objected to this latest development. 'I thought it was a foolish piece of waste', he said. 'I don't know what they gained by losing the *Enterprise*, other than a moment in a film. The *Enterprise* was really one of our continuing characters.'

Part of the climactic action of *The Wrath of Khan* had been cooked up between Harve Bennett and Leonard Nimoy on set during filming. Just before Spock takes action to save the *Enterprise*, thus leading to his death, he delivers the notorious Vulcan nerve pinch to Dr McCoy, so the medic will not interfere. Bennett had come from episodic television, and was aware that *Star Trek* might well return for a third episode. Laying possible story threads that could be picked up in the next movie, Bennett (with Meyer's reluctant agreement: he wanted Spock's death to be final) had Spock perform a mind-meld on McCoy, with the crucial line of dialogue – 'Remember' – suggested by Nimoy himself. This also served to provide a response to Roddenberry's main criticism of the film, namely the apparent death of Spock. Few knew at that point how – or if – the implications of that brief moment might be picked up in another *Star Trek* film.

Bennett had to first persuade Nimoy to return once again if they were to seriously pursue the option of resurrecting Spock. After each *Star Trek* movie Nimoy had considered himself to be finished with the character. The actor always had a confused relationship with his Vulcan creation (to the extent that he issued two autobiographies at different times, one called *I Am Not Spock* and another titled *I Am Spock*). If Nimoy had not fully grasped the implications of the brief 'Remember' scene, he did understand the meaning of the surprise appearance of Spock's burial tube on the Genesis planet (a scene added by Paramount and not shot by Meyer) in the closing moments of *The Wrath of Khan*: he would be wanted once again to play Spock.

The two key *Star Trek* stars who returned for *The Wrath of Khan* managed to gain pay-or-play deals (meaning they would be paid whether the projects proceeded or not) for two additional non-*Star Trek* acting projects from Paramount as part of their negotiations. Nimoy knew what his deal-breaker would be this time around: he wanted to direct. Nimoy recalled that he (and Shatner) had campaigned for the opportunity to direct episodes of the original *Star Trek* TV series back in the 1960s – but had been consistently turned down, although Shatner was scheduled to helm a late season three instalment that was never made due to the show's cancellation. Now Nimoy saw his opportunity: in return for reviving Spock in *Star Trek III*, he wanted to direct the movie.

Expecting to meet studio resistance, Nimoy was pleasantly surprised to find much support for the idea among the Paramount executives, including Harve Bennett (Nimoy had previously directed a TV movie that Bennett had produced, *The Powers of Matthew Starr*). Perhaps more surprising was the support of studio boss Michael Eisner. According to Nimoy's *I Am Spock* memoir, Eisner immediately latched on to the promotional aspects of the idea: 'Leonard Nimoy directs the return of Spock? I love it!' Nimoy noted of Eisner's reaction, 'He was so enthusiastic, I went totally slack-jawed.' Eisner even asked Nimoy if he'd like to write the script, but the actor was content to leave that task to Harve Bennett.

Picking up the story threads planted in *The Wrath of Khan*, *The Search for Spock* reveals that the 'Remember' scene saw Spock implant his 'katra' (his essential essence) within McCoy's psyche during the mind-meld as a back-up, in case he perished attempting to save the *Enterprise*. Realising this, Kirk and his crew steal the *Enterprise* in order to retrieve Spock's body from the Genesis planet and reunite it with his katra. In the process they come into conflict with hostile Klingons, led by Kruge (Christopher Lloyd), who are after the secrets of the Genesis device. Kirk's newly found son David Marcus is killed, and the *Enterprise* is destroyed.

As far back as *The Motion Picture*, William Shatner and Leonard Nimoy had enjoyed a 'favoured nations' clause in their contracts, meaning each would be offered the same benefits as his co-star. Shatner therefore expected to also direct a film in the *Star Trek* movie series, regarding that as a benefit to be shared. Starting work on *The Search for Spock*, Shatner admitted to finding being directed by his co-star difficult and awkward until he got used to the situation. The absence of Spock from much of the movie allowed Nimoy to focus on his work behind the camera. The third film in the series finally offered a prominent role to DeForest Kelley as Dr McCoy, the incongruous and unexpected carrier of Spock's katra. The rest of the regular *Star Trek* cast all had their moments, but none beyond the three central bridge characters really had a chance to make any significant impact.

Once again Bennett's TV production habits kicked in and he decided to open the film with a series of clips from the previous movie to remind audiences of the key story threads, the same way a TV series might open a new episode that built on last week's developments. The difference with the *Star Trek* movies was that audiences would go years between instalments. In writing the screenplay, Bennett had the film's ending in mind from the beginning. It was obvious that the crew would find and resurrect Spock, so Bennett came up with the 'Your name is . . . Jim' line to signal that Spock's consciousness had survived. As a result the movie is perhaps rather predictable with all the dramatic high points fairly well telegraphed, even though Bennett took the opportunity to feature the Klingons as big screen adversaries.

Following the ageing and death themes of *The Wrath of Khan*, Bennett introduced a more optimistic friendship and commitment theme to *The Search for Spock.* The film would be about the central trio of *Star Trek* characters' commitment to each other. Kirk is prepared to break the rules to save Spock, while McCoy – despite his comic antagonism to his Vulcan friend – takes on the burden of carrying his katra. For his part, Spock had enough faith in Kirk and McCoy to trust them to bring him back from beyond death. While Roddenberry objected to story developments such as the destruction of the *Enterprise*, he remained silent about the apparent introduction of Christian sacrifice and resurrection themes to his previously usually anti-religious series.

Produced on a slimline $16-million budget, *Star Trek III: The Search for Spock* opened on 1 June 1984, competing with other summer blockbusters that year including *Indiana Jones and the Temple of Doom*, *Gremlins* and *Ghostbusters*. Breaking the record-making weekend gross of the second *Indiana Jones* movie released the week before, *The Search for Spock* recovered its production budget in its opening weekend. The movie went on to gross $76.5 million in the US, reaching a total of $87 million worldwide.

The third *Star Trek* movie was not as widely acclaimed as *The Wrath of Khan*, with critics praising its sense of grand space opera, while commenting on the movie's lower production values. Roger Ebert, in the *Chicago Sun-Times*, called the movie 'Good, but not great', while *USA Today* praised the film as the best of the three and the closest in spirit to the original TV series. Nimoy's direction was approved of by the majority of critics, with *Newsweek* acclaiming *The Search for Spock* as the best-paced of the three movies to date. However, the shock dramatic developments of David's death and the destruction of the *Enterprise* were criticised by some as obvious and manipulative moves. Fans broadly welcomed the further adventures of the *Enterprise* crew, but for most the third film did not trump *The Wrath of Khan* as the best *Star Trek* movie.

Many of the ideas developed for the first *Star Trek* movie had involved time travel. One of the best episodes of the TV series – Harlan Ellison's 'The City on the Edge of Forever' – had seen Kirk, Spock and McCoy travel to Earth's past for an adventure. For the fourth *Star Trek* movie, which would conclude the trilogy begun with *The Wrath of Khan*, Bennett resolved to send the *Enterprise* crew back to contemporary Earth. This gambit would not only give the often otherworldly *Star Trek* series a direct connection to its contemporary audience, but it would also help with the budget if scenes could be shot in an environment requiring no 'futuristic' set dressing.

Working on the story together, Leonard Nimoy (who would again direct following the success of *The Search for Spock*) and Harve Bennett set out to develop a film with an environmental theme: not only were environmental problems gaining mainstream attention in the mid-1980s, but the idea seemed to fit with one of *Star Trek*'s original successful ploys. The new film would tackle a contemporary subject in the futuristic dressing of *Star Trek*, just as many episodes of the original series had taken on 1960s social and political concerns wrapped up in a space opera setting.

Another thing both storytellers agreed on was that *Star Trek IV* needed a more light-hearted tone than the high drama of the previous two movies. While the stakes would be high and there'd be plenty of incident, it was felt that the *Star Trek* characters had been put through the emotional wringer in *The Wrath of Khan* and *The Search for Spock*, so the fourth movie would go lighter on them. All the pair had to do was settle on what the story would actually entail – they only knew that some element from their past (the audiences' present) would need to be retrieved by the *Enterprise* crew to save their future.

Before much further progress was made on these ideas, however, the project was dealt a body blow. William Shatner was no longer interested in playing Kirk. 'I was being "difficult", at least according to the studio', wrote Shatner in *Star Trek Movie Memories*. 'I steadfastly refused to sign on the dotted line for our new film, holding out partially in an effort to make up for two decades' worth of nonexistent residuals [payments for repeat screenings of TV episodes] and merchandising revenues. [I cited] the fact that our previous three films had earned the studio well over a quarter of a billion dollars.'

Initially it looked like Shatner's gambit would not pay off. A change at the top of Paramount meant that new executives were in charge of the *Star Trek* movies. Michael Eisner and Jeffrey Katzenberg had both left to run Disney, and Barry Diller had gone to Fox, finally achieving the dream of Paramount's fourth TV network elsewhere. The new head of the studio was distribution man Frank Mancuso, with Ned Tanen supervising motion pictures and Dawn Steele appointed head of production. While all were committed to continuing the *Star Trek* motion picture franchise, none of them was wedded to the successes and failures of the past movies, so they were open to new directions.

Faced with a missing-in-action Admiral Kirk, Nimoy and Bennett had to come up with an alternative plan. Bennett's first suggestion was one that would resurface many times over the next two decades in connection with a variety of *Star Trek* projects. He suggested a prequel movie chronicling Kirk and company's time at Starfleet Academy, their pre-*Enterprise* adventures. This would require the characters to be younger, thus entailing recasting the core *Star Trek* crew, solving the Shatner problem. Nimoy could even appear in the movie as the older Spock, either as a narrator in a narrative wraparound or through some time travel device, allowing him to actually take part in the action. The new executive team at Paramount was apparently open to taking the *Star Trek* movies in this direction.

They also had other, more outré ideas for *Star Trek*. One of the biggest stars Paramount had in the mid-1980s was Eddie Murphy. Nimoy had actually approached Daniel Petrie Jr, writer of Murphy's star-making movie *Beverly Hills Cop* (1984) to work on *Star Trek* when the concept of featuring Murphy in the *Star Trek* movie was tabled. Outgoing Paramount executive Jeffrey Katzenberg described this as 'either the best or worst idea in the world'. Nimoy and Bennett were tempted by the notion as a way of attracting non-*Star Trek* fans to the fourth movie, although they were also wary of the fact that Murphy's comedic presence might unbalance the film and even lead to *Star Trek* being ridiculed. Murphy himself claimed to be a huge *Star Trek* fan and was very positive about the idea of being included in the film. Writers Steve Meerson and Peter Krikes worked on a Murphy-centric screenplay that would see him play a contemporary college professor who believes in aliens and meets the *Enterprise* crew in a series of comedic encounters. In the end, Murphy opted to make *The Golden Child* (1986), having decided he didn't like the *Star Trek* role offered, claiming he'd rather play an alien or a Starfleet officer. It also seems that business sense ruled the day at executive level at Paramount – there was little point combining two multi-million-dollar franchises (*Star Trek* and Eddie Murphy) into one when separately they'd bring in twice as much revenue.

The Eddie Murphy detour cost seven months of development time in 1985, and in the end Nimoy and Bennett returned to their 'time travel to the past to save the future' idea, this time with Admiral Kirk part of the action as Shatner was back on board, having negotiated a larger financial compensation package (which Nimoy also benefited from, thanks to their shared 'favoured nations' clause). Writer–director Nicholas Meyer was brought back into the *Star Trek* fold to help script the fourth movie after opting out of number three as he felt 'I didn't want to resurrect Spock' as such a move 'attacked the integrity and the authenticity of the feelings provoked by his death. However, by the time we got to *IV*, Spock was alive, it was a de facto thing, and on top of that my friends were in trouble.'

The first order of business was to decide exactly what the 'MacGuffin' – Alfred Hitchcock's term for an otherwise insignificant plot motivator – from the past needed to save the future would be. Several things were considered, including violin-makers and oil drillers, or the cure to a disease that could only be found in the rainforests (extinct in the future). It was Nimoy's reading of a book about the extinction of animal species that set them on the path to whales. Having humpback whales extinct in the future, but needing to retrieve some from the past, seemed like an idea that would give the film a wide appeal beyond just *Star Trek* fans. The addition of mysterious whale song to the film helped to secure the story: a destructive space probe in the future threatens the Earth while seeking an answering whale song to its signal. Kirk, the newly resurrected Spock, McCoy and the crew use the Klingon Bird-of-Prey ship to slingshot around the sun in an effort to travel to the past in order to bring some living whale samples back to the future. Everyone involved in the project recognised that the opportunity for culture clash moments between the twenty-third-century humans and those from 1986 would allow for a lot of natural comedy without the star casting of Eddie Murphy.

So it proved: *Star Trek IV: The Voyage Home* was released on Thanksgiving weekend, 26 November 1986, to huge critical acclaim and astonishing box office receipts. The first five days saw the movie gross $39.6 million in the US, against the production budget of just $21 million. Globally, the film was a huge success, totalling $133 million at the worldwide box office. Originally scheduled for release at Christmas, Paramount head Frank Mancuso had suggested bringing the film forward to

Thanksgiving, a switch that gave the film greater life in the holiday period leading up to Christmas.

The fourth *Star Trek* movie was a huge crossover success with the plight of the whales, the contemporary setting and the accessible character humour all attracting a sizeable non-fan audience to the film. The *Washington Post* dubbed the picture 'immensely pleasurable Christmas entertainment', while the *New York Times* felt the latest instalment had 'done a great deal to ensure the series' longevity'. Again, there was much comment on how the film was true to the critics' memories of the TV series, while having the characters play up to their reputations in the popular imagination proved a masterstroke in bringing in a wider audience. An easy to engage with contemporary issue in the possible extinction of the whales (and other species) made the film relevant to broad 1980s audiences, without being environmentally preachy. Above all, *The Voyage Home* was a great slice of entertainment that would be well remembered by all who saw it.

Following *The Voyage Home* was always going to be difficult. Given that Leonard Nimoy had directed two hugely successful entries in the franchise, it might have been expected that he'd continue with the fifth. However, due to the parity between Nimoy and his *Star Trek* co-star, it was clearly now Shatner's turn to be the driving force behind a *Star Trek* movie. It seems likely this was part of the negotiation that had brought Shatner back on board to star in *Star Trek IV* – that he'd be the one behind the camera on *Star Trek V*. Shatner also took the opportunity to develop the storyline for the fifth movie, as Nimoy had done for the fourth. Overseeing the production, as on the previous movies, was Harve Bennett, even though he had attempted to opt out of the series after *The Voyage Home*.

In developing his storyline, Shatner was inspired by the sight of growing numbers of tele-evangelists prospering in American culture. Shatner was entranced by the fact that people like Jim and Tammy Faye Baker and Jimmy Swaggart were not only hoodwinking (in his opinion) millions of

Americans into believing their Christian-inspired storytelling, but also getting many of them to part with their hard-earned cash so the tele-evangelists could live high on the hog. Shatner combined the figure of a preacher who hears the word of God with one of Gene Roddenberry's earliest ideas for a *Star Trek* film – the *Enterprise*'s quest for God – to come up with a plot for *Star Trek V*. The 'God' eventually discovered would be an all-powerful alien being that Kirk and company would have to defeat.

This idea, and the resulting script from writer David Loughery (*Dreamscape*), did not meet the same positive reception from the studio and *Star Trek* cast members as the previous movie. Under Shatner's initial direction Loughery had crafted a story that promoted Kirk at the expense of the other main characters: while they fell for the proselytising of the unicorn-riding, Vulcan mystic Zar (later revised to be Sybok, the previously unknown half-brother of Spock), Kirk was the sole hold-out for reason and the only one who could save them all. Specifically causing discontent were the scripted actions of Spock and McCoy, who allow Sybok to take command of the *Enterprise* because they buy into his mystical vision. In the process they betray Kirk, although he has to rescue them from themselves by the climax. Naturally, Leonard Nimoy and DeForest Kelley were not impressed by this take on their characters and (as Shatner had done on *Star Trek IV*) they asked for substantial script revisions.

Having previously objected to the death of Spock in *The Wrath of Khan* and the destruction of the *Enterprise* in *The Search for Spock*, this time Roddenberry objected to the entire basis for William Shatner's *Star Trek* movie in a series of memos and letters. Writing to Shatner, Roddenberry stated, 'I simply cannot support a story which has our intelligent and insightful crew mesmerised by a 23rd-century religious charlatan.' In a memo to Harve Bennett, Roddenberry was even blunter in his assessment of the proposed storyline: 'It is not *Star Trek*! [This] will destroy much of the value of the *Star Trek* property.' He also sent a summary of his feelings on the matter to his lawyer,

Leonard Maizlish, to prepare him for any dealings with Paramount. 'The errors of property format, science and fact in this movie story are nothing less than shocking', wrote Roddenberry. In a later memo to Shatner and Bennett, he explained that in his opinion the suggested story 'demeans and degrades *Star Trek* with subject matter that it has assiduously avoided in the past ... Please abandon this story laden with mesmerisation, pop psychology, flim flam betrayal, a lack of power, a lack of humour. Please do something with the ingredient that is the hallmark of *Star Trek* . . . believability.' Roddenberry even recruited authors Isaac Asimov and Arthur C. Clarke to his cause, but it was all to no avail. While Roddenberry could clearly see that Shatner's storyline for *Star Trek V* was in no way a suitable follow-up to the crowd-pleasing and immensely successful *The Voyage Home*, no one else at Paramount appeared to agree (or at least appeared willing to take on the might of Shatner's contractual arrangements and considerable ego). Although the script went through many revisions and was improved in Roddenberry's eyes, the fundamental basis of the storyline was so flawed he felt the film was beyond salvaging.

There were other pressures on Paramount. The studio was keen to capitalise quickly on the success of *The Voyage Home* with another movie, while the looming 1988 Writers Guild of America strike was threatening to curtail any new film's development time. They also had a new *Star Trek* TV series in *The Next Generation* to promote and wanted the film to drive viewers to the TV show, and vice versa. The rush into production, with an underdeveloped script and an inadequate budget and time scale meant that the finished film suffered immensely, just as Roddenberry had foreseen it would. The original climax on the 'planet of God', Sha Ka Ree, (meant to sound like Sean Connery, the former James Bond whom Shatner hoped would play Sybok) was to feature an attack upon the *Enterprise* crew by a rock monster. The effects used to create the sequence were, however, considered too poor for a major motion picture and this climax was abandoned. Shatner later admitted of his rock man, 'Our guy in the silly rubber suit ultimately just looked like . . . well, a guy in a silly rubber suit. I realised that the already compromised ending of my movie was now in serious trouble.' In post-production Shatner attempted to save the scene: 'My God effect looked cheesy, and the hastily concocted light blob, designed to replace our disastrous rock man, was truly disappointing. Harve [Bennett] and I tried to scrape up the funds to reshoot the ending, but found the studio purse strings tightly knotted. [This] hastily thrown together ending left us dead in the water. It was the ruination of that film.'

As with the release of *The Wrath of Khan*, the new *Star Trek* movie was up against sequel films featuring Indiana Jones and the Ghostbusters in the summer of 1989. Although upon opening on 9 June *Star Trek V: The Final Frontier* achieved the highest opening gross of any *Star Trek* film to that date, taking $17.4 million, the film's initial success was not to last. With a production budget of $27 million (the highest yet for a *Star Trek* movie, excluding *The Motion Picture*), *The Final Frontier* grossed just $52 million in the US and reached a worldwide total of only $70 million, almost half of the $133 million taken by *The Voyage Home*. Despite this disappointment, the movie was still the tenth highest grossing film of the year.

A series of very critical reviews contributed heavily to the significant underperformance of a movie Paramount had been privately projecting could gross in excess of $200 million. The *Washington Post* called the movie 'a shambles', while the *Chicago Sun-Times* critic Roger Ebert was scathing of Shatner's directorial efforts: 'There is no clear line from the beginning of the movie to the end, not much danger, no characters to really care about, little suspense, uninteresting or incomprehensible villains, and a great deal of small talk and pointless dead ends.' Fans generally regard *The Final Frontier* as the worst of the *Star Trek* movies by far, second only to 2002's *Star Trek Nemesis*.

For the final *Star Trek* film to feature the original 1960s cast all together, the man who'd previously saved the *Star Trek* movie franchise twice was called back into action. After *The Motion Picture* tanked, Nicholas Meyer had revived *Star Trek* with *The Wrath of Khan*. After *The Search for Spock* failed to be as exciting as its predecessor, Meyer had written the screenplay for the most popular *Star Trek* film to date, *The Voyage Home*. Now, after William Shatner's encounter with God in *The Final Frontier* had proved to be something of a damp squib, the producers turned to a tried and tested storyteller: Nicholas Meyer was once more seen as the only man who could save *Star Trek*.

In 1991, *Star Trek*'s twenty-fifth anniversary was looming, so Paramount wanted something special. Harve Bennett had once more touted his long-cherished idea for a Starfleet Academy movie (dubbed by detractors and supporters alike as '*Top Gun* in space'), only for it to be dismissed once again in the face of a hostile reception for the idea from *Star Trek* fans and the (no doubt self-interested) cast of the current movie series. The rejection of his idea for the second time resulted in Bennett quitting the *Star Trek* films and withdrawing from the role of producer on *Star Trek VI*.

Instead, the successful idea for *Star Trek VI* came from Leonard Nimoy, who as he had done with *The Voyage Home* – suggested that the film should take its theme from contemporary political or social issues, reflecting the often successful gambit of *The Original Series*. In response to the fall of the Berlin Wall in 1989 and the end of the Cold War, Nimoy asked, 'What would happen if the Wall came down in space?' To this were added aspects of the Chernobyl nuclear disaster of 1986, recrafted as the environmentally devastating destruction of the Klingon moon Praxis. This event throws the Klingon Empire into turmoil, resulting in the prospect of a peace treaty with the United Federation of Planets. However, other factions are at work that will use assassination to prevent the peace from happening in a bid to further their own aims. The story puts the safety of Klingon Chancellor Gorkon (David Warner) in the hands of Kirk, whose son was killed by Klingons in *The Search for Spock*.

The Paramount studio executives had one proviso for

writer–director Meyer: this sixth movie should serve as a swan song for the original *Star Trek* television cast, who were now considered too old to front an action-adventure movie franchise. Meyer brought in Denny Martin Flinn to co-write the screenplay, deliberately layering in those contemporary political references. The Cold War and Chernobyl aspects made sense, thought Meyer, as the Klingons had always been *Star Trek*'s stand-ins for the Russians. The assassination plot was felt suitable, as leaders who sue for peace (as Chancellor Gorkon – modelled on Russian leader Mikhail Gorbachev – would do) often found themselves attacked by their own side (or others) serving their own entrenched self-interests.

To keep costs down, much of the film was shot on the *Enterprise* sets then in use by *The Next Generation* TV series, redressed and lit differently for the film. Because many of Paramount's studio stages were also in heavy use at the time of the film's production, much of the movie would be shot on location around Los Angeles. Shatner, Nimoy and Kelley all agreed to cuts in their respective fees to keep the budget low, opting instead to be paid from the film's net profits.

Once again, as with so many of the films in the *Star Trek* series after *The Motion Picture*, Gene Roddenberry disapproved of *Star Trek VI: The Undiscovered Country* (using the title Meyer had originally intended for *The Wrath of Khan*). He and Nicholas Meyer had a fundamentally different take on the future as depicted in *Star Trek*. While Roddenberry had long spoken of an idealistic future where bigotry and prejudice did not exist, Meyer believed such traits – often the basis of dramatic conflict needed in good storytelling – would never be eliminated from human nature. Even though Roddenberry was revered as the Great Bird of the Galaxy and *Star Trek*'s originator, long-standing fans enjoyed and approved of much of Meyer's fresh take on Roddenberry's creation. Of the six original *Star Trek* movies, *The Wrath of Khan*, *The Voyage Home* and *The Undiscovered Country* are widely regarded as the best, and all featured the heavy involvement of natural storyteller Nicholas Meyer.

Released on 6 December 1991, *Star Trek VI: The Undiscovered Country* opened to another record-breaking weekend for the *Star Trek* series, taking $18 million at the box office. The film went on to gross $74.8 million in the US, totalling a worldwide take of $96.8 million overall. It was a significant improvement over the dismal *The Final Frontier*, justified by a significantly improved film, but it could not match the runaway mainstream popularity of *The Voyage Home*. Critics found the movie to be a welcome step up from its predecessor, and many saw it as a suitable sign off for the venerable *Star Trek* crew of the 1960s, who by the 1990s were being eclipsed by their younger counterparts on television's *The Next Generation*. The Australian newspaper the *Herald Sun* welcomed the film's 'suspense, action and subtle good humour', while *USA Today* commented that 'this last mission gets almost everything right – from the nod to late creator Gene Roddenberry to in-jokes about Kirk's rep as an alien babe magnet'.

The undiscovered country from whose bourn no traveller returns was the final destination of *Star Trek* creator Gene Roddenberry, shortly after he viewed a near-complete rough cut of the film before release. Roddenberry died of heart failure on 24 October 1991, aged seventy. He'd been in ill health for his final years, but he had remained fully committed to and involved in his creation. A dedication to the creator of *Star Trek* was added to the film before its December release, and it brought much hearty applause across movie houses from the *Star Trek* fans in the audience. While he had opposed much of the material included in the *Star Trek* film series – rightly, in the case of Shatner's misguided *Star Trek V* – Gene Roddenberry knew it was the amazing success of the movies that had allowed his return to television production with *The Next Generation*. While his storytelling talents hadn't been needed by the makers of the movies, Roddenberry knew that he could still weave magic with his words. Challenged by a Paramount executive who'd told him he couldn't capture lightning in a bottle twice, Gene Roddenberry had set out to prove the doubters wrong.

# Chapter 7

## Far Beyond the Stars:
## *The Next Generation*

'*Roddenberry had created quite a complex and at times mysterious character. Guarded, cautious, careful in showing his feelings, in expressing his ideas about many things – I found that very interesting.*' Patrick Stewart

For years, executives at Paramount had been happy to maximise their income from what some had termed 'the seventy-nine jewels', the original three years of *Star Trek* episodes. The show had lost money during the years it was in production and on the air, but the afterlife of seemingly endless reruns the series enjoyed during the 1970s – and the growing popularity of the show – ensured that those seventy-nine episodes generated a healthy income for the parent company (and anyone lucky enough to be on residuals).

That surprising afterlife, and the fact that Paramount was finally convinced there was an audience for more *Star Trek*, led to the hugely successful movie series. Science fiction was in vogue again following *Star Wars*, and after the tortuous diversion into the development of the *Star Trek: Phase II* TV series, Paramount had finally made a commercial success of *Star Trek*. As the original crew aged on screen, Paramount began to think about bringing *Star Trek* back to television again, with an all-new crew in all-new adventures.

September 1986 saw the twentieth anniversary of the debut of the original *Star Trek* series. Paramount celebrated with a lavish party, which many involved thought was unusual for a studio that had never previously shown much interest in the series. Many put the unexpected focus on *Star Trek* down to the upcoming fourth movie and the fact that episodes were now being sold on videotape to a growing audience. No one suspected that a major resurgence of *Star Trek* on television was mere months away. In October 1986, a month prior to the release of *Star Trek IV: The Voyage Home* (the most popular of the original cast *Star Trek* movies), Paramount announced a new first-run syndicated TV show entitled *Star Trek: The Next Generation*.

Gene Roddenberry had made several failed attempts to get a new science fiction show on air during the 1970s, resulting in a collection of TV movie pilots. That decade generally had not been a good one for SF TV in the US, consisting of interchangeable adventure shows like *The Six Million Dollar Man*, produced by Harve Bennett. Towards the end of the 1970s, in the wake of the success of *Star Wars*, space opera shows began to appear, prime among them being *Battlestar Galactica* (1978–80) and *Buck Rogers in the 25th Century* (1979–81). This boom in 1970s SF movies and TV series had led to the work on *Star Trek: Phase II* resulting in *Star Trek: The Motion Picture* and the successful 1980s series of *Star Trek* films. The early 1980s saw a TV mini-series adaptation of Ray Bradbury's *The Martian Chronicles*, followed by a surprisingly successful blockbuster alien invasion TV series: *V*. The 1983 mini-series led to a 1984 sequel dubbed *V: The Final Battle*. The battle wasn't all that final, though, as a short-lived regular episodic series followed in the 1984–5 season. *Battlestar Galactica* producer Glen A. Larson was tapping a then-unserved appetite for fantasy adventure with series like *Knight Rider* (1982–6), *Manimal* (1983) and *Automan* (1983–4), but none was particularly accomplished. It was into this environment that the new *Star Trek* TV series would debut.

Since *The Motion Picture* Gene Roddenberry had been side-lined from any significant creative input into the ongoing *Star*

*Trek* movie series, and he (initially at least) apparently had little
interest in producing a weekly television series again. He recalled
the negative effect that producing the original *Star Trek* had had
on his life, at a time when his two young daughters were growing
up. He was not prepared to make that kind of exhausting commitment of time and creative effort again. However, the temptation
to reclaim *Star Trek* for himself, and this time 'get it right' was
overwhelming. The $1-million bonus (plus ongoing salary)
offered for simply signing the contract with Paramount to create
and creatively guide the series was perhaps another factor in
Roddenberry's decision to board the *Enterprise* once more.
'When Paramount came to me and said, "Would you like to do a
new *Star Trek*?" I said no', Roddenberry claimed on a 1988 radio
show. 'I wanted no part of it.' He had previously likened producing a new weekly television series as being the equivalent of
turning out 'half a motion picture' every week. 'Television is
twelve hours a day, miserably hard work', he told an audience at
an event at New York's Museum of Broadcasting in March 1986,
just months before signing on to *Star Trek: The Next Generation*.
'I wouldn't produce a television series again myself.'

Did Paramount need Roddenberry for *Star Trek*, or did
Roddenberry himself need *Star Trek* more? The studio's experience with the maverick producer during the course of the four
(to that date) *Star Trek* motion pictures had not been great and
although the studio executive team had changed, most knew of
the problems laid at Roddenberry's feet during the creation of
*The Motion Picture*. However, there was a danger fans and
general audiences alike would somehow regard a new *Star Trek*
without Roddenberry's approval as somehow illegitimate – and
there was the further danger that if he was not involved,
Roddenberry would be free to criticise the project from outside,
as had been feared at the time of *The Wrath of Khan*. It was a risk
Paramount was not willing to take, although they would not put
Roddenberry in sole charge of a twenty-four-episode series
where each episode was projected to cost around $1.2 million.

Roddenberry's involvement became a central point of the

original announcement of the return of the show: 'Although this is a new starship *Enterprise*, with a new cast and new stories, the man at the helm is still the same: the creator of *Star Trek*, Gene Roddenberry. And we're going to have him once again supervising all aspects of production', said Mark Harris, then President of Paramount Television.

Paramount had in fact begun the project entirely without Roddenberry, hiring writer–producer Gregory Strangis to develop a new take on their old *Star Trek* property. Strangis was a supervising producer on the glossy evening soap opera *Falcon Crest*, hired to work out characters and situations for a show set 100 years after *The Original Series* – among the new characters Strangis developed was a Klingon officer working within Starfleet. Also approached, given his creative work on the *Star Trek* movie series, was Leonard Nimoy. The actor turned the project down, citing his reluctance to get involved in the production of a weekly TV series just at a time when his non-*Star Trek* feature film directing career was taking off.

Already worried that a new *Star Trek* without Kirk, Spock and McCoy might have difficulty attracting an audience, talks were reluctantly started between Paramount and Roddenberry. It seems likely that the studio hoped the producer would rule himself out of any involvement, as his recent public statements seemed to imply he would. Roddenberry recalled the studio executive's taunt about how he wouldn't be able to 'capture lightning in a bottle twice', and that he'd probably be better off not getting involved – but this only made Roddenberry more determined to prove that he was *Star Trek*, and that the new show would require his involvement if it was to succeed. To win his support, Paramount had to offer him full creative control of the series. 'The reason I have some say on *Star Trek*', Roddenberry told a convention fan audience in 1989, 'is that Paramount is a little afraid that all of you would commit revolution.'

With Roddenberry's arrival, Strangis was out – with a sweetheart deal to produce a TV series sequel to the 1950s movie *The War of the Worlds*. Roddenberry commented that it was just as well, as Strangis' outline for the series was another variation on Harve Bennett's long-suggested Academy Years idea, with the *Enterprise* crewed by a troupe of youthful space cadets. All Roddenberry had to do now was produce a successful update of the much-loved *Star Trek* concept.

Although Paramount's first instinct was to place its new *Star Trek* show with an established network, as had been done with the original series on NBC, they initially targeted the newly established Fox network, now home of *The Simpsons*, which launched just the day before the October 1986 announcement of the new *Star Trek* series. Fox would only commit to thirteen episodes, however – not enough for the producers to recover what would be enormous start-up costs in creating the show. Terms could not be agreed, so Paramount decided to take the further risk of debuting the new show in syndication, where the original seventy-nine episodes had prospered. This meant placing the show with the independent stations linked up as the second-run syndication network on an advertising revenue-sharing basis.

In order to meet the September 1987 debut date for the series, Roddenberry had a huge amount of work to do, with less than a year from creation to broadcast. Roddenberry saw the new show as a chance to learn lessons from *The Original Series*, to achieve some of the ambitions he didn't manage first time around, and to produce a show that was more in keeping with his views of the world as the new decade of the 1990s loomed. Rather than just rely on his own thoughts, Roddenberry took a collegiate approach, canvassing ideas from a 'brains trust' of previous *Star Trek* luminaries, including David Gerrold, Robert Justman, D. C. Fontana and Edward K. Milkis. Out of this process came the idea of an older, less active starship captain who would not go on 'away missions' to new planets. That action role would be filled by a younger first officer, thus presenting two strong but different characters at the head of the show, in the hope of avoiding the William Shatner–Leonard Nimoy rivalry that has so plagued the original.

Roddenberry went on to hire some of those pioneering *Star Trek* contributors, though most would depart during the troubled first season. Paramount would not trust their expensive flagship new show to Roddenberry alone, so placed studio executive Rick Berman on the series with ultimate responsibility for making it work. Previously a producer of children's entertainment, Berman had joined Paramount in 1984 supervising current TV programming such as *Cheers* and *MacGyver*. Alongside producers Maurice Hurley and Michael Piller, Berman would help rein in Roddenberry's more outré or outdated ideas, while also steering *Star Trek* towards the millennium and beyond.

Roddenberry spent some time catching up on recent science fiction TV series and films, watching movies such as James Cameron's *Aliens* (1986) in the studio screening rooms. Drafting a series 'bible', Roddenberry developed some new crewmembers to fill the *Enterprise* alongside the older captain and all-action first officer. A female military figure (seemingly drawn from his viewing of *Aliens*) was included, alongside Lieutenant Commander Troi, a 'four-breasted, over-sexed hermaphrodite', and a wise figure similar to Yoda from the *Star Wars* movies named Wesley Crusher. Although the names would be retained, these characters were seen by others involved in the production as too radical for a weekly television series, even in the late 1980s.

Robert Justman's ideas for the series included having children on the *Enterprise*, speculating that such long space voyages would include families. He also suggested that the ship should have an android among the crew 'with all the characteristics of Spock fused with the leadership and humanistic qualities of Captain Kirk'. This character would eventually evolve into Data – with David Gerrold suggesting a golden hue to the android's artificial skin. Justman also conceptualised the 'holodeck', a recreational virtual reality device that he saw as a source for many potential storylines (a similar technology had previously appeared in an episode of *The Animated Series*). He also picked up Strangis' thought of having a Klingon among the team on the bridge of the *Enterprise*, developing Worf, a character Roddenberry would later gleefully take sole credit for, despite initially resisting the idea. Even the depiction of a journey through the solar system that featured in the main titles was down to Justman. He left the show at the end of the first season, effectively retiring from a forty-year career in film and television.

The involvement of key creative crewmembers from the original *Star Trek* helped Roddenberry's mission to give the new series some authenticity in the eyes of fans. D. C. Fontana named the new *Enterprise* captain Jean-Luc (compared to Roddenberry's suggestion of Julien) and argued against the Great Bird's four-breasted counsellor character with the comment (in a memo): 'Don't be silly'. Few of the old hands lasted on the series beyond the first season, and Roddenberry himself, due to his failing health, took a lesser role on the show as the 1990s dawned.

The show Roddenberry and his team came up with was an extension of the *Star Trek* people knew, but with some subtle new twists. 'Gene had to create a new television show from twenty-five years of mythology that had grown up over an old one, and he had to do it out of whole cloth', said Rick Berman in Edward Gross and Mark Altman's thirty-year *Star Trek* history, *Captains' Logs*. 'Gene felt the obsessive necessity to put his own print on everything.'

Roddenberry was back on the Paramount lot once more, with an office in the Hart Building. He concerned himself with developing a script for the two-hour pilot movie and the following twenty-four episodes, just as he had done in the days of *Star Trek: Phase II* over a decade before. Practical production matters on the series were largely handled by Berman and his team of writer–producers. Filling the *Enterprise* with new characters would require an all-new cast.

Casting directors and television executives always cast a wide net in trying to find just the right actor to fill a leading role. The new captain of the *Enterprise* was to be named Jean-Luc Picard, a man of French descent who would be a more intellectual, older figure than Kirk had been. Among the actors considered – as listed in a 1986 Paramount memo – were Roy Thinnes, the star of 1960s alien invasion series *The Invaders*; Yaphet Kotto, who had appeared in Ridley Scott's *Alien* (1979); and Patrick Bachau, who had appeared in the James Bond movie *A View to A Kill* (1985). Also on the list was balding British Shakespearean actor Patrick Stewart. Choosing Stewart over nearest rival Bachau was a huge risk for the production. He was another important part of the series development that was down to Robert Justman, who'd seen the actor performing at UCLA and recommended him to Roddenberry and Berman.

Roddenberry had his own thoughts about who should captain the new *Enterprise*. His preferred choice was Stephen Macht, from *Knots Landing* and *Cagney & Lacey*. Berman remembered that Roddenberry was 'very stubborn about who he wanted to be Picard. Bob [Justman] discovered Patrick Stewart and brought him to the attention of Gene, but Roddenberry said "No". I met Stewart and said to Bob, "We have to convince Gene to use this guy."' Unaware of Roddenberry's reputation for never changing his mind, Berman nevertheless went to work on the executive producer, fighting to have Patrick Stewart as Picard. 'I was the guy who basically bugged Gene into realizing that Patrick was the best Picard', said Berman.

The heroic, action-oriented first officer role of William Riker was the most Kirk-like character (given away by his near-anagram, sound-alike surname, and the fact the character shares a first name with Kirk actor Shatner). Among those to make the shortlist were Ben Murphy, star of *Alias Smith and Jones* and *The Gemini Man*. Perhaps considered too old for the role, he had been a regular on *The Love Boat* in the early 1980s. His rivals for the part were Gregg Marx, a soap star on *All The World Turns*, and Michael O'Gorman, an actor with few credits to that date – although the memo noted him as a favourite: 'He's sort of an atypical choice for the role, however a good one'. Also short

of credits was Jonathan Frakes, who finally won the part. Frakes
was a frequent TV guest star actor who'd enjoyed regular roles
on soap *Falcon Crest* and the Civil War TV mini-series *North
and South* (1985). Again, Berman had to battle with Roddenberry
over this role. The series' creator's preferred choice was Bill
Campbell, who would go on to star in *The Rocketeer* (1991) – it
was only when Campbell turned the part down that Roddenberry
agreed to even see Frakes.

*Star Trek: The Next Generation* aimed to break new ground by
featuring a character with a disability as part of the main ensemble. Geordi La Forge would not only be blind, but he'd also be
the ship's navigator. Considered for the role were Wesley Snipes,
Tim Russ (later Vulcan Tuvok on *Voyager*), and *Predator* actor
Kevin Peter Hall. *Roots* (1977) star LeVar Burton won the part.

The new doctor on the *Enterprise* would not be Southern –
like McCoy – but would instead be female. Considered for the
role of Dr Beverly Crusher were *An American Werewolf in London*
(1981) actress Jenny Agutter, and actress and choreographer
Cheryl (later known as Gates) McFadden, who won the role.

Security Chief Tasha Yar and ship's counsellor Deanna Troi
were originally cast the opposite way around, with Denise Crosby
as Troi and Marina Sirtis playing Yar. According to Berman, it
was Roddenberry's idea to swap the actresses around. Others
considered for Yar were Rosalind Chao (later a regular on *Deep
Space Nine*) and Julia Nickson, later a featured character on *Deep
Space Nine* rival series *Babylon 5*. The part of Worf, the *Enterprise*'s
Klingon officer, was filled by Michael Dorn, while Crusher's son
Wesley was Wil Wheaton, who'd featured in the acclaimed movie
*Stand by Me* (1986). Young Wesley Crusher would be the prime
representative of the fact that the *Enterprise* now carried families
aboard, but he quickly came to be seen as an irritant (to the audience as well as to Captain Picard) whose high intelligence led to
him saving the ship on multiple occasions during the first four
seasons. His name was drawn from Roddenberry's middle name,
Wesley, and the character was seen as something of a 'Mary Sue'
figure – a wish-fulfilment role reflecting the show's creator.

The most challenging part to cast was that of android Data, the series' Spock substitute. Among those considered was the six-foot-nine-inch actor Kevin Peter Hall (also being considered for La Forge); Mark Lindsay Chapman, a TV movie regular; and Eric Menyuk, later to play the otherworldly 'Traveler' figure on the show. Ironically, most of the actors who auditioned for the role were well over six foot in height, indicating that the original conception for the android was more of a Gort-type character from *The Day the Earth Stood Still* (1951), or the Norman android seen in *The Original Series* episode 'I, Mudd'. A change came about when the character was perceived as more of a Pinocchio like figure, an artificial man who wants to be 'a real boy'. That allowed the casting of the far shorter, but much more exuberant Broadway musical star Brent Spiner. He would bring a different approach to the Spock-like role of the non-human character who spends the series discovering and exploring his own 'humanity'.

There was a change in feel for the new *Enterprise*. Instead of a functional, military-style vehicle, the new starship would be more like a flying city, carrying families of serving officers. This would mean all the support facilities (including leisure) that any city would have, such as schools, health facilities, entertainment centres and so on. Even the bridge had a more 'domestic' makeover, with wall-to-wall carpeting and a less functional look, giving it the feel of an upmarket hotel foyer.

'Some people were afraid of the new *Star Trek* because the old people wouldn't be in it', recalled Justman. 'I don't think that lasted too long. People resist change [but] the great thing about people interested in science fiction is that they have open minds. They're eager for new ideas.'

*The Next Generation* had to deliver the same but different – it had to be *Star Trek* as audiences would recognise it, but brought up to date for the 1980s, and it also had to compete to some degree with the *Star Trek* movies. New production techniques and new technology, especially in the field of special effects, helped the show look more sophisticated than the tired 1960s

version. However, some of Roddenberry's ideas – which he held
to stubbornly – got in the way of good dramatic storylines.
Roddenberry had long contended that humanity in the future
would be free of interpersonal conflict (ironically, an edict he
had fought on *The Lieutenant*). The problem was (as Rick
Berman realised) that this does not make for engaging drama.
Conflict is at the heart of most drama, whether between the
central characters of a TV show or between 'our' team of heroes
and some external threat or danger. 'We had to manufacture
our conflicts from other than interpersonal conflicts among our
characters and that does make it very difficult to write', said
Berman. 'With *Star Trek* you've got two sets of rules: the rules of
science and the rules of *Star Trek*. Writers have to be willing to
follow both sets of rules. It's difficult.'

The first thirteen episodes of the new series were widely
considered to be rather disappointing, especially given the high
hopes for the show. There was a 'revolving door' policy towards
writers as the production team – and Roddenberry in particular
– struggled to bring *Star Trek* up to date. Many writers would
contribute one or two episodes during the first season before
their services were no longer required. It took a while for the
show to evolve into its comfort zone, a process that did not
really happen until after Roddenberry's involvement ended and
Berman took full control.

The double-length pilot episode, 'Encounter at Farpoint',
had to lay out the basics of the new show. D. C. Fontana – who'd
written several episodes of the original series – scripted the
opening instalment, with heavy rewriting by Gene Roddenberry.
As well as establishing the new crew of the *Enterprise* (and
allowing the actors to become familiar with their characters and
each other), the opening episode had to tell an engaging story
– one that would bring back a curious audience for the following episodes. The episode featured Roddenberry's long-running
obsession with alien beings who appear God-like in the character of the omnipotent, manipulative 'Q'. John de Lancie's
character would feature throughout the series (and spin-offs) as

an antagonist (and occasional ally) to Captain Picard. He would be pivotal in the series' final episode, which would see a return to events at Farpoint Station. The opening episode features the maiden voyage of the *Enterprise* NCC-1701-D, introduces the crew and throws them into conflict with Q, who tries to warn them that man's exploration of space has gone far enough. The new crew find themselves put on trial for the wrongs done by humanity in space exploration. Picard successfully argues that the situation at Farpoint Station should be used to test man's worthiness to continue venturing outward into space. It's a talky show that spends more time worrying about setting up the series than trying to entertain.

Fontana and Gerrold felt badly treated by Roddenberry in the development of *The Next Generation*. Gerrold had effectively written the series bible, which Roddenberry claimed as his own, and had incorporated suggestions from others such as Justman. Fontana essentially served as de facto story editor, alongside Gerrold, working on developing scripts – although neither received the appropriate credits and remuneration for those jobs (in breach of Writers Guild rules), while Roddenberry claimed the credit for his 'vision' of *Star Trek*.

During this time Roddenberry's lawyer Leonard Maizlish became involved in the creative side of the series, accompanying the 'Great Bird' to meetings and serving as his messenger whenever bad news had to be delivered. Over time, as Roddenberry's health began to fail, Maizlish would become even more prominent, supposedly representing Roddenberry's views on all things *Star Trek*, delivering comments on scripts and even attempting his own rewrites (again, in contravention of Writers Guild rules).

Many on the production would later tell tales of Roddenberry's erratic conduct during the early years of *The Next Generation*. The creator was rightly protective of his creation, but to some it seemed as though Roddenberry had taken up permanent residence in the twenty-fourth century. His poor health contributed to temper tantrums and confused feedback on story outlines and scripts. At other times Roddenberry seemed distant or vacant during meetings, or sometimes did not recognise colleagues when passing them in corridors. Joel Engel's unauthorised biography itemises a lengthy list of drugs, prescribed and illegal, that Roddenberry was using at this time, on top of a copious alcohol intake. He speculates that the 'Great Bird' may have suffered some form of brain damage related to his diabetes, high blood pressure and alcoholism. Certainly, whatever the direct causes, Roddenberry's failing health at the end of the 1980s contributed to his eccentric behaviour in the production offices of *The Next Generation*.

Despite that, for many of the writers and young staffers on *The Next Generation*, the chance to work with an idol like Gene Roddenberry was irresistible. However, during the first three years of the series, twenty-four different writers or writer–producers arrived at and departed the show in rapid succession, three times as many as might be expected on any average series. Many found it difficult working for Roddenberry, or failed to match their work to his concepts for *Star Trek*. It was a shocking discovery for many of the series' aspiring writers that their idol had feet of clay and was, in fact, an obstruction to them getting their work done. Roddenberry re-adopted his 1960s habit of rewriting everything that came in – after all, he was Mr *Star Trek* – but more often than not he would make the script worse through his interference. Other producers would have to rescue scripts they thought could be brought to the screen, working around Roddenberry's unwanted input. 'No one but Gene could be recognised as a contributor to ideas for the show. No one else could write a final draft . . . Perfectly good scripts [were] rewritten by Gene into something far less . . . in the space of nine months no fewer than eight writing-staff members left the series', remembered D. C. Fontana of the situation in the writers' room.

*The Next Generation* would 'live long and prosper', surpassing its confused origins and outliving the Great Bird of the Galaxy himself. The first season introduced Q, the Ferengi and explored the possibilities of the holodeck in 'The Big Goodbye'. The character of Data was expanded, with the introduction of an evil 'brother' dubbed Lore in 'Datalore', while Starfleet Academy finally became a focus of *Star Trek* as Wesley Crusher applied to become a cadet. The character of Worf allowed for the beginning of an exploration of Klingon culture that would expand in later years, and a major character – Tasha Yar – was killed off towards the end of the first season in 'Skin of Evil'.

The second season improved dramatically on the first, with a new doctor – Katherine Pulaski played by Diana Muldaur, who'd featured in two original series episodes, 'Return to Tomorrow' and 'Is There in Truth No Beauty' – replacing Beverly Crusher. Whoopi Goldberg a huge *Star Trek* fan joined the series as mysterious *Enterprise* bartender Guinan. A writers' strike cut the episodes from twenty-four to twenty-two, with scripts originally developed for *Star Trek: Phase II* revived and reshaped for *The Next Generation*, including the opening episode 'The Child'. Character development received new attention from incoming producer Maurice Hurley, with story and character arcs meaning that the *Enterprise* crew developed and changed rather than following the end-of-episode 'reset' button that often returned things to 'normal' on the original *Star Trek* series. The episode 'Q- Who?' introduced new alien adversaries the Borg (derived from Cyborg, meaning artificial human). Data received a lot of attention, as did the slowly expanding Klingon culture, very little of which had been seen on *The Original Series*.

By the third season in 1989, Roddenberry had more or less withdrawn from any creative input. For the first time Rick Berman and Michael Piller were able to take active control of the show without Roddenberry, resulting in a maturing of the series' storytelling and the production of more sophisticated episodes such as 'Yesterday's *Enterprise*'. *The Next Generation* was a series that had begun to grow up. Ira Steven Behr joined the show in the third year and would go on to become a driving force behind the second spin-off series, *Star Trek: Deep Space Nine*.

Season four saw Brannon Braga and Jeri Taylor join the show
– they would later go on to run spin-off *Star Trek: Voyager*.
Season three had ended on a dramatic cliffhanger – a first for a
*Star Trek* season finale – with 'The Best of Both Worlds' seeing
Captain Picard captured and transformed by the Borg. Opening
episode of the fourth season, 'The Best of Both Worlds, Part II',
both resolved the storyline and became the episode that saw *The
Next Generation* pass the seventy-nine episodes produced for
*The Original Series*. Unlike the *Star Trek* of the past, the effect of
Picard's experiences was explored as the damaged captain came
to terms with his confrontation with the Borg in the next episode
of season four, 'Family'. The series reached 100 episodes with
the fourth season finale, 'Redemption'.

The remaining three seasons of *The Next Generation* extended
and deepened the new *Star Trek* mythology that the show had
built up. Klingon and Vulcan storylines would come to dominate, with Worf involved in a Klingon civil war, while the two-
part story 'Unification' depicted an attempted reconciliation
between the Romulans and the Vulcans. The episodes featured
a guest appearance by Leonard Nimoy as Spock in a promotional tie-in with the sixth *Star Trek* movie, *The Undiscovered
Country*. Nimoy's Spock was the last of four original series
characters to appear on *The Next Generation*. 'Encounter at
Farpoint' had seen DeForest Kelley reprise the role of an elderly
Dr McCoy, giving a seal of approval to the new 1980s show.
Mark Lenard later appeared as Spock's father, Sarek, in an
episode built around his character, while 'Relics' would see
James Doohan's Scotty arrive in the twenty-fourth century
thanks to a transporter malfunction.

By the end of seven years on air, *The Next Generation* returned
to its beginning. Double-length season finale 'All Good
Things . . .' revisited the events of 'Encounter at Farpoint' with
the return of the malevolent Q. In the wake of the new *Star Trek*
series came a new generation of science fiction television shows,
such as *Quantum Leap* (1989–93), *Sliders* (1995–2000), and the
epic *Babylon 5* (1993–8), as well as fantasy series like *Buffy the*

*Vampire Slayer* (1997–2003). Of course, the show also spawned three additional *Star Trek* spin-offs in *Star Trek: Deep Space Nine* (1993–9), *Star Trek: Voyager* (1994–2001) and *Star Trek: Enterprise* (2001–5).

The command crew characters of *The Next Generation* were closer to Gene Roddenberry's original ideas for the 1960s series, which had been seriously derailed by the popularity of Spock and the dominance of the Kirk–Spock–McCoy triumvirate. However, the characters on the bridge of the *Enterprise* continued to be split down the traditional *Star Trek* opposition of science versus emotion. In Picard there is something of the Vulcan in his unemotional aloofness that often sets him apart from the rest of the crew. With Riker filling the womanising action-hero role previously filled by Kirk (all emotion), *The Next Generation* allows the captain to step back from the immediate crisis and have a broader overview. When Picard meets Spock in the 1991 episode 'Unification II', Spock sees much of his Vulcan father in the human captain of the *Enterprise* (Sarek and Picard shared that most intimate of connections, the Vulcan mind-meld). It is only through mind-melding with Picard that Spock finally understands his father's true feelings for his half-human, half-Vulcan son.

Picard leads the non-emotional grouping of characters: those who look to ideas and pragmatic solutions rather than acting on instinct. Among this group are Data (searching for a way to experience emotions that Spock suppresses, Data discusses their opposite views of humanity in 'Unification II'); the Crusher family, consisting of Dr Beverly Crusher (who returned to the show in the third season, also a long-term romantic interest for Picard), youthful prodigy Wesley Crusher (although Picard initially dislikes having children on board his ship) and Chief Engineer Geordi La Forge.

Riker heads up the emotional group, those who might leap before looking, whose actions are driven by instinct and feelings. Among this latter group are (of course) the ship's telepathic half-Betazoid counsellor Deanna Troi, and security chief Worf (whose Klingon aggression is a problem to be overcome, as was Spock's half-humanity in the original series).

*The Next Generation* took a more sophisticated view of encounters with other species than the original series managed. In many episodes, the *Enterprise* appears to be the space equivalent of the United Nations, negotiating disputes or mediating between alien species in search of conflict resolution. This was a very 1990s obsession (following perestroika in Russia, the fall of the Berlin Wall in 1989 and the end of the Cold War), and departs from the cliché of 1960s *Star Trek* in which Kirk was thought to shoot his phaser first and ask questions later. This approach to storytelling was even reflected in the design aesthetic of the new *Enterprise*, which appeared to be an intergalactic conference centre, with its colour schemes, décor and design all reminiscent of a public building or international chain hotel.

Whereas Kirk emphasised human values as correct above all else, Picard and co were more respectful of life (or consciousness), whatever form it might take. A story like 'The Devil in the Dark' from *The Original Series* – in which a 'monster' threatening miners is found to simply be a mother protecting its young – would not be possible in *The Next Generation*, since the crew would not be as blind as Kirk and Spock initially are to the creature's virtues just because of its appearance and actions. The 1960s values are replaced by Roddenberry's oft-sought 'perfect' humanity, where professionalism (in exploring space and making contact with alien species) trumps human limitations (fear of the alien 'other') at all times.

This is a universe seventy-five years after Kirk's time, where the Prime Directive of non-interference in other cultures is taken a lot more seriously, at least by Picard. The Cold War idea of offering aid to countries that might be allies in the fight against Communism (or military 'advisors' to those who need a little 'persuasion', as in *The Original Series* episodes 'Errand of Mercy' and 'A Private Little War') was replaced by a more understanding approach to relative cultural values, even where these conflict with the values of humanity. Changes to a civilisation's mores or culture might be suggested by Starfleet or the Federation (embodied in Picard), but were very rarely imposed through the use of overwhelming force (or subterfuge, as might have been employed by Kirk).

In the post-Cold War world of *The Next Generation*, the simple oppositional politics of the original series (Klingons = Russians) had to be rethought in a more complex world of mosaic-like politics, where different interest groups vied for dominance and alliances became conditional and shifting. Instead of the Klingons and the Romulans (although both featured and were further developed in the series), *The Next Generation* introduced new, more relevant antagonists such as the Ferengi, signifiers of 1980s 'Greed is good' (to quote Gordon Gekko in *Wall Street* (1987)) unregulated capitalism. Although intended as serious antagonists for the Federation, the Ferengi rapidly developed into comic figures (later rehabilitated in *Deep Space Nine*).

A more serious enemy – and one not susceptible to reasoned negotiation – were the Borg. Literally single-minded (through their sharing of one hive-mind) and not open to pleas of mercy or rational debate, the Borg's sole purpose is to conquer and assimilate other life forms in order to secure their spread throughout the galaxy. Their mantra of 'resistance is futile' represents their unstoppable nature. The crew of the *Enterprise-D* first encounter the Borg in the episode 'Q-Who?', thanks to the meddling Q, who boosts the ship to an unexplored sector of space as a warning of some of the threats awaiting humanity as they continue to expand ever outwards (echoing the purpose of Q's debut appearance in 'Encounter at Farpoint'). This very act, of course, brings Picard, the *Enterprise* and humanity in general to the attention of the Delta Quadrant-inhabiting Borg, making them a target. The Borg are a riff on *Doctor Who*'s 1960s cybernetic creatures the Cybermen, whose 'You will be like us' catchphrase and cyber-conversion modus operandi were restated in the Borg's process of physical assimilation.

Communication and contact with other cultures was always central to *Star Trek* and it provides the dramatic thrust to some of the best episodes of *The Next Generation*. Iconic among them is 'Darmok', essentially a two-hander between Stewart's Picard and an alien starship captain, Dathon (Paul Winfield, heavily disguised under alien make-up). In a set-up reminiscent of *The Original Series* episode 'Arena', 'Darmok' sees two antagonistic captains beamed to a planet where they must cooperate (or, in *The Original Series*, fight) to survive. The *Enterprise* has encountered the Tamarians, a race whose language cannot be translated sensibly by Starfleet's universal translator (a gimmick used to get over the question of why everyone in space speaks American English). Forced to communicate with his opposite number, Picard deduces that the Tamarian speaks in metaphors drawn from his planet's heroic myths. In trying to communicate with the representatives of the Federation, Dathon is trying to recreate one of his planet's mythic battles in order to give the humans a shared reference point, and in doing so he and Picard create a new legend of their own. It's a complex episode, the likes of which would never have been attempted on *The Original Series*, and many fans regard it as one of the best in the entire *Star Trek* canon, including the spin-off shows that came after.

The original *Star Trek* often focused on finite resources: failing dilithium crystals, colonies running out of supplies or in need of medical aid. *The Next Generation*, however, takes place in a universe of plenty where 'new' technology like the replicator and the holodeck caters to everyone's immediate needs. Turning raw energy into matter, the replicator can provide anything needed by the *Enterprise* crew, from foodstuffs such as 'Earl Grey, hot' (as frequently ordered by Picard) to heavy machine parts to repair the ship. Where the original *Star Trek* was outward-looking, with a willingness on Kirk's behalf to ignore the Prime Directive and interfere in the affairs of other planets (for their own good, of course), *The Next Generation* was more inward-looking, dealing with 1990s concerns like emotional therapy and bodily health (whether that be the human – or alien – body or that of the *Enterprise* itself).

Screened at a time when fear of AIDS was at its height and computers were beginning to make their way into homes and workplaces as tools regular people could use, several episodes of *The Next Generation* saw the metaphor of invasion (by biological or computer virus, alien species or unconscious contagion) drive many episodes. Nanites, parasites and bacteria infect the *Enterprise* and her crew with regularity (in episodes such as 'Evolution', 'Phantasms', 'A Matter of Honor' and 'Contagion'). Counsellor Troi represented the touchy-feely Californian 'talk about your feelings' strain of self-help therapy rampant from the 1970s to the 1990s. Troi is as much about helping others as she is about suffering mental crisis herself, thanks to her telepathic nature. Such disruption of the crewmembers' otherwise perfect mental states allowed for the kind of character conflict that Roddenberry's dictates about the twenty-fourth century did not generally allow.

*The Next Generation* took ongoing character development more seriously than the previous show had, in keeping with wider television trends across the 1990s. Characters were treated more like real people than they had been on the formulaic action-adventure shows of the 1970s. Television became more serialised in nature, where incidents had consequences and characters changed rather than reverting to type by the conclusion of any individual episode. *Babylon 5* would be the prime exponent of this in science fiction, while *Deep Space Nine* would take a similar approach in its later seasons.

However, *The Next Generation* made its own moves in treating its characters more like real people with emotions, wants and desires. Prime among the crew for this serious treatment is Captain Picard. The opening episodes of the show's fourth season resolved 'The Best of Both Worlds' cliffhanger, and Picard was freed from Borg control. However, the show then presented an episode ('Family') entirely based around Picard's emotional reaction to his experience. In his tribute to Gene

Roddenberry, *Family Guy* creator Seth McFarlane noted: 'The people [on *The Next Generation*] were not militant cardboard soldiers, far more they behaved like people you'd work with in your office, except they were thousands of light years from Earth. I remember watching the famous two-part episode where Captain Picard is captured by the Borg – it was exciting, thrilling, beautifully put together. Then next week the writers brilliantly followed it up with an episode that contained no sci-fi element at all: it focused on Picard returning to his home in France to sort out the psychological ramifications of the experience while reconnecting with his estranged brother. In two weeks I felt like I'd gone from *Star Wars* to *Upstairs, Downstairs* – I never knew what I was going to see, and I loved it. How many science fiction franchises are so well-founded they can tell a purely character-based story with no pyrotechnics? Gene knew *Star Trek* was about the people and the ideas.'

Another example of this in-depth character exploration of the captain came in the late fifth season instalment 'The Inner Light'. Picard is targeted by an alien probe and awakens as a man named Kamin. He goes on to apparently live a full life as part of the extinct Ressikian culture, falling in love and producing a loving, extended family of the kind he does not have in 'real life'. On the *Enterprise*, Picard is unconscious for only a short time but in his mind he experiences decades of this alternative life, one that is both as real to him as his life on the ship yet as artificial as a holodeck experience. For Picard, the life he lived and the experiences he enjoyed were 'real', and they and the long-gone Ressikian culture live on within his memory. Such events were not forgotten by the show, and served to deepen characters such as Picard, making them more relatable among all the crowd-pleasing space hardware and alien zapping that was a necessary part of a *Star Trek* show.

Other characters were also well developed, such as Worf and Data. However, others still had episodes that focused on them, but across the show's seven-year run it could be argued that secondary lead characters did not fare well in this respect

– especially Riker and Troi, who more often than not were called upon to exhibit their basic characteristics and little else. The general approach, however, was a great step forward from the dramatic reset button of *The Original Series*.

*The Next Generation* was the most successful of all the *Star Trek* television incarnations, proving a hit with general viewers and fans alike. It updated Gene Roddenberry's concepts about the future of humankind and put them through a filter of the real world of the 1990s to great effect. Paramount, however, failed to realise that such in-depth exploration of issues and characters prospered effectively in the format of ongoing television story arcs, rather than in the less than two hour format of movies. Like *The Original Series* before it, *The Next Generation* would be heading to the big screen – but with far less success than its predecessor.

# Chapter 8

## Future's End:
## *The Next Generation* Movies

'*The Borg are the greatest nemesis of all things* Star Trek. *It made* Star Trek *not only an action-adventure movie, but made it a horror movie as well.*' Jonathan Frakes

The cast of the original *Star Trek* had signed off (literally in the end credits) with *Star Trek VI: The Undiscovered Country*. Age, a theme first explored in *Star Trek II: The Wrath of Khan*, had finally caught up with them. Now a new crew was waiting in the wings to take their place. After seven years of exploratory voyages on television, the bridge crew of *Star Trek: The Next Generation* were ready to step up to the movies – with a helping hand from William Shatner's Captain Kirk.

The baton of *Star Trek* on television was being carried forward by *Star Trek: Deep Space Nine* (soon to be joined by *Star Trek: Voyager*) so Paramount believed they could continue the big screen incarnation of *Star Trek* by promoting *The Next Generation* crew. After almost half a decade longer on air than the original series managed, the cast and creative crew of *The Next Generation* were rather tired. The show had gone out on a high and most of the cast were looking to move on to something new. The speed with which they were switched to the big screen proved to be a problem for some, not least Captain Picard himself, actor Patrick Stewart. 'I wish we had not had to go into the movie quite so quickly as we did. I had four days off between wrapping the series and stepping aboard the *Lady Washington* in Santa Monica bay [for a holodeck-set sequence]. Luckily, I did not have to do too much character research'.

A movie version of *The Next Generation* had been gestating since 1993, when Paramount had suggested the idea to Rick Berman, who'd been responsible for the show from the second season following the enforced retirement of Gene Roddenberry due to the latter's ill health. As happened with the original pilot episodes of *Star Trek*, Berman was asked to develop two possible movie stories for *The Next Generation* with two different writing teams. The writers going head to head in this friendly competition were all *Star Trek* TV veterans: Maurice Hurley, who'd done so much to shape *The Next Generation* in the early days, and the team of Brannon Braga and Ron Moore. The only rule laid down by the studio was that each story should feature the appearance of a character (there was no specification as to who) from the original *Star Trek* series. Given that Spock, McCoy and Scotty had all appeared in cameos in *The Next Generation*, the obvious choice was Captain James T. Kirk. Sulu would feature in an episode of *Voyager* two years later.

Braga and Moore won the internal screenwriting 'contest'. They'd prepared by watching the preceding six *Star Trek* movies, some of them more than once. 'We watched *IV* (*The Voyage Home*) closely', said Moore, '[and] we watched *The Wrath of Khan* several times, because it's my favourite and I think the best as far as story and execution. We wanted to get a feel for how *Star Trek* translated to the big screen.'

The writers were used to working within the limitations of television, where a space battle requiring special effects shots would be strictly limited to a couple of exterior shots, occasional phaser strikes and a lot of camera shake to simulate action. The same restriction would not apply to a big-budget movie with a different approach to special effects. Riffing on the title of one of the best-remembered *The Next Generation* episodes, the writing team of Braga and Moore set out to capture 'the best of both worlds' in fusing the humour of *The Voyage Home* with the high drama and charismatic villain of *The Wrath of Khan* in their *The Next Generation* movie.

They were also aware that popular though *The Next Generation* was on television, the *Star Trek* movies had to appeal beyond those core viewers to an even wider potential audience, who might not be as familiar with the set-up and characters of *The Next Generation* as they were with the original *Star Trek* series. The movie had to be more of a stand-alone action-adventure story featuring *The Next Generation* characters than a tale caught up in seven years' worth of serialised back-story and mythology.

'We knew Kirk was going to be in it', said Braga of the film that eventually became *Star Trek Generations*. 'We knew what we wanted to do with Data. Coming up with the space-time Nexus and what the villain was up to was not a struggle. Because it is a movie you can take bigger risks with characters, because you are not obligated to do another episode the next week. We ended up with a lot of humour, but a dark film as well. The theme does deal with death: Picard suffers a terrible tragedy, while Kirk is facing profound regret. There are some sombre moments.'

Bringing the two generations of *Star Trek* crews together was always going to be a narrative challenge. Their first instinct was to put the two crews in conflict, inspired by a draft movie poster concept of two *Enterprise*s engaged in combat. Common sense rapidly prevailed, however, when the writers discovered that coming up with a plausible reason for such a situation was more difficult than they'd imagined. They also ruled out a time travel story (something they'd done several times on *The Next Generation*, and a Brannon Braga speciality), and they didn't want *The Original Series* characters to appear in the twenty-fourth century as ancient versions of themselves, like McCoy had in 'Encounter at Farpoint'. It was Rick Berman who suggested a story spanning both time zones, beginning in the twenty-third century of Captain Kirk and then continuing seventy-eight years later in the world of *The Next Generation*.

The one thing everyone agreed had to happen was a meeting

between the two iconic *Star Trek* captains, Kirk and Picard. The desire for that meeting to take place on neutral ground led to the development of the Nexus, a kind of 'nowhere' place outside regular time and space within which both captains would find themselves trapped.

Unlike the choice of an experienced Hollywood director in Robert Wise to helm *Star Trek: The Motion Picture*, the first film for *The Next Generation* crew would be directed by a name familiar from the TV series. David Carson was a veteran of many TV pilots, including the $12-million opening episode of *Deep Space Nine*. His selection came only after Rick Berman had approached Leonard Nimoy. 'We had a difference of opinion about the script', noted Nimoy, who was also offered a cameo role in the movie. 'It didn't work for me.' The benefits Carson brought to the project were many – he was very familiar with the *Star Trek* universe, cast and crew; he was equally at home directing the actors as well as handling the special effects requirements; and he had huge directorial experience across a range of different television shows. The step up from the *Deep Space Nine* pilot to a $26-million feature film was not that huge, and Berman regarded Carson as a known quantity, one that would avoid all the problems Roddenberry had faced working with Wise back in 1979.

Many of the behind the scenes crew from seven years of *The Next Generation* moved smoothly onto working on *Generations* as the series segued directly into the movie. Although the requirements of a feature film versus a TV episode were often somewhat different, Berman was glad that most of his experienced team were able to step up their game for the big screen *Enterprise*.

Initially, the plan was to feature the entire original series crew in the opening sequence of *Generations*, but several of the actors felt they had said a more than suitable farewell to their *Star Trek* characters in the more meaningful conclusion of *The Undiscovered Country*. Missing from the film therefore were Leonard Nimoy, DeForest Kelley, George Takei and Nichelle

Nichols. They realised that the story was built around the meeting between Captain Kirk and Captain Picard, making their roles largely superfluous. In the end, joining William Shatner in the film were James Doohan as Scotty and Walter Koenig as Chekov.

With only two hours to tell a movie story, rather than the twenty-six hours of the average season of *The Next Generation* on TV, Rick Berman was clear that story choices had to be made. The film would be primarily about Picard, Kirk and Data, relegating everyone else from both *Star Trek* crews to secondary status. Unexpectedly finding themselves sidelined by this focus were some of the cast of *The Next Generation*, including Marina Sirtis (Troi) and Michael Dorn (Worf). Even Jonathan Frakes, as Picard's right-hand man Will Riker, suffered. 'It's like a big Picard episode, with those on the Away Team being the B-story', said Frakes. 'Maybe I'll have more to do in the next movie?'

This was to be a problem for all *The Next Generation* films going forward: how to translate the ensemble nature of the TV series to the big screen, with only one two-hour story every few years, but a large group of characters to feature. The additional decision to feature Whoopi Goldberg's Guinan character heavily (after all, she was a more experienced movie star than someone like Sirtis), and the villain Soran (Malcolm McDowell), further limited the screen time of the more incidental regular *The Next Generation* characters.

In the opening of the film, Kirk is teamed up with Scotty and Chekov, rather than Spock and McCoy as had originally been planned. 'It was very odd', said Shatner. 'I felt very lonely without my two buddies.' The three veterans of Starfleet are in attendance at the launch of the *Enterprise-B* when a distress call is received from a vessel transporting El-Aurian refugees to Earth. Proceeding to the rescue, the new *Enterprise* crew witnesses an energy distortion – the Nexus – that seemingly claims the life of Kirk as he saves the ship. Long-lived El-Aurian refugee survivors of the distortion include Guinan and Dr

Soran, who encounter the *Enterprise-D* seventy-eight years later. Soran plans to enter the temporal Nexus, at the cost of many innocent lives, so he can recreate his lost family. In an attempt to stop Soran, Picard is drawn into the Nexus where he discovers Captain Kirk, whom he recruits to help defeat Soran. The pair is able to leave the Nexus at a time before they entered, thus stopping Soran, but Kirk's life is the price.

The death of Kirk was to be a central part of *Generations* from the beginning, following the same treatment of Spock in *The Wrath of Khan*. Paramount insisted the writers consult with Shatner before taking such a dramatic step, and they were surprised when he agreed quite readily to the development (although Shatner would later resurrect Kirk in novel form in a series of co-written stories). Other characters were further developed too, with Picard suffering a family tragedy and Data exploring his capacity for emotions, giving both actors dramatic challenges and new ways to look at their very familiar TV characters.

Hoping for a Khan-like villain in McDowell's Soran, the writers of *Generations* further raided the *Star Trek* movie back-catalogue by lifting the destruction of the *Enterprise* from *The Search for Spock*. This time it was *The Next Generation*'s sleek *Enterprise-D* that would be wrecked – allowing for the long-planned saucer separation sequence that had been little seen on TV (most notably way back in 'Encounter at Farpoint'). 'It was something we always wanted to do [more] on the series, but didn't', admitted Braga. 'Saucer separation was expensive and elaborate.' The resulting sequence, in which the saucer section of the *Enterprise* crashes to the planet Veridian III, was achieved using somewhat old-fashioned physical model techniques at a time when many movies were exploring the possibilities of computer-generated imagery (CGI), ironically something *Star Trek* had pioneered in the second and fourth original cast movies.

'We wanted to explore mortality', said Braga of *Generations*, '[but not] in the religious way that *Star Trek V* [did]. The film is

about time – Picard is obsessed with what his future holds, and
his impending death [while] Kirk is a man looking at what he
did or didn't accomplish in life. The Nexus in space-time gives
both men a chance to cheat death, until they realize it's part of
life. It's really about how these different characters come to
terms with their personal dilemmas.'

Released in November 1994, just six months after the final
episode of *The Next Generation* aired on TV (compared to the
decade it took *The Motion Picture* to reach the screen), *Star Trek
Generations* opened to a mixed reception from fans, critics and
the wider public alike. The film had racked up a production cost
of $35 million – having started off with a budget of $26 million:
controversial reshoots of the climactic battle to the death
between Kirk and Soran and enhanced special effects shots
added $4 million, following a failed test screening in September.
However, the movie grossed $75 million in the US and $118
million worldwide, following a $23-million US opening week-
end. The *New York Times*' Janet Maslin complained that
'*Generations* is predictably flabby and impenetrable in places,
but it has enough pomp, spectacle and high-tech small talk to
keep the franchise afloat', indicating that the makers had failed
in their objective of making a film that would appeal to a non-
*Star Trek* audience in the style of *The Voyage Home*. Roger Ebert,
writing in the *Chicago Sun-Times*, thought *Generations* was
'undone by its narcissism. [It is] a movie so concerned with
Trekkers that it can barely tear itself away long enough to tell a
story. I was almost amused by the shabby storytelling'.

Lessons would be learned from the critical failure of
*Generations*. With the obligation felt by *The Next Generation*
creators to the crew of the original *Enterprise* discharged by this
movie, the next film would be entirely theirs and it would involve
no 'shabby storytelling'.

One of the problems with *Star Trek Generations* may have been
its very proximity to the TV series that spawned it. *Star Trek*
fans were desperate for a new movie in 1979, as it had been a

decade since the *Enterprise* crew had been seen on the big screen, apart from in a two-dimensional animated form. The struggle to revive *Star Trek* throughout the 1970s had been followed closely by fans who witnessed the project mutate from a movie to a new TV series and back to a movie again. When *Generations* was released in 1994, it came mere months after the conclusion of seven years of TV adventures, while *Star Trek* on television was an ongoing concern in the shape of *Deep Space Nine* and the upcoming *Voyager*. While Paramount had been keen to trade on *The Next Generation* momentum with a new movie following 1991's *The Undiscovered Country*, fans were not nearly as starved of *Star Trek* material in 1994 as their 1979 counterparts had been. This potential 'franchise fatigue' (the fear that there was just too much *Star Trek* available) would become a serious problem for later *Star Trek* TV shows and movies.

The second *The Next Generation* movie (the eighth in the series overall) would enjoy a different reception upon release in November 1996, two and a half years on from the end of the series. By this time, fans of *The Next Generation* had seen enough time pass since their heroes beamed away from regular television episodes to be excited about seeing Picard and his team in action once again. In addition, this time they'd be up against one of the television series' iconic foes, the Borg.

*Generations* had been a muddled movie, trying to achieve too much in just one film. It was yet another send-off for (some of) *The Original Series* crew, an introduction for *The Next Generation* team to the big screen, a chance for series' icons Kirk and Picard to meet, and it had to tell a story of its own. *Star Trek: First Contact* would be different – this time *Star Trek* would be an all-out blockbuster action movie.

Rick Berman was still in charge of Paramount's *Star Trek* franchise, and he turned once again to *Generation*'s scriptwriters Brannon Braga and Ron Moore for story ideas, suggesting he'd like to see something involving time travel. 'All of the *Star Trek* films and episodes I have been most impressed with – *The Voyage Home*, 'Yesterday's *Enterprise*', 'The City on the Edge of

Forever', and I could give you half a dozen more – have all been
stories that deal with time travel', said Berman. 'In a way,
*Generations* dealt with time travel. Nick Meyer's wonderful
movie *Time After Time*, dealt with time travel. The paradoxes
that occur in writing, as well as in the reality of what the characters are doing and what the consequences are, have always been
fascinating to me. I don't think I've ever had as much fun as
being involved with 'Yesterday's *Enterprise*', and having to tackle
all the logical, paradoxical problems that we would run into and
figure out ways to solve them.'

It was Braga and Moore who wanted to bring the cybernetic
Borg to the big screen. Their first attempt to incorporate the
time travel aspect saw consideration being given to stories set in
the American Civil War and Roman times. However, the most
developed idea was for a trip to the European Renaissance for
Picard and the Borg, under the title *Star Trek Renaissance*. Ron
Moore recalled the story involved Picard investigating a village
under siege by hideous monsters. 'We begin to realize that these
horrific monsters were the Borg. We track them down to a castle
near the village where a nobleman runs a feudal society. We
suspect the Borg are working in there, but no one can get in. So
Data becomes our spy, impersonating an artist's apprentice . . .
Data became friends with Leonardo da Vinci, who at the time
was working for the nobleman as a military engineer . . . you
would have sword fights and phaser fights mixed together, in
fifteenth-century Europe . . . it risked becoming really campy
and over-the-top.'

Saner heads saw the film's setting relocated to the twenty-first
century, allowing the story to explore the origins of the *Star Trek*
universe through the development of warp drive technology
and humanity's 'first contact' with the Vulcans. Out to foil these
events would be the Borg, setting out to assimilate the past.
Brannon Braga recalled: 'The one image that I brought to the
table is the image of the Vulcans coming out of the ship. I wanted
to see the birth of *Star Trek*. We ended up coming back to that
moment. That, to me, is what made the time travel story fresh.

We get to see what happened when humans shook hands with their first aliens.'

Following the elevation of Leonard Nimoy into the director's chair for *Star Trek III* and *IV*, Picard's 'number one', Jonathan Frakes, was invited to direct *First Contact*. Frakes had the innate understanding of *Star Trek* that Nimoy had enjoyed (which gave the Paramount brass confidence), but in its more modern guise of *The Next Generation*. He had directed a variety of the show's episodes on television, including the acclaimed 'Cause and Effect' (and would go on to direct *Deep Space Nine* and *Voyager* episodes, as well as appearing in the series finale of *Enterprise*).

The loss of the *Enterprise D* in *Generations* necessitated the creation of a new, more streamlined ship for use in *First Contact* and future movies. Long-time *Star Trek* production designer Herman Zimmerman came up with the new, sleek movie *Enterprise*, while the Borg were redesigned to stand up to the greater scrutiny they'd be under on giant movie screens. After Paramount executives criticised early drafts of the script (under the title *Star Trek Resurrection*) for making the Borg come across as little more than space zombies, a leader was created, in the style of the assimilated-Picard Locutus of Borg, seen in the Borg's best-known TV appearance 'The Best of Both Worlds'. The Borg Queen would be a figurehead for the collective, as well as an audience identification point and a Borg with whom the crew of the *Enterprise* could communicate, allowing for clear and simple exposition of major plot points that might otherwise be difficult to get across.

Like *The Wrath of Khan* before it, *First Contact* drew its central character from an episode of *The Original Series*. Zefram Cochrane had been played by Glenn Corbett in the episode 'Metamorphosis', discovered by Kirk on an isolated asteroid after having been missing for 150 years. Cochrane was an important figure in the creation of the Federation as the inventor of the first warp-capable ship, the *Phoenix*. In the episode, Cochrane's youth has been maintained by a female alien 'companion' creature. The movie would explore Cochrane's creation of the pivotal warp drive technology, and his encounter with Picard's *Enterprise* crew and the Borg. Although Tom Hanks – a well-known *Star Trek* fan in Hollywood – had expressed interest in playing the role, he wasn't available due to directorial commitments, so the part went to acclaimed actor James Cromwell. Oscar-nominated for *Babe* in 1995, Cromwell was a *Star Trek* veteran, having previously appeared in two episodes of *The Next Generation* and in an instalment of *Deep Space Nine*, two out of the three times under heavy alien make-up. Cromwell would play the part of Cochrane once again in the pilot episode of *Enterprise*, 'Broken Bow'.

The action-oriented role of Lily Sloane, a twenty-first-century woman working with Cochrane who battles the Borg on the *Enterprise* alongside Picard, went to actress Alfre Woodard, another Oscar nominee. South African-born Alice Krige filled the challenging role of the Borg Queen, who kidnaps and tries to convert Data to the Borg point of view. Krige would reprise the role on *Voyager*'s series finale 'Endgame'. Comic relief was provided by the character of Barclay, a clumsy, fearful *Enterprise* crewmember played by *The A-Team*'s Dwight Schultz, and Robert Picardo as an alternate version of *Voyager*'s Emergency Medical Hologram. *Voyager*'s Ethan Phillips also appeared in the movie in a small, uncredited role.

Just as *The Wrath of Khan* was a more accessible and enjoyable *Star Trek* adventure than *The Motion Picture*, so *First Contact* was an easier, more straightforward adventure for a non-*Star Trek* fan audience to connect with. The film cost about $10 million more than *Generations* at $45 million, but took $92 million at the US box office, a sum well in excess of *Generations*' $75-million US take. *First Contact* pulled in an additional $57.5 million worldwide, and scored a $30.7-million US opening weekend, taking the number one spot in the top ten. The reviews were widely positive, with Roger Ebert leading the charge: 'One of the best of the eight *Star Trek* films', he wrote in the *Chicago Sun-Times*. '*Star Trek* movies are not so much about action and effects as they are about ideas and dialogue. I doubted the original *Enterprise* crew would ever retire because I didn't think they could stop talking long enough . . . [Director Frakes] achieves great energy and clarity. In all of the shuffling of time-lines and plotlines, I always knew where we were. *Star Trek* movies in the past have occasionally gone where no movie had gone, or wanted to go, before. This one is on the right beam.' Writing in the *Los Angeles Times*, critic Kenneth Turan felt that *First Contact* 'does everything you want a *Star Trek* film to do, and it does it with cheerfulness and style'. James Berardinelli, of website ReelViews, wrote that the film 'single-handedly revived the *Star Trek* movie series, at least from a creative point of view'.

The cast and creative crew could rightly bask in the appreci-ation being heaped upon *Star Trek: First Contact* – although it wouldn't last, with the *Star Trek* movies about to enter a down-ward spiral.

There was considerable momentum behind *Star Trek* following the blockbuster success of *First Contact*. Somehow, over the next two films the creative brains behind the movies managed to squander that momentum, along with fan and public goodwill, by turning out two very disappointing movies in *Star Trek: Insurrection* and *Star Trek Nemesis*.

The writers of the two previous films, Braga and Moore, were unavailable for the third *The Next Generation* movie as they were committed to both ongoing *Star Trek* TV series, *Deep Space Nine* and *Voyager*, as well as scripting *Mission: Impossible II* for Paramount. Michael Piller was brought in by Rick Berman to work on the project after he'd lost out on the opportunity to write *Generations*. Piller's reaction to *First Contact* was that it was 'too dark' for a *Star Trek* movie and he wanted to move things in a lighter direction.

Piller had explored a concept he called 'the Roddenberry box', meaning the limitations that Gene Roddenberry had initially set for *Star Trek* and had adhered to most strictly on the early years of *The Next Generation*, but which each subsequent series had strived to work around. Roddenberry's rules for life in the twenty-third and twenty-fourth centuries were not fixed in stone – he often revised them as he went along – but they were his rules. Writers trying to create dramatic conflict often fell foul of these 'rules' as they seemed to inhibit many of the standard dramatic techniques used by screenplay writers for film and television. Unlike many, Piller quite liked the restrictions of working within 'the box', believing that *Star Trek* fans were drawn to that universe precisely because of the rules that Roddenberry had developed. Part of that was portraying the future in an optimistic manner: 'The strength of *Star Trek* depends upon making people feel good about the future', said Piller. The next *Star Trek* movie would, therefore, be a 'feel-good' movie.

Various ideas came together in the discussions between Piller and Berman. Piller was conscious of his own ageing process, and like the themes contained in the earlier *Star Trek* movies of the 1980s, he was keen to tackle the subject again, perhaps in the form of a quest for the 'fountain of youth'. Berman was also thinking in terms of a quest, but more along the lines of Joseph Conrad's *Heart of Darkness*, a loose inspiration for the structure of Francis Ford Coppola's *Apocalypse Now* (1979). In an interview on startrek.com, Berman addressed Piller's early work: 'He wanted to tell a story of Picard ending up being stripped of everything, losing his ship, his crew, his commission in Starfleet, losing everything but his sense of what was right and his integrity, and being left with nothing but that. When the studio read the story, they had the same reaction I had, which was that it was just nothing close to what a *Star Trek* movie should be.'

The problem for Piller was that *First Contact* had effectively used up *The Next Generation*'s best villains in the Borg. He couldn't return to them, but neither was it wise to try and develop an even more powerful adversary. His decision was to make a different kind of movie, something that wouldn't try to compete directly with the previous *Star Trek* film. His initial attempt – under the title *Star Trek: Stardust* – had Picard pursuing a renegade Starfleet officer who'd taken it upon himself to attack the

Romulans. During the chase, the crew of the *Enterprise* find themselves getting younger as they get closer to a mysterious area of space that seems to function as a fountain of youth. *Star Trek* had reverted its casts to childhood on several occasions on TV, in the episodes 'The Counter-Clock Incident' (*The Animated Series*) and 'Rascals' (*The Next Generation*) – as well as making them extremely aged in 'The Deadly Years' (*The Original Series*) and 'Encounter at Farpoint' (*The Next Generation*).

Script revisions resulted in the rogue Starfleet officer being replaced by Data, in the Colonel Kurtz role from *Apocalypse Now*, and the fantasy-like fountain of youth notion was dropped altogether. The idea of Picard pursuing his rogue android friend seemed to work well, but Piller and Berman knew that Data would have to have very good reasons for turning on Starfleet. The result of their thinking through the problem was to posit an upcoming alliance engineered by powerful forces between the Federation and the Romulans. This outline again met with resistance from Paramount executives, who considered the proposed film too political, and from star Patrick Stewart who wanted to continue the development of Picard as an action hero as seen in *First Contact*.

Stewart – credited as an associate producer on the film – had some other ideas for the movie. He agreed with Piller's desire to produce a lighter film that would show the crew having more fun, but he also felt that the stalled romance Picard had enjoyed with Alfre Woodard's Lily in *First Contact* had not gone far enough. Stewart was also keen on the discarded fountain of youth idea, perhaps feeling that Picard should face the same ageing issues as Kirk had previously. 'The script ended up having input from Patrick Stewart, from the studio, from me, and slowly the story started changing', remembered Berman. 'I think maybe it's a little like that old story about a camel being a horse made by committee. Instead of setting it aside and coming up with another story, we took that story and started bending it, twisting it, changing it and making it more upbeat. I don't think the script ever quite solidified.'

Piller worked on a new script, confining Data's rebellion to the opening of the film only (and excusing his actions by having him really on an undercover mission on behalf of Starfleet, investigating a rebel faction), while the villains became the Son'i, a race persecuting the child-like Ba'ku and in league with renegade Federation officers to steal the power of rejuvenation their planet seems to provide. Final changes saw the Son'i become the Son'a; the Ba'ku turned into adults; the addition of a love-interest figure for Picard in the Ba'ku woman Anji (filling the Alfre Woodard romance role); and the action quotient was increased dramatically.

Jonathan Frakes returned to direct the film, although he was later to express concerns about what he saw as weaknesses in the screenplay. As the villainous Son'a leader, Frakes cast F. Murray Abraham as Ru'afo, the latest in a series of *Star Trek* movie villains who would live in the shadow of *Star Trek II*'s Khan. Starfleet renegade Admiral Dougherty was played by Anthony Zerbe, while 'love interest' Anji was Donna Murphy. Despite a budget in the region of $58 million, *Star Trek: Insurrection* (as the film was dubbed after the titles *Prime Directive* and *Nemesis* were rejected) managed to look like a very cheap film, or – in the view of many critics – an overextended television episode.

Rick Berman later admitted that *Star Trek: Insurrection* was 'a less-than-stellar follow-up to *First Contact*, which had been so up and so exciting'. Critics agreed, with the *Chicago Sun-Times*' Roger Ebert dubbing the movie 'Inert and unconvincing. The plot grinds through the usual conversations and crisis . . . there's a certain lacklustre feeling.' Ebert's more serious criticism concerned the basic premise of the movie: that the rights of 600 indigenous people should outweigh the potential of immortality for all, the 'greatest good for the greatest number of people. The filmmakers have hitched their wagon to the wrong cause'. *Variety* agreed, comparing the film unfavourably with the previous, action-packed movie: 'a distinct comedown after its immediate predecessor, the smashingly exciting *First Contact*.

[It] plays less like a stand-alone sci-fi adventure than like an expanded episode of *Star Trek: The Next Generation*.' It had long been a struggle for those behind the *Star Trek* movie to find stories 'big enough' for cinema, compared to the often low key (but nonetheless fascinating) moral dilemmas faced by the various *Enterprise* crews on television. It had been an issue that had plagued Paramount executives in the ten-year development of *The Motion Picture* and it would be an issue that would trouble director J. J. Abrams in the creation of his second *Star Trek* film. Many fans would regard *Star Trek: Insurrection* as the movie that was 'truest' to the television series that spawned it precisely because it came across as a television-scale instalment, rather than an action movie like *First Contact*. The *San Francisco Chronicle* review was a little more upbeat, describing the film as a 'tight, highly-entertaining spectacle' with 'fascinating ideas, mind-blowing visuals', but the *Los Angeles Times* thought the film was let down by a lack of 'adrenalized oomph'. Even without much 'oomph', *Star Trek: Insurrection* claimed $70 million at the US box office (a $22-million drop from *First Contact*) and $112 million worldwide (a whopping $34 million less than the previous film).

One of the rejected early ideas for *Star Trek: Insurrection* was a riff on *The Prisoner of Zenda*, which would have seen a doppelganger of Picard threaten to take over his role as commander of the *Enterprise*. The idea was revisited for *Star Trek Nemesis*, even though Rick Berman had initially (under the studio's direction) begun to explore the possibility of the tenth *Star Trek* movie not featuring *The Next Generation* cast at all. 'There was an attitude that I should go out and find a new Tom Cruise', Berman told startrek.com of the drive to find a younger crew for the *Enterprise* in response to the relative failure of *Star Trek: Insurrection*. 'I felt strongly against that for two reasons. One reason was that when we were developing this movie, the *Enterprise* [TV] series was coming out. So the *Star Trek* audience was about to get introduced to a whole new cast of young characters on television.

For us to simultaneously introduce them to a whole new cast of young characters in a movie seemed to be insane to me. The other reason was I felt that after a four-year absence from the screen, the fans really wanted to see Patrick, Brent, Jonathan and company again.'

It was Patrick Stewart and Brent Spiner who brought screen-writer John Logan to Berman's attention. Logan had been Oscar-nominated for his work on *Gladiator* (2000) and was a very much in-demand screenwriter – but crucially he was also a big fan of *Star Trek*. 'I thought this was exciting', said Berman. 'Rather than going with people who'd been involved with *Trek* television for so many years, here we had a fresh, A-list, Hollywood writer who happened to be a gigantic fan of *The Next Generation*.' The only strong stipulation from the studio that Berman had to adhere to was to use acclaimed film editor and director Stuart Baird (*Executive Decision*, *U.S. Marshals*) to direct the film, further taking the movie away from the creative involvement of those who knew *Star Trek* intimately (Frakes later directed children's movies *Clockstoppers* (2002) and *Thunderbirds* (2004)). *The Prisoner of Zenda* idea resurfaced, according to Berman, in 'the whole idea of a Picard clone. It went from Picard's son to a Picard clone that was the same age as Picard, where Patrick would play both characters. Finally, it ended up being the Tom Hardy character that was a clone of Picard, but not a look-alike. There was a lot of suspension of disbelief in the choice of actor.'

Hardy – then known for the TV mini-series *Band of Brothers*, but later better known for movies such as *Bronson* (2008) and *Inception* (2010) – was cast as the movie's villain, Shinzon. He's a Reman clone of Picard, plotting to take over the Romulan Star Empire and take his revenge on Picard and the Federation for their perceived abandonment of him. In this motivation, the confrontation between two equally matched protagonists and in the submarine-like space battle scenes, *Nemesis* was heavily modelled on *The Wrath of Khan*, but somehow failed to be anywhere near as engaging.

The movie's sub-plot built on *Insurrection* with its focus on Data, and originated from actor Brent Spiner (who gained a story credit on the film). The discovery of a prototype version of Data (dubbed B-4) set the scene for the Spock-like self sacrifice of Data to save Picard and the *Enterprise-E* at the movie's climax. Data variants had appeared before on *The Next Generation*, including evil 'brother' Lore ('Datalore', 'Brothers', 'Descent', 'Descent Part II') and his 'daughter' Lal ('The Offspring', 'Inheritance'). The introduction of B-4 was probably intended as a safety-net way of reviving Data (through a download of his pre-*Nemesis* cortex) in any future *The Next Generation* films, in the same way that Spock was brought back after depositing his consciousness within McCoy's brain.

The production of *Star Trek Nemesis* did not go as smoothly as that of the other *The Next Generation* films. Several of the cast members put this down to Stuart Baird's unfamiliarity (and seeming wilful failure to engage) with the *Star Trek* mythos. 'I'm not an aficionado', admitted Baird to the BBC. 'There were little hiccups here and there when some people were offended I didn't quite understand the back story. It's incredibly important to them, so some of them would think directing this one, you surely should know it all. But God almighty, I wasn't going to look at 178 episodes.'

Baird was an action editor and director who saw his job as simply being to produce a fast-paced space adventure movie. He didn't concern himself with the details of the *Star Trek* universe – he felt that was the writers' and actors' job. Baird told the BBC: 'It's big entertainment, but I know the fans take it hugely seriously. I took it very seriously to give you two hours of entertainment, with as much bang for your buck, and thrills, spills, emotion, and humour. That was my task, and not to get too precious about it.'

Logan, whether by his own design or the demands of others, had stuck too closely to *The Wrath of Khan* as a template for the new movie, producing a poor imitation of the original – just as Shinzon turns out to be a poor imitation of Picard. The feeling that *Nemesis* could have been any old SF action movie pervaded the final product, and it seemed to *Star Trek* fans that the film somehow lacked that very hard to define *Star Trek* magic that Gene Roddenberry had always gone to great lengths to protect.

The release of *Star Trek Nemesis* was a calamity, with a US box office take of only $18.5 million over the opening weekend in December 2002 – the film was up against the latest instalments in other franchises such as *Harry Potter* (*The Chamber of Secrets*), *James Bond* (*Die Another Day*) and *The Lord of the Rings* (*The Two Towers*), and was beaten to the number one spot by the Jennifer Lopez comedy *Maid in Manhattan*. Total US box office take was $43 million (less than *Star Trek V*, making *Nemesis* the lowest grossing *Star Trek* movie, although totalling $67 million worldwide) – a huge collapse from *Insurrection*'s $70 million and *First Contact*'s $92 million. Apart from the strong competition from other movies that Christmas season, Rick Berman had little to offer in the way of explanation for the dramatic failure of *Star Trek Nemesis* with audiences. 'Everyone from the studio to me thought we'd crafted a really good movie. And nobody came to see it. It wasn't even a question of not getting good reviews. Any *Star Trek* movie opened and it'd have a huge opening weekend, but this one didn't. To this day, [I] have some difficulty understanding why it met with such a poor reception. The movie backfired and there's certainly a lot of room for discussion of why. It was sad and a little baffling to me.'

In an interview conducted at the Atlanta, Georgia fantasy convention DragonCon, in September 2005, both Marina Sirtis and LeVar Burton were very critical of the final two *The Next Generation* movies. *Nemesis* failed, said Burton, 'because it sucked', while Sirtis in response suggested, 'It didn't suck as much as *Insurrection*. I fell asleep at the premiere of *Insurrection*.' Burton clearly blamed Baird, noting that for the first six weeks of production he'd referred to Burton as 'Laverne' instead of LeVar, while Sirtis claimed Baird 'didn't even watch a single episode of *Next Gen*. [*Star Trek: The Next Generation*]'.

Baird's defence of his film was simple, even if the actual movie had failed: 'My intention since I was a virgin to it all, was I wanted to make a movie that stands alone and doesn't rest on all the past history.' Sirtis claimed that approach doesn't work on *Star Trek*: 'There is a history, there is a legend. There are [*The Next Generation*] characters that have been around for fifteen years and have relationships with each other. Gene always used to say it's a people show, it was about the people on the ship. [Baird] didn't really take that into account.'

The *Star Trek* movie series, from the arrival of *The Motion Picture* to the 2009 reboot, received fourteen Academy Award nominations (albeit mainly in technical categories), but didn't win any until J. J. Abrams' *Star Trek* (2009). The most successful and most popular of the films featuring the original television casts had been *The Wrath of Khan*, *The Voyage Home*, *The Undiscovered Country* and *First Contact*. The first three had Nicholas Meyer in common (as either writer or director), while *First Contact* went down the populist action movie route with the Borg as dynamic and destructive villains. They all brought characterisation to the fore and featured ideas mixed with action, sticking faithfully to Gene Roddenberry's initial prescription for *Star Trek*. It was to be a lesson learned by J. J. Abrams when the time came to reinvent *Star Trek* once again for a twenty-first-century mainstream movie audience.

# Chapter 9

## New Ground: *Deep Space Nine*

*'Roddenberry created characters that he purposely chose not to put in conflict. There's no good drama without conflict.'* Rick Berman

The creators of *Star Trek: Deep Space Nine*, the second TV spin-off from *The Original Series*, deliberately conceived the show as the 'anti-*Star Trek*'. David Carson, who directed the two-hour pilot episode, said of the show's creators: 'I think what they're striving for is to look at the people in the 24th century who are not so much at peace with themselves as the crew of the *Enterprise* was in *Star Trek: The Next Generation*.' *Deep Space Nine* would diverge considerably from what Michael Piller called 'Roddenberry's box' of restrictive storytelling rules and would take *Star Trek* in a new direction. The new storytellers who would map this unexplored territory included Ira Steven Behr and Ron Moore.

The show debuted in 1993, during the sixth season of *The Next Generation*, and it was more a spin-off from that show than from the original *Star Trek*. Set in the same twenty-fourth-century time period, it featured many of the same characters, including Miles O'Brien (Colm Meaney) and, from the fourth season onwards, Klingon Worf (Michael Dorn). The show would match its progenitor for longevity, running for seven seasons to 1999, but would not make the step up to feature films like the previous two series.

From the beginning, *Deep Space Nine* was intended to be different. Executive producers Rick Berman and Michael Piller signalled this difference in the most dramatic way possible the show would not feature a Federation starship engaged in exploration. Instead, the title referred to an isolated space station to which the drama of each episode would come. Fan jokes at the time had the station (and potentially the series) boldly going nowhere.

Controversy dogged this 'darker' *Star Trek* series from the outset, with J. Michael Straczynski, creator of the similarly space-station-set *Babylon 5* (which began airing mere weeks after *Deep Space Nine*), heavily suggesting that the development of Paramount's new *Star Trek* show had been influenced by his proposal. Straczynski had attempted to sell his space station series to Paramount as early as 1989, complete with series bible, pilot script and outlines for a first season of twenty-two episodes, including development artwork and character histories. Paramount rejected this detailed proposal, but only announced *Deep Space Nine* after Warner Bros. TV picked up Straczynski's *Babylon 5*. For his part, Straczynski remained convinced that *Babylon 5* must have influenced the development of *Deep Space Nine*, something that all involved have long denied. Straczynski decided to rise above the controversy, knowing that suing Paramount would probably not help his own career. '[Paramount] know what happened, and I know what happened', Straczynski posted to his internet forum in 1996. 'The fact that the two shows were so similar at that time – one a nobody show from nowhere, the other bundled with the *Star Trek* name – came within an inch of killing *Babylon 5*. We were told "The syndie [syndication] market can't sustain two shows like this; you're gonna get creamed."'

In fact, *Babylon 5* went on to secure a five-season run (although as with the original *Star Trek*, renewal was always tricky, complicated by the fact that Straczynski had set out to tell a complete five-year story). The series even spawned its own *Star Trek*-style spin-offs in the form of a series of TV movies and *Crusade*, a one-season follow-on. *Babylon 5* deliberately set out to challenge the *Star Trek* storytelling style, to overcome the end-of-episode narrative reset button that reasserted the status quo, and to present storylines and characters that were constantly changed by the narrative developments of the series. It was a storytelling approach *Deep Space Nine* would itself come to embrace in later seasons.

The new show would have the most ongoing storylines of all *Star Trek* series, with character conflict at its core. Not only did it trash 'Roddenberry's box' of narrative restrictions, it made a positive virtue of ignoring them. 'To a lot of people [*Deep Space Nine*] is not what *Star Trek* is', admitted producer Rick Berman. 'These two shows [*Deep Space Nine* and *The Next Generation*] were to run concurrently, so there was no question we needed to come up with something different, a little darker and with a lot more conflict.'

From first considering a second spin-off in 1991, Paramount executives knew the new show had to be distinctive, yet somehow still *Star Trek*. Thoughts turned to a series set within the Klingon Empire, explored in episodes of *The Next Generation*, but the fear of exorbitant make-up costs quickly put paid to that notion. George Takei had long been lobbying for a show of his own, featuring Sulu as the captain of his own starship. Takei had a strong fan following, but Paramount had already decided the new show would be set in the same time period as *The Next Generation*. Other ideas explored briefly included Harve Bennett's old concept of Starfleet Academy, an option bolstered by *The Next Generation* episode 'The First Duty', featuring Wesley Crusher at the Academy, and Bennett's lobbying for the concept to form the basis of *Star Trek VI*. Another notion was for a series set on a Federation Starbase or a colony planet. Starbases had cropped up in *Star Trek* since *The Original Series* (notably in the episode 'The Trouble With Tribbles'). They were re-supply and maintenance bases, like motorway service stations or trading posts in the US old West. An entire series set among the crew and visitors to a Federation Starbase might have strong dramatic potential, as it would be a destination or way-station for many non-Starfleet characters, thus allowing the writers to introduce a higher degree of conflict than might be allowed (or expected) from among a 'perfect' crew on yet another starship. The colony planet idea was discarded due to the amount of location-based filming that would have been required, and the space station concept was developed.

Setting the series on a space station rather than a starship had many implications for the drama. The location implied a degree of commitment to dealing with consequences perhaps missing from the starship shows: the people on *Deep Space Nine* could not simply fly away from their problems. Additionally, characters would get married or enjoy lengthy relationships, an additional level of commitment and source of character drama. The fact that non-Starfleet characters would feature heavily gave *Deep Space Nine* a different feeling, too, with alternative viewpoints being explored and having an impact on the show's regular characters. As people lived their lives, their fixed location and wider relationships would inform their decision-making, with galaxy-wide consequences.

With the death of Gene Roddenberry in 1991, and his lessening involvement in *The Next Generation* before that, Rick Berman was freer than ever before to do something different with *Star Trek* without the Great Bird of the Galaxy hovering over his shoulder – although Roddenberry had been involved in some of the earliest discussions of what would become *Deep Space Nine*. As far as Roddenberry had been concerned, he was the only person who could create and cast a *Star Trek* TV series or movie – an argument he'd used to prevent Harve Bennett's Starfleet Academy proposal from proceeding. Berman took a different view of things: 'Before he died I worked closely with Gene for five years. I learned his language and his religion and his outlook. I have been obsessively true to it. Gene's involvement in *The Next Generation* had been minimal since the first year of the show. [*Deep Space Nine*] will be absolutely true to that vision, it's a show that rests on Gene's idea of the future.'

Despite his assertion, the storytellers working under Berman would deliberately undermine his stated adherence to Roddenberry's strictures, setting out to create in *Deep Space Nine* the anti-*Star Trek* they believed modern television audiences required.

Various titles were developed for the new show, including the rather bland *Starbase 362* (most Starbases featured in various episodes of the two preceding *Star Trek* series had numerical identifiers) and the oft-suggested *Star Trek: The Final Frontier*. Inspiration for the exact setting and dramatic situation of the new series would be drawn from a handful of specific episodes of *The Next Generation*.

*The Next Generation* episode 'Ensign Ro' had introduced the planet Bajor and the Maquis rebel faction, both developed further in *Deep Space Nine*. Bajor had suffered under the oppressive rule of the Cardassians for generations, with the orbiting space station Terok Nor recently vacated and reoccupied by the now freed Bajorans alongside Starfleet personnel, led by Commander Benjamin Sisko (Avery Brooks). 'Ensign Ro' introduced the character of troubled Bajoran Ro Laren (Michelle Forbes), intended to be a regular on *Deep Space Nine*. However, Forbes declined the offer, making way for the station's First Officer Kira Nerys (Nana Visitor). The joint control of the station was intended to pave the way for Bajor to join the Federation, with the station renamed *Deep Space Nine*.

The Maquis rebel faction grew out of *The Next Generation* episode 'Journey's End'. That saw a group of Native American settlers refuse to leave their colony world when it is reassigned to the Cardassians under the terms of a treaty. Unusually for *Star Trek*, the Maquis (the name taken from French Resistance guerrillas during World War II) were a human resistance group made up of Federation citizens, many of them working within Starfleet. They would later reappear in *Star Trek: Voyager*.

An additional element was the discovery of a stable wormhole, with the station residing between the wormhole and Bajor.

The wormhole offered access to the largely unexplored Gamma Quadrant of the galaxy, so was strategically important. This development saw the return of the Cardassians, who had stripped the station during their withdrawal from Bajor. Interested in accessing (or controlling) the wormhole as much as the Bajorans and the Federation, the Cardassians would become recurring villains.

A further complication saw the wormhole perceived by the religious Bajorans as fulfilling a long-held prophecy. The alien beings inhabiting the wormhole and living beyond linear time and space are seen as gods by the Bajorans. In their religion, the wormhole is the Celestial Temple, while the aliens are dubbed the Prophets. Sisko is seen an emissary of the Prophets after he survives an encounter with the wormhole inhabitants and he subsequently acts on their behalf. *Deep Space Nine* started with a much more complicated and more sophisticated set-up than *The Next Generation* had only a few years previously.

Another break with the past was taken in the casting of leading character Commander Benjamin Sisko (the equivalent to Captains Kirk and Picard). It was decided to spearhead *Deep Space Nine* with an African-American actor, although thought was also given to casting a woman. Experienced movie names Tony Todd (*Candyman*) and Michael Clarke Duncan (*The Green Mile*) were considered, but the leading role went to acclaimed stage actor Avery Brooks (known to US TV audiences for the sidekick role of Hawk on *Spenser: For Hire* and its short-lived spin-off *A Man Called Hawk* in the 1980s). 'Today, many of our children, especially black males, do not project that they will live past the age of 19 or 20', Brooks told Michael Logan of *TV Guide* in 1993. '*Star Trek* allows our children the chance to see something they might never otherwise imagine.' Brooks was following in the footsteps of such *Star Trek* role models as Whoopi Goldberg and LeVar Burton, who'd both stated that the existence of such characters in *Star Trek*'s future had fuelled their own ambitions.

The other regular roles on *Deep Space Nine* were filled by a variety of television actors who were not particularly well known. Two of the most experienced – Armin Shimerman and Rene Auberjonois – had their faces disguised by heavy alien make-up as Quark, a Ferengi, and Odo, a shape-shifter. Movie star Famke Janssen turned down the role of alien Trill Jadzia Dax, allowing Terry Farrell to take the part, but only after the pilot had been filming for over a week. Siddig El Fadil (now Alexander Siddig) played the genetically boosted Dr Bashir, the station medic.

This ensemble cast allowed *Deep Space Nine* to escape from the focus on a core triumvirate of characters (like Kirk–Spock–McCoy and Picard–Data–Riker), allowing for a wider range of representation. Odo channelled the split nature of Spock, being a shape-shifter living among humans, and Kira Nerys anchored the Bajoran–Cardassian story nexus, while Sisko's character arc explored issues of power, responsibility and faith, especially through his relation to the wormhole aliens and the fact that he was essentially engineered by them to battle the evil Pah-Wraiths.

At a cost of $12 million, the pilot episode of *Deep Space Nine* was the most expensive television pilot then made. The episode featured Patrick Stewart to cement the connection to parent series *The Next Generation*. The fledgling show found it difficult during the first year, with writers who'd written for a previous *Star Trek* driven by exploration, having to revamp stories for a station that went nowhere and a cast of characters who – by virtue of their circumstance – were more reactive than active.

It always takes a new series a while to find its feet. *Deep Space Nine* both benefited from and was hampered by being under the wing of *The Next Generation* for its first two seasons. The show spent very little time as the only *Star Trek* series on air, though, as halfway through its third year it was joined by the more traditional (for *Star Trek*) *Voyager*.

Beyond the elements set up in the pilot show, 'Emissary' – Bajor, the wormhole and the role of the Maquis – *Deep Space Nine* would explore areas that made for a darker *Star Trek* series than any that had gone before. In many ways the show initially struggled to find an identity, but the third season (the show's first without *The Next Generation* around) saw the development of a strong military space opera storyline with the Dominion War arc (contrasting heavily with *Voyager*'s traditional exploration-driven narrative). Writer–producer Ira Steven Behr was a key storyteller behind this development, initially set up by a mention of the Dominion in an otherwise comic episode of the second season, 'Rules of Acquisition'. The aim with the Dominion was to clearly differentiate the Gamma Quadrant from the more familiar *Star Trek* 'home turf' of the Alpha Quadrant. Those who hailed from the Gamma Quadrant were the 'anti-Federation', an alliance of alien races who were the opposite of the 'enlightened' Prime Directive-following Federation, a kind of 'axis of evil' in space.

The second season finale episode, 'The Jem'Hadar', properly introduced the Dominion, a military power from the Gamma Quadrant led by the Founders, a race of shape shifting changeling aliens. Odo (Auberjonois), the station's amnesiac alien security officer, discovers he is one of the Founders and that his race is in a battle for dominance with the 'Solids', as they call creatures of fixed form like humans. It was writer–producer Michael Piller who made the connection between this new race and Odo, solving the existing mystery of the character's origins. This development gave what had previously been a rather mysterious and underdeveloped character a strong role in stories going forward, and built right through to the series' overall finale. It elevated Odo to the role of the character with split loyalties that had previously been filled by Spock and Worf. The Founders use a pair of genetically altered races, the Vorta and the Jem'Hadar, as their foot soldiers. Both races worship their 'creators' as gods. Fear, rather than the Federation's friendship, was the tool used to cement alliances and hold these races together in their malevolent (at least to Federation thinking) aims. It's evident from their name that in developing the Founders, *Deep Space Nine*'s key storytellers – Behr, Robert

Hewitt Wolfe and Peter Allan Fields – had been looking to Isaac Asimov's *Foundation* trilogy of 'deep history' novels. Asimov had been a friend of Roddenberry's and was someone he often consulted via letter in the days of the original *Star Trek*. For all involved, the development of a new iconic *Star Trek* villain, following the original series' Klingons and Romulans and *The Next Generation*'s Borg, had been incredibly difficult. Wolfe admitted that they'd fallen back on the old idea that had informed the Romulans – the history of the Roman Empire – in some of their thinking about the nature of the Founders.

The third season not only brought the threat of an all-out Dominion attack, but also saw *Deep Space Nine* acquire its own ship, the USS *Defiant*, a small prototype originally created to combat the Borg. This allowed the characters to more easily get off the station and fulfil the traditional *Star Trek* mission of 'boldly going'. An influx of writing talent from the now defunct *The Next Generation* also boosted the series' storytelling from the third year. *Deep Space Nine* had always embraced serialisation and the possibility that characters could change – both strong 'anti-*Star Trek*' elements. These aspects differentiated it from everything that had come before and were even stronger from the third year. The original intention – according to Berman – was for the Dominion War story to play out over a handful of episodes. So rich were the storytelling possibilities, however, that the decision was taken to extend the plotline for as long as good stories could be developed. It would actually run right through to the end of the series. An additional factor was the arrival of *Star Trek: Voyager* which took up much of Berman and Piller's attention, meaning that Behr and his collaborators running *Deep Space Nine* had more creative space in which to work, allowing the series to move further away from Roddenberry's idealistic view of the *Star Trek* universe.

According to an interview with TrekWeb.com, Behr saw *Deep Space Nine*'s mission as 'getting back to telling character-oriented stories, getting back to having conflict between human beings; plot at the service of character. We created a much more complete universe in which you can have all these characters with all these back stories, all these races, all these supporting characters. You knew more about Garak or Gul Dukat, ultimately, than you knew about Riker. We brought back money, greed, racial bigotry, war – all the stuff that [had] disappeared [from *Star Trek*]. I began to see opportunities that I hadn't seen before. We certainly took the series where [co-creator] Michael Piller would freely admit he hadn't thought of [taking it].'

Building up the existing villains, the writers put the deposed Cardassians in an alliance with the Dominion, resulting in a state of all-out war by the fifth season's finale episode, 'Call to Arms'. Shifting loyalties and alliances kept the story elements fresh, but for any *Star Trek* fans not enamoured with military science fiction the strong shift in this direction was off-putting. Even *Star Trek*'s long-time enemies turned friends the Klingons got caught up in the Dominion War (on the Founders' side), while the Romulans stuck by the Federation. Whatever viewers' feelings about *Star Trek* turning military, there can be no doubt that this was a unique storytelling gambit and it certainly provided much story potential that had been denied the more straight-laced *The Next Generation*, which had been firmly stuck within Roddenberry's storytelling 'box'.

*Deep Space Nine* seriously explored the horrors of war more than any other series, even *The Original Series* that had regularly highlighted the issue in the shadow of the Vietnam War. Inspired by contemporary events in the Balkans, the later seasons of *Deep Space Nine* deliberately set out to reflect some very 1990s concerns. President Clinton had committed American military forces to preventing genocide in central Europe following the break-up of Yugoslavia at the start of the decade. Ethnic tensions had increased among Bosnian Serbs and Bosnian Croats, resulting in an international armed conflict between 1992 and 1995. The show drew on this, and the earlier Gulf War of 1990–1, to inspire storylines of conflicting religious ideologies, the rise of international terrorism, the role of nation-building after conflict, the threat of bio-weaponry and the dangers of ethnic cleansing and potential genocide, all in a 'dark' *Star Trek* context. The show took a more serious approach than *The Original Series* episode 'A Private Little War' had managed, an analogy of the Vietnam conflict with the Klingons representing America's Cold War opponents. The seventh season episode 'The Siege of AR-558' saw regular Ferengi character Nog (Quark's nephew) seriously injured in battle and lose a leg as a result. The greed of the Ferengi is highlighted when Quark quotes the 34th Rule of Acquisition to Ezri Dax: 'War is good for business'. Faced with the personal outcome of war when his nephew suffers, Quark is forced to reconsider his opinion. Sisko ends the episode recalling that the people who lose their lives in war are all individuals, leaving behind family and friends. 'They're not just names', he says. 'It's important to remember that – we *have* to remember.'

Moral ambiguity was also more prevalent in *Deep Space Nine*, with the station's resident Cardassian character – a tailor named Garak (Andrew Robinson), who befriends Dr Bashir – revealed as a former secret policeman turned spy. The ending of the Dominion War largely depended upon a very un-Starfleet-like deception enacted by Sisko with Garak's help. In the season six episode 'In The Pale Moonlight', Sisko participates in a conspiracy to bring the Romulans into alliance with the Federation, but which also leads to Garak committing murder on his behalf – an event covered up to preserve the greater good. It's a subversive take on the usually very black and white moral universe of *Star Trek*. According to writer Michael Taylor, this episode 'showed how *Deep Space Nine* could really stretch the *Star Trek* formula. It pushes the boundaries in a realistic way, because the decisions Sisko makes are the kinds of decisions that have to be made in war. They're for the greater good.'

Another sign of *Deep Space Nine* breaking taboos was the way in which the series undermined the purity of the Federation, something *The Next Generation* had only briefly toyed with (in the episode 'Conspiracy', and later in the movie *Insurrection*). 'Conspiracy' was the penultimate episode of *The Next Generation*'s first season. The first story ideas had a group of warmongering

Starfleet officers try to provoke war with the Klingons. Revised following Roddenberry's intervention, the episode instead featured an alien-driven conspiracy in which Starfleet Admirals were possessed by alien parasites, as he felt Starfleet officers themselves would never turn against the Federation. A suggestion that the alien creatures might become recurring adversaries was never followed up. *Insurrection* saw Picard turn against a wing of the Federation Council, which was conspiring to steal the secret of long life. Neither of these stories suggested that Starfleet had a secret intelligence wing, although it might be supposed that despite such enlightened future times such a thing would not be impossible. *Deep Space Nine* would spend several episodes exploring the implications of just such an organisation within an organisation.

Dr Bashir was the centre of the Section 31 episodes. Introduced in the sixth season's 'Inquisition', Section 31 was depicted as a Starfleet agency operating without oversight, represented by Sloan (William Sadler). It is clear to Bashir that Section 31 is violating long-established Federation values, a position defended by Sloan as ethical compromises necessary to defend those same values in times of war. This drew on real-life 1990s concerns about the activities of US and other intelligence agencies that used the excuse of defending liberty to justify inhumane actions such as torture. As alien security officer Odo comments in the episode 'Dogs of War': 'Interesting, isn't it? The Federation claims to abhor Section 31's tactics, but when they need the dirty work done, they look the other way. It's a tidy little arrangement, wouldn't you say?' Odo's scepticism is interesting, especially as it would later transpire that Section 31 both created and provided the cure (once Bashir extracts it from Sloan's mind) for the 'morphogenic virus' affecting Odo and the Founders. Sharing the cure with the Founders helps bring about the end of the Dominion War, and it's an action Odo takes in defiance of Federation policy. Complex shades of grey dominate morality in *Deep Space Nine*'s complex storytelling.

Gene Roddenberry's view of *Star Trek*'s future would have

little room for such a covert organisation as Section 31, seeing it as unnecessary in a utopia. The creators of *Deep Space Nine*, however, had truly escaped Roddenberry's box and had bypassed his storytelling limitations while still trying to stay true to the heart of *Star Trek*. Behr limited Roddenberry's view to Earth, refusing to accept that things might be the same on an outpost such as *Deep Space Nine* in the middle of a war. 'We decided that Earth is paradise – we'll buy into that [Roddenberry notion]. I don't quite understand it, but we'll buy it. "It's easy to be a saint in paradise," Sisko said in "Maquis, Part II". To have a Federation person say that as opposed to a Cardassian, Ferengi or Bajoran was telling, because Sisko was learning. *Deep Space Nine* was the series that refused to play it safe. We all knew it, every writer was behind it. It was an exhilarating place to be creatively.'

Section 31 dealt with threats to the Federation that could not be tackled successfully in more acceptable ways, but gave those involved plausible deniability. For Section 31 operatives like Sloan, the end always justified the means and if that meant breaking a few rules along the way, so be it. This was not a viewpoint Bashir (representing Roddenberry) could agree with and he refused to be co-opted (at least willingly) by the organisation. Despite Bashir's interest in espionage narratives, displayed through his James Bond-like fantasy holodeck activities, real-world spying and betrayal was not for him. Section 31 would reappear in several episodes and the organisation's origins would eventually be revealed in the *Star Trek* prequel series *Enterprise*.

*Deep Space Nine* even looked back to the original *Star Trek* series for ideas to develop, hitting upon the mirror universe of 'Mirror, Mirror' as ripe for exploitation. That episode saw a transporter malfunction send Kirk, Spock, McCoy and Uhura to an alternate universe where the benign Federation is an evil Terran Empire. Each of the *Enterprise* crew has their Machiavellian counterpart, launching the cliché that alternative universe evil twins sport goatees.

The second season *Deep Space Nine* episode 'Crossover' provides a direct sequel to 'Mirror, Mirror', revealing that Kirk's intervention led to the fall of the Terran Empire, with mirror Spock as a reforming leader. *Deep Space Nine*'s series of mirror universe stories (encompassing the episodes 'Through the Looking Glass', 'Shattered Mirror', 'Resurrection' and 'The Emperor's New Cloak') allowed actors to play alternate, more extreme versions of their usual characters. It also allowed for even darker stories to be told, perhaps revealing the kind of show *Deep Space Nine* might have been if Roddenberry's *Star Trek* restrictions had been thrown off entirely.

This time an accident within the wormhole sends the characters to the mirror universe, around 100 years after Kirk's intervention. Here a Klingon–Cardassian alliance dominates and the station is still Terok Nor, with Bajor under the control of Bajorians who own human slaves. Terrans are seen by those on Terok Nor as the bad guys, called ruthless barbarians by Kira Nerys' opposite number, the sultry Intendant. With the help of the displaced inhabitants of *Deep Space Nine*, the human ore miners of Terok Nor are able to form a resistance movement, led by Sisko's mirror alternate, and free themselves from Bajoran domination.

*Deep Space Nine* also rescued the Ferengi from their status as comic relief characters in *The Next Generation*. Originally intended as serious villains, their hobgoblin looks had meant that the capitalistic Ferengi instead became caricatures. It was easy for writers to use them in a comedic way to comment on very human traits – such as greed – that the supposedly enlightened twenty-fourth-century humans had left behind. The Ferengi became more complex in *Deep Space Nine*, with a number of regular characters – especially the bartender Quark (Shimerman) – being well developed. Just as Worf on *The Next Generation* had allowed the writers to explore and elaborate on Klingon culture (and use it to mirror human culture and history), so *Deep Space Nine* gave the Ferengi a depth previously missing, especially in the war-related fate of Quark's nephew,

Nog. Issues of capitalism's exploitation and perceived sexual norms were tackled through the depiction of the Ferengi, with Quark often involved in major events on his home world.

Initially, critical reaction to the arrival of *Deep Space Nine* was very positive. *TV Guide* described it as 'the best acted, written, produced and altogether finest' *Star Trek* series. However, George Takei was one of many who felt that the show had moved too far from Gene Roddenberry's view of the future. 'The people that really understand and love *Star Trek* are no longer there', he told *iF Magazine* in 2007. 'When Gene Roddenberry passed, that really was the end of *Star Trek* as we knew it. The series that came on immediately after was *Deep Space Nine*, which was the polar opposite of Gene's philosophy and vision of the future, so *Star Trek* lost its way then.'

Others viewed this controversial *Star Trek* rather differently. Original series story editor and writer D. C. Fontana felt that Roddenberry would appreciate *Deep Space Nine*'s war-based tales, due to his experience of World War II. 'I think Gene would have liked it ultimately even with the darker themes', she told TrekMovie.com in 2007. 'Let's face it, Gene lived and fought through World War II and those were pretty dark days so he has to know they occur. He was around when we were in the middle of the muck of Vietnam. He would like to think that humanity would be better than that, but we made the same mistakes over and over again and until we learned from history. I suspect we are going to keep on doing it.'

Fan campaigner Bjo Trimble, who'd led the letter-writing campaign to save the original *Star Trek*, agreed with Fontana that Roddenberry would have appreciated the different approach. 'I feel that Gene might have come to like *Deep Space Nine*, had he lived to see it', Trimble told trekplace.com. 'There might have been some changes. The only reason there were not full [space] battles in early *Trek* was lack of funds to pull it off, and lack of technology to show it. Otherwise, [Gene] would certainly have added it; he knew what audiences liked.'

In 2002, writer–producer Ronald D. Moore (who would go on to revamp the 1970s show *Battlestar Galactica*) expressed the view that *Deep Space Nine* had taken the *Star Trek* concept as far as it could go without breaking it. Interviewed for the documentary *Ending an Era* on the season seven *Deep Space Nine* DVD set, he noted: 'You have *The Original Series*, which is a landmark – it changes everything about the way science fiction is presented on television, at least space-based science fiction. Then you have [*The*] *Next Generation* that, for all of its legitimate achievements, is still a riff on the original. It's still another starship and another captain . . . Here comes *Deep Space* [*Nine*] and it says "OK, you think you know what *Star Trek* is? Let's put it on a space station, and let's make it darker. Let's make it a continuing story, and let's continually challenge your assumptions about what this American icon means." I think it was the ultimate achievement for the franchise. Personally, I think it's the best of all of them . . . an amazing piece of work.'

One specific area that marked *Deep Space Nine* out from all the other television versions of *Star Trek* was its attempted exploration of sexuality within Gene Roddenberry's universe. While *The Original Series* had been a pioneer in depicting a mixed-race crew almost without comment (and it boasted that Kirk–Uhura kiss), the various iterations of the franchise had been less successful in dealing with sexuality. The original series had Kirk as the intergalactic ladies' man and occasionally Spock would melt a woman's heart, but it was a very traditional, almost macho heterosexuality – very much in the image of Roddenberry, whose attitudes to women and sex seemed more suited to the 1950s than the 1960s.

When the show branched out into its various TV spin-offs, there was a chance to filter the sexuality of these characters from the future through the prism of the 1980s, 1990s and 2000s, while keeping within the bounds of what was permissible on American television. *Deep Space Nine* was perhaps the most successful of the *Star Trek* series in representing the diversity of human (and alien) sexuality.

One of the notable achievements of early *Star Trek* fandom was the creation of a genre that came to be known as 'slash fiction'. The name came from the 'slash' between the pairing of Kirk/Spock. Many fans took it upon themselves to read more into the Kirk/Spock relationship than had ever been hinted at on screen. In the early days of fanzines, some were dedicated to amateur fan stories that explored various facets of this non-canonical relationship. This was never recognised on screen, and in general *Star Trek* has been heavily criticised for its relative failure – at a time when the television landscape was becoming ever more diverse – to depict lesbian, gay, bisexual or transgender (LGBT) characters or to craft stories dealing with the issues of LGBT rights – a hot topic in real-world society, especially in the 1990s when *Deep Space Nine* was on air. Given that *Star Trek* had always been a show that reflected real-world human rights struggles – such as the 1960s racial equality and gender equality battles – why was it shying away from the topic of non-traditional sexuality?

Despite his sometimes reactionary views, Roddenberry was enlightened enough to promise the depiction of gay characters in *The Next Generation* – although his promise was never properly fulfilled. 'My attitude toward homosexuality has changed', Roddenberry admitted in an interview in the *Humanist* in 1991. 'I came to the conclusion that I was wrong. I was never someone who hunted down "fags", as we used to call them on the street. I would sometimes say something anti-homosexual off the top of my head because it was thought in those days to be funny. I never really deeply believed those comments, but I gave the impression of being thoughtless in these areas. I have, over many years, changed my attitude about gay men and women.'

He went on to add that 'in the fifth season [of *Star Trek: The Next Generation*] viewers will see more of shipboard life [including] gay crewmembers in day-to-day circumstances', although this statement came at a time when his actual influence over the show was virtually non-existent and he was entering the final few months of his life. *Star Trek* – the forward-looking, groundbreaking, taboo-busting show that depicted a 'perfect' future – had fallen way behind in television portrayals of diverse sexuality by the 1990s. The majority of pre-1970s negative portrayals of homosexual characters had been eliminated, with shows taking positive steps to depict gay characters as they would any other. Spoof soap opera *Soap* had been more ground-breaking than *Star Trek*, featuring a gay character in 1977, while other similar shows followed suit – *Dynasty* in 1981 and *Melrose Place* in 1992. Prime-time sitcom *Ellen* featured a lesbian main character from 1997, leading to *Will and Grace* and a same-sex kiss in teen show *Dawson's Creek*. Series that followed often featured gay characters and relationships without comment.

Where was *Star Trek* in all this? The show was stuck in its own past, refighting old battles over racism (a regular theme in *Deep Space Nine*, via Sisko and other characters) and gender equality (through Captain Janeway in *Voyager*, and countless other female characters). *The Next Generation* had made some rather half-hearted attempts at addressing the issue, as if from a sense of duty. In the romance episode 'Qpid', omnipotent alien trick-ster Q realises that Vash has the key to Picard's heart. He comments that 'She has found a vulnerability in you . . . a vulnerability I've been looking for, for years. If I had known sooner, I would have appeared as female', making a lame joke of his potential sexual polymorphism. In the episode 'The Host', the *Enterprise* doctor (and sometime love interest for Picard) Beverly Crusher strikes up a relationship with an alien 'male' who comes from a species (the Trill, later featured as regular characters on *Deep Space Nine*) capable of co-joining with different genders. The Trill symbiont inhabits a willing human-oid host, and so can exist within a male or female body. When the male body is killed (and after a period inhabiting Commander Riker), the Trill Odan is reinstalled in a female body, and Crusher feels unable to continue the relationship she had devel-oped with the male version of Odan. Episode director Marvin Rush rejected the idea that this represented a form of homo-phobia. 'Some commented that they were unhappy with the ending because it left a question. There was, or could have been, a sort of homosexual aspect to it and we chose not to go that route. I felt it was more about the nature of love, why we love and what prevents us from loving. To me the best analogy is if your beloved turned into a cockroach, could you love a cockroach? Rather than deal with the fact it was because of any homosexual bent per se, it's just that in our culture and our society people who are heterosexual want the companionship of a male because they are female, [and] wouldn't be able to deal with that opposite situation.'

Another fumbled attempt to tackle the issue in *The Next Generation* concerned the J'Naii, in the episode 'The Outcast'. This time Riker falls in love with a member of an androgynous race of aliens who has chosen, against custom, to be female. The J'Naii were all played by female actors, a crucial decision that resulted in the episode appearing to be set on a planet of lesbians. 'We had wanted to do a gay rights story', said teleplay writer Jeri Taylor of 'The Outcast'. 'We'd not been able to figure out how to do it in an interesting science fiction, *Star Trek*-ian way. As a woman, I know what it feels like to be disenfranchised'. Despite that positive intention, Riker actor Jonathan Frakes felt the point would have been strengthened if the role of Soren, his love interest, had been played by a male, not a more televisually acceptable female. 'I didn't think they [the producers] were gutsy enough to take it where they should have', he said. 'Soren should have been more obviously male.' Michael Piller thought the episode had finally done the job of addressing the gay issue in *Star Trek*: 'We decided to tell a story about sexual intolerance.' However, many fans continued to feel that a previously groundbreaking show had simply continued to sidestep a key issue of the late twentieth century.

Picard faced similar gender cross-dressing trouble in 'Liaisons', as he found himself involved with an alien male Lyaaran disguised as a female human who uses Picard to experience the emotion of 'love'. The episode was more of a spoof of Stephen King's *Misery* – as Picard is essentially kidnapped by

an obsessed alien – than a serious look at cross-gender relationships. It was further watered down by the introduction of two of
the same species, who spend time on the *Enterprise* experien-
cing other human emotions via the crewmembers.

This was the problem with *Star Trek* in the eyes of the LGBT
community, the majority of whom simply wanted the series
to introduce an otherwise unremarkable gay character or two.
Instead, the series attempted to produce 'issue' stories, written
(or more often 'constructed') by people who did not have a
clear understanding or any personal involvement in the issues.

One person who did understand from his personal experience of being gay was David Gerrold, writer of *The Original
Series* episode 'The Trouble With Tribbles', who'd also been
involved in establishing *The Next Generation*. He'd developed a
storyline for an early episode entitled 'Blood and Fire', an allegory about the then-prominent explosion of AIDS among the
gay community. The outline featured a clearly gay male couple
and the effect on them of alien bloodworms, and Gerrold was
confident of getting it made as at the time Roddenberry was
saying positive things about how the new show should continue
the diversity of *The Original Series*. Returning from holiday,
Gerrold found that his story was not to be made after all, as
Roddenberry's idealism had run up against the reality of broadcasting business concerns. Paramount felt that as the show was
syndicated and could be seen in the afternoon in some markets,
such subjects were not suitable for 'family entertainment'. This
incident was a major contribution to Gerrold's leaving the series
early in its run.

Some progress was made on *Deep Space Nine* with the first
romantic same-sex kiss in the episode 'Rejoined', further exploring the nature of the co-joined Trill. In the mirror universe
episodes the alternate Kira Nerys, the Intendant, is clearly
bisexual. Even the once comic Ferengi got in on the act, with
the female Pel disguising herself as male to progress in society,
but falling in love with Quark. The bartender rejects Pel's
advances – even when he discovers she is female – on the

grounds that having a female business partner is frowned upon
in Ferengi society. In 'Profit and Lace', Quark is himself surgi-
cally altered to become female in an attempt to enlist the help of
a powerful businessman in reshaping Ferengi society. In this
guise the show depicts *Star Trek*'s first male same-sex kiss,
although Quark's exact gender status is ambiguous at that point.
Sometimes the issue was addressed in throwaway lines, such as
the comment that a character in the episode 'Field of Fire' has a
'co-husband' as well as a wife, although the sexual implications
of this are not explored.

*Deep Space Nine* writer Ron Moore suggested in an interview
from 2000 that an executive on the show was against exploring
the issue of sexuality. 'There is no answer for it other than people
in charge don't want gay characters in *Star Trek*, period . . . The
studio is not the problem here. The studio is going to let you go
wherever you want to go, as long as they believe it's good work.'

The problem with the invisibility of homosexuality among
Federation crewmembers in *Star Trek*, and especially in *The
Next Generation*, is that it leaves the viewer with the impression
that by the twenty-fourth century it has somehow been 'cured',
'corrected', 'bred out' or otherwise banished. Some of the key
people involved expressed their embarrassment and disappointment that their shows had failed on this front. Speaking with
*The Advocate* in 1995, Patrick Stewart said: 'It would be very
appropriate if *The Next Generation* movies made it their business to have gay characters.' Kate Mulgrew, who played Captain
Kathryn Janeway, claimed to have been trying to move things
forward on *Voyager*, but admitted to having failed, hoping that
perhaps the next show, *Enterprise*, might be more successful.
'I've approached [Berman] many, many times over the years
about getting a gay character on the show – one whom we could
really love, not just a guest star. Y'know, we had blacks, Asians,
we even had a handicapped character – and so I thought, this is
now beginning to look a bit absurd. And he said, "In due time."
And so, I'm suspecting that on *Enterprise* they will do something. I couldn't get it done on mine, and I am sorry for that.'

The issue of homosexuality on *Star Trek* was back in the spotlight in 2005 when Sulu actor George Takei publicly confirmed his own homosexuality. Although Takei had never hidden the fact it had been an open secret among *Star Trek* fans since the 1970s, and he was active in various LGBT organisations – his move brought further attention to *Star Trek*'s failure to tackle these issues in a satisfactory way. Takei said: '[LGBT people] are masculine, we are feminine, we are caring, we are abusive. We are just like straight people, in terms of our outward appearance and our behaviour. The only difference is that we are oriented to people of our own gender.' After all, for black and Asian actors later involved in the series, seeing characters like themselves portrayed in earlier episodes had confirmed they had a place in the future of *Star Trek*. To many gay fans, it seemed as though they did not.

*Deep Space Nine*'s successor, *Enterprise*, did not significantly advance the issue, despite suggestions that regular character Malcolm Reid (Dominic Keating) might be depicted as gay. At a convention in Portland in 2002, Keating confirmed the idea had been briefly discussed and quickly rejected. Eventually, in 2011, Brannon Braga admitted that those involved in *Star Trek* in the 1990s might have a different view of the topic today. '[There was a] constant back and forth about how do we portray the spectrum of sexuality. There were people who felt very strongly that we should be showing casually two guys together in the background in [*Enterprise* bar] Ten Forward. At the time the decision was made not to do that. I think those same people would make a different decision now. I have no doubt that those same creative players wouldn't feel so hesitant about a decision like that.' Whatever the producers may have felt on the subject, it is clear that in terms of progressive depictions of sexuality on television, *Star Trek* in the 1990s failed to take the kind of leading position expected of such an apparently forward-looking show.

*Deep Space Nine* had never enjoyed the *Star Trek* televisual space to itself – its entire run was accompanied by the last two seasons

of *The Next Generation* and the first five years of 'back to basics'
*Star Trek* show, *Voyager*. This allowed the series to do its own
thing within the shadow of those other shows, something storyteller Ira Steven Behr took fine advantage of, but it also resulted
in it being overlooked by some *Star Trek* fans and critics. It was
also the first *Star Trek* series to fail to graduate to movies, and it
may have had trouble retaining more casual viewers thanks to
its heavily serialised nature, especially from the fourth season
through to the end. However, within all these restrictions, the
show offered a space for storytellers like Behr and Ron Moore
to take a fresh look at *Star Trek* and move the franchise in a
different direction.

   *Star Trek: Deep Space Nine* cannot be faulted for its ambition
and was a concentrated attempt by a new generation of young
writers and producers to do something different with the *Star
Trek* legacy within the shadow of Gene Roddenberry's creation.
It may have been a series that was simply too complex for
episodic television to cope with, and it may have tried to follow
too many story strands and too many characters across seven
years, but the world of *Star Trek* would be far duller without it.
Created in reaction to the Roddenberry utopianism of *The Next
Generation* and the ongoing *Star Trek* movie series, *Deep Space
Nine* took risks unlike any other *Star Trek* TV show or movie
had done before.

# Chapter 10

## Business as Usual: *Voyager*

'Voyager *had a different dynamic because we were not speaking everyday to Starfleet and we had a female captain. That set this show apart from the others ... It had the core belief of Star Trek in terms of excitement and action and in terms of the provocative ideas that Star Trek has always been known to present.'* Rick Berman

Just as the creation of *Deep Space Nine* had been a reaction against the successful storytelling traditions of *Star Trek* and *The Next Generation,* so the creation of *Voyager* was both a reaction against *Deep Space Nine*'s more static and darker take on *Star Trek* and to the fear that *The Next Generation* fans and more casual viewers were missing a starship-set *Star Trek* show. *Deep Space Nine* would become increasingly serialised and darker with the Dominion War arc, but the hope at Paramount was that *Voyager* would recapture some of the forward-looking optimism of the 1960s original. The show came amid a slew of late 1990s recreations of 1960s icons, including movies based on old British TV series (*The Avengers, The Saint*), a big-budget revamp of *The Wild, Wild West* and a series of films based on *Star Trek*'s old Desilu stablemate, *Mission: Impossible.* Everything old was new again, and so it was with *Star Trek: Voyager.*

The fourth *Star Trek* television series was the second to be created without the direct involvement of Gene Roddenberry. Despite that, *Voyager* would be (initially at least) an attempt to return *Star Trek* to basics, with a diverse crew of a starship exploring the unknown. The show was co-created by Rick Berman, Michael Piller and Jeri Taylor, who would bring much to the creation of *Star Trek*'s first female leading character. It would be Brannon Braga, however, who would emerge as the prime storyteller, driving *Voyager* forward to the past.

*Voyager* – which had various working titles during development, including *Far Voyager*, *Outer Bounds* and *Galaxy's End* – was an attempt to return *Star Trek* to its traditional mission to 'boldly go where no man has gone before'. This was achieved in an extreme way, with a Federation starship propelled to the far reaches of the galaxy, and the journey home likely to take longer than a human lifespan. TV shows had adopted this idea before, from *Lost in Space* (the clue is in the title), to *Space: 1999*, but *Voyager* would use it in a unique *Star Trek* context. As well as the survivors of the Federation crew, the ship would be carrying Maquis rebels who would be forced to function as part of the crew if they were all to survive, a sure source of character conflict.

Unlike *The Next Generation* and *Deep Space Nine*, *Voyager* would not debut in syndication but would help launch the United Paramount Network (UPN), the long-sought dream of a network of independent stations under the Paramount banner, which had dated right back to the mid-1970s development of *Star Trek: Phase II*. Finally, in 1995, that ambition would be achieved and *Voyager* would be the flagship show.

The Intrepid-class *Voyager* would be a smaller starship than the various incarnations of the *Enterprise*, dedicated primarily to scientific exploration. On a mission to locate a missing Maquis vessel lost in the galactic 'badlands', *Voyager* and the Maquis ship are thrown across the galaxy thanks to the intervention of an alien being dubbed the Caretaker. Now seventy-five years' journey time from home, the two crews join together and attempt to find a way back to the Alpha Quadrant.

The set-up promised much, not least a degree of *Deep Space Nine*'s trademark conflict among the ship's surviving crew, due to their diverse origins. However, the show quickly folded the

Maquis rebels (including Native American First Officer Chakotay and half-human, half-Klingon chief engineer B'Elanna Torres) into the Federation crew and any differences were smoothed over. The character of Tom Paris, initially a wayward trouble-maker, was quickly reformed and fitted back into acceptable Starfleet norms. Areas ripe for exploration and many storytelling opportunities were quickly squandered by the fledgling series closing down these avenues so soon.

However, *Voyager* broke new ground by following up *Deep Space Nine*'s African-American captain with *Star Trek*'s first female series lead in Captain Kathryn Janeway, played by Kate Mulgrew. Producer Rick Berman saw the decision as a break-through for *Star Trek*. 'When it came time for *Voyager*, we knew we had to do something different. The decision was to develop a show that had a female captain', he said on 'Braving the Unknown: Season One', an extra feature on the *Voyager* season one DVD. 'The feeling was that the best direction for us to go – in terms of trying new things, being socially responsible, which *Star Trek* has always been – was to go for a female captain.' Jeri Taylor admitted that, 'The search for the captain was a long and difficult one. This is the person that gets the white-hot glare of publicity as the first female ever to head [a] *Star Trek* series and she had to be just right.' Berman added, 'We didn't want to just create a captain and cast it with a female. We wanted to create a female captain who was somewhat more nurturing and a little bit less swashbuckling than Captain Kirk, a little bit less sullen than Captain Sisko, and a little bit more approachable than Captain Picard. And Kate [Mulgrew] delivered a feminine nurturing side and, at the same time, a sense of strength and confidence.'

Mulgrew was a late replacement for French-Canadian actress Genevieve Bujold as Captain Nicole Janeway, who'd dropped out of the series after just two days' filming. The public reason for her departure was that the actress was more used to the slower pace of moviemaking than the more hectic production process of weekly episodic television. Other suggested reasons were that Bujold disliked her character and the producers may have been dissatisfied by her early performance. In *TV Guide* in October 1994, Berman simply described Bujold as 'not a good fit' for *Star Trek*.

The rest of the cast was largely made up of unknowns, most of whom had appeared in many episodic TV guest spots over the years. Robert Beltran played Chakotay and Tim Russ was Vulcan security officer Tuvok. Russ had previously screen-tested for the role of Geordi La Forge on *The Next Generation* and played minor background roles on *The Next Generation*, *Deep Space Nine* and the movie *Star Trek Generations*. He was something of a knowledgeable *Star Trek* fan, who came to the series well aware of Vulcan lore. Robert Duncan McNeill played the rebellious Tom Paris, and would go on to direct episodes of the series as well as follow-on *Star Trek* show *Enterprise*. Roxann Dawson was Torres, and she followed McNeill's example by moving into directing *Voyager* and *Enterprise* episodes. The young and inexperienced Operations Officer Harry Kim was played by Garrett Wang, while Ethan Phillips portrayed the ship's cook and morale officer Neelix, disguised under heavy alien make-up. Jennifer Lien played the alien Kes during the first four seasons, while Robert Picardo filled the Spock/Data role as the holographic ship's doctor who would explore issues of humanity. A later addition to the cast was Jeri Ryan, playing a freed Borg drone dubbed Seven of Nine who joined the *Voyager* crew and became a key character, also fulfilling some of the Spock/Data function in commenting on humanity.

The jumping-off point for the location of the series was 'Q-Who?', *The Next Generation* episode that had been used to set up the arrival of the Borg. Malevolent God-like being Q had caused the *Enterprise* to be propelled into unknown space and face an encounter with the Borg in an attempt to warn humanity of the dangers 'out there'. When creating *Voyager*, Michael Piller noted, 'We remembered the episodes, many episodes, where Q would show up and throw one of our ships or one of our people off to a strange part of the universe. And we'd have to figure out why we were there, how we were going to get back, and ultimately

– by the end of an episode – we'd get back home. We started to talk about what would happen if we didn't get home. That appealed to us a great deal . . . You have to understand that Rick, Jeri and I had no interest in simply putting a bunch of people on another ship and sending them out to explore the universe. We wanted to bring something new to the Roddenberry universe. The fans would have been the first people to criticize us if we had not brought something new to it. But everything new was a challenge in the early stages of development of *Voyager*.'

One of the early promises of *Voyager* was that due to being located in an unknown area of space, it would escape all the familiar trappings of *Star Trek* beyond the ship and crew. There would be no Federation, no Starfleet, no Klingons, Romulans or Borg. New alien species and menaces would need to be created. Co-creator Jeri Taylor noted, '[It's] a new universe. We have to come up with new aliens, we have to come up with new situations. We knew we were taking some risks. We decided, in a very calculated way, to cut our ties with everything that was familiar. This is a dangerous thing to do. All that wonderful array of villains that the audience has come to love and hate at the same time will no longer be there.'

Although setting out with these radical intentions, the production team clearly found them very challenging to achieve in practice. As the series progressed, more familiar *Star Trek* elements gradually found their way into *Voyager*: the crew itself included a (half-) Klingon and a Vulcan to start with, and Romulans had appeared by the series' sixth episode. By the series' end seven years later, the Cardassians and the Ferengi had appeared in the supposedly unknown and unexplored Delta Quadrant, while the show itself had come to rely very heavily on repeated reappearances by the Borg (and liberated Borg crewmember Seven of Nine).

Another failing of the series was an unwillingness to seriously tackle questions of resources. The ship is essentially lost at sea, with no way of replenishing supplies or infrastructure, despite the presence of the seemingly magical replicator device – even that must get its raw matter and energy from somewhere. The episode 'The Cloud' paid lip service to this with the crew issued 'replicator rations', but it was never central to the series. The holodeck seemed to be in almost constant use, with no indication of where it was powered from and whether this was a good use of resources, given the wider situation. Across the series, there should have been a gradually worsening situation shipboard for the crew of *Voyager*, with the search for resources being part of the drive of the series (something both the revamped *Battlestar Galactica* – under *Star Trek*'s Ron Moore – and *Stargate Universe* would tackle head-on). *Voyager* addressed the concept in the radical season four two-part episode 'Year of Hell' (originally planned as a season-long story arc, but nixed by Paramount). By focusing on selected days across a period of a full year, the story explored the impact on *Voyager* of a conflict with a Krenim military scientist who uses time as a weapon. Although the use of the traditional reset button at the end restores everything to normal, the year in which *Voyager* and the crew struggle to survive provides an example of how the series might have tackled the question of dwindling resources in a more realistic and dramatic manner.

Captain Janeway insisted from the moment the ship was lost in space that the crew would adhere to Starfleet rules and discipline, despite their circumstances. In the series finale, a time-travelling older Janeway would criticise her younger self for making this choice, but it was the only one the show could make if it was to remain recognisably *Star Trek*. A glimpse of what *Voyager* could have been if it had taken a harder-edge look at the 'reality' of the ship's situation was seen in the two-part 'Equinox'. The fifth season finale saw *Voyager* encounter another lost Federation ship, the USS *Equinox*, captained by Rudolph Ransom (John Savage). Half the crew of the *Equinox* are dead and the ship is seriously damaged. Discipline and Starfleet protocol has broken down, with the remaining crew simply focused on their own survival. As a result they have set aside the ethical questions around using a nucleogenic life form as fuel for the ship in their efforts to return home. Resolving the story in the sixth season opener, 'Equinox Part II', Ransom and Janeway must cooperate to save the ships' respective crews from the wrath of the aliens. In the process, Ransom is sacrificed and his ship destroyed, but many of his remaining crew are saved by transferring to *Voyager*. With another push of the reset button, the surviving (presumably traumatised) *Equinox* crew are assimilated into the *Voyager* crew, closing down another potential line of rewarding storylines.

Failing to learn from *Deep Space Nine, Babylon 5* or the on-going narratives of *The X-Files, Voyager* regularly employed this plot reset button. Usually by the end of each episode the status quo would be re-established, no matter what had happened. Characters rarely evolved and changed from the opening episode onwards, with the significant exceptions of Seven of Nine and the holographic Doctor, whose whole purpose was to grow and change, to become more human. Very few consequences flowed through the stories from episode to episode. *Voyager* was a return to the 1960s storytelling of the original *Star Trek*, where each episode was more or less self-contained and although the surrounding universe grew through the accumulation of stories (just as it had done in the 1960s), the serialised storytelling and significant character development of *Deep Space Nine* was delib-erately avoided, much to the show's detriment.

Another problem with *Voyager* was the way it locked itself into telling clichéd *Star Trek* stories – sometimes the same ones over and over again. As the fourth iteration of a franchise stretching from the 1960s to the 1990s, *Voyager* suffered by sticking too closely to the traditional *Star Trek* formula that *Deep Space Nine* had done so much to shatter. The show didn't boast the sense of wonder that had powered *Star Trek* and *The Next Generation*. Despite Janeway being a scientist–captain, there seemed a distinct lack of curiosity about the unexplored space through which their ship was travelling. The overriding desire of most of the crew was simply to return home to Earth as soon as possible.

Some of the actors involved – specifically Kate Mulgrew and Robert Beltran, the more senior members of the cast – later complained about the inconsistent writing of their characters, while writer–producer Michael Piller had departed the series by the end of the second year, disappointed that the show was not living up to its potential. Jeri Taylor followed at the end of the fifth year, leaving Brannon Braga – a writer obsessed with time warps, spatial anomalies and gimmicky 'sci-fi' plots – as the driving force for the series' final two years.

Part of the series' difficulties may have come about due to the forced nature of its initial creation. *Voyager* did not grow organically, it was created in response to a request (or a demand) from Paramount to producer Rick Berman for another *Star Trek* show – any *Star Trek* show. For the studio, it was about creating product to fill airtime and sell advertising (with the addition of guaranteed significant home video revenues by the mid-1990s). The creative team were working within that restriction, rather than coming up with something that had been driven by their need to express themselves and tell new *Star Trek* stories. More than any other series, *Voyager* was just another manufactured instalment in what was now clearly an ongoing franchise, and was recognisably the product of a long-running – perhaps even tired and worn-out – concept.

One particular second season episode of *Voyager* was notorious both among fans and the production team for being, in the words of teleplay writer Brannon Braga, 'a royal, steaming stinker'. In 'Threshold', Tom Paris investigates whether it is possible to break the warp ten starship speed limit in an attempt to get back home to Earth quicker. As a result, he and Janeway are mutated into lizard-like life forms that then breed.

The idea for the episode came from a good intention: what if one of Roddenberry's long-ago imposed limits was changed, even if just for one episode? Jeri Taylor noted: 'Gene made the determination at the beginning of *The Next Generation* that warp ten would be the limit, and at that point you would occupy all portions of the universe simultaneously – which always seemed like a wonderfully provocative notion. Then the question is "What happens if you do go [to] Warp Ten, how does that affect you?" We came up with this idea of evolution and thought that it would be far more interesting and less expected that instead of it being the large-brained, glowing person, it would be full circle, back to our origins in the water. [We're] not saying that we have become less than we are, because those creatures may experience consciousness on such an advanced plane that we couldn't conceive of it. It just seemed more interesting.'

The explanation of those bizarre final images in the episode was apparently lost in the rewriting process, according to Braga. The result was a confused and confusing script that baffled series star Robert Duncan McNeill. 'When you try to tell the story – [Paris] breaks Warp Ten, starts shedding skin, kidnaps the captain and then he becomes one with the universe, [he and Janeway] are salamanders, and have a baby – it sounds ridiculous.'

Brannon Braga said of his much-derided work on 'Threshold': 'It's very much a classic *Star Trek* story, but in the rewrite process I took out the explanation, the idea behind the ending, that we evolve into these little lizards because maybe evolution is not always progressive. Maybe it's a cycle where we revert to something more rudimentary. That whole conversation was taken out for various reasons. That was a disaster because without it the episode doesn't even have a point . . . none of [the evolutionary theorising] came across. All we were left with were some lizard things crawling around in the mud. It was not my shining moment.'

'Threshold' was symptomatic of many of the problems with *Voyager*'s storytelling in attempting both to recapture the 1960s glory of the original *Star Trek* and, in some ways, continue *Deep Space Nine*'s self-declared mission of breaking Roddenberry's taboos. The result was that the show was neither innovative nor progressive (in terms of *Star Trek*), nor was it simply a nostalgic replay of the adventures of Captain Kirk (something that would be attempted, with some success, in franchise prequel series *Star Trek: Enterprise*).

*Voyager* did get some things almost right, though. Its third year on air coincided with *Star Trek*'s thirtieth anniversary, allowing both that show and *Deep Space Nine* to celebrate with special episodes. *Deep Space Nine* produced the innovative 'Trials and Tribble-ations', an imaginative sequel to the original *Star Trek* fan favourite 'The Trouble With Tribbles'. Incorporating much footage from that 1960s episode featuring the original *Star Trek* cast, the episode cleverly worked several of the *Deep Space Nine* characters into the background of the original adventure as they pursued an independent adventure of their own. Television technology had progressed far enough that through a combination of video effects, clever shooting and the use of doubles and specially built sets, the integration of the *Deep Space Nine* crew with that of the original *Enterprise* is almost seamless.

One major member of the original cast was missing from 'The Trouble With Tribbles', so could not be featured in *Deep Space Nine*'s 'Trials and Tribble-ations'. George Takei was off shooting a role in the movie *The Green Berets* alongside John Wayne when the episode went before the cameras at Desilu Studios in the 1960s. Little could Takei have known the kind of afterlife that particular episode would enjoy with fans and casual viewers alike. As part of *Voyager*'s contribution to *Star Trek*'s thirtieth anniversary, it was decided to make up for this by building an entire episode around the further adventures of Takei's Sulu, thus also answering a growing clamour among some *Star Trek* fans to see Sulu with his own command.

The resulting third season episode was cheekily entitled 'Flashback', and took the shape of a flashback story experienced by Vulcan Tuvok of his time serving aboard the USS *Excelsior* alongside Captain Sulu. The episode also tied in closely with the events of the last original cast movie *Star Trek VI: The Undiscovered Country*. Rather than use another time travel plot to have the *Voyager* characters involved with original series characters as *Deep Space Nine* was doing, the writers drew upon an already existing idea for a story that would explore problems with Tuvok's failing memory. Brannon Braga recalled the team wanted to 'to do a time travel story without doing time travel, by doing a [mind-] meld. Tuvok's old enough that we can go way back, to Sulu's ship and events that happened in *Star Trek VI*. That was what we combined.'

Having lobbied for a return to the series in some form, and helped foment the fan calls for the same, Takei was only too happy to play Sulu once more. 'I thought it was a very imaginative idea to bring a connection between Sulu and Tuvok. It turns out that he was on the bridge of the *Excelsior* when the Praxis incident [in *Star Trek VI*] happened, and so there we had a story, making Captain Sulu, Tuvok and Janeway all organic parts of the same episode.'

After all the high hopes that *Voyager* would be a return to the exploration of the unknown, the writers and producers had quickly fallen back on the use of races, characters and situations developed in previous incarnations of *Star Trek*. Chief among them was the Borg, lifted from *The Next Generation* and taken to the next level of development in multiple *Voyager* episodes.

By the middle of season three, the decision had been taken to bring the Borg into *Voyager*. The aim was to create an event episode for the February 1997 'sweeps' period, when ratings would determine the value of ad slots for the series, and capitalise on the anticipated success of *First Contact* in cinemas. Staff writer Kenneth Biller began working on an episode – eventually entitled 'Unity' – in May 1996, with the aim of bringing the Borg back to *Star Trek*. He also felt it was an opportunity to expand upon what had been done with the Borg in *The Next Generation* and the then-upcoming movie *First Contact*. 'When you think about the Borg', he told *The Official Star Trek:Voyager Magazine*, 'they're interesting and cool, but they're just relentless and keep coming at you. How do you get under their skin? That was the question I had to ask.'

Realising that the Borg were a hive-mind community, Biller wondered if a group of Borg could be freed from the collective together, and if so, what would become of them once their individuality returned? He also saw resonances with fairly recent contemporary events on the world stage, namely the disintegration of the Soviet Union into smaller individual sovereign states at the end of the 1980s. By the mid-1990s there was an odd nostalgia for the old, unified Communist super-state among those who'd gained independence, so Biller wondered if the same would apply to a group of ex-Borg: would they miss the collective experience of being a Borg, despite gaining their individual freedom?

The result was his script for 'Unity' that saw Chakotay trapped on a planet after answering a distress call. Tended to by a benevolent community, he discovers they are de-assimilated Borg drones, survivors of the Battle of Wolf 359 (as featured in *The Next Generation*'s 'The Best of Both Worlds' and the *Deep Space Nine* pilot 'Emissary'). An electro-kinetic storm had broken their link with the Borg hive-mind, leaving them to cooperate and survive on their own. Helping to heal Chakotay (who is separated from his own 'collective' on *Voyager*) with a neural link, he experiences their memories. In an attempt to re-establish their collective nature, the survivors reactivate the crashed Borg ship and awaken its still-Borg inhabitants. With the help of *Voyager*, the ship is destroyed but the planet's ex-Borg survivors are able to retain their newly restored collective nature without being part of the wider Borg collective.

'Unity' raised a series of thoughtful issues, and paved the way for the Borg to become a major part of *Voyager* through to the end of the series, nicely set up by the discovery of a Borg corpse by the *Voyager* crew in the immediately preceding episode, 'Blood Fever'. A line in 'Unity' speculates whether this group of Borg were defeated by an even more powerful enemy, which would lead to the reveal of Species 8472, an inter-dimensional 'fluidic' race, in the third season finale, 'Scorpion'. This episode grew out of a discarded idea from 'Unity', with Brannon Braga keen on the concept of a 'Borg graveyard' with the Borg eventually re-animating and posing an ongoing threat to *Voyager*, while building on both 'Unity' and the movie *First Contact* (as well as providing an economical opportunity to reuse costumes and set pieces from the movie).

In 'Scorpion' parts I and II, episodes that spanned the end of

*Voyager*'s third year on air and the start of the fourth, the crew of *Voyager* travel through 'Borg space' in their continuing attempt to return to Earth. Encountering fifteen Borg cubes, only the intervention of an unknown alien race saves the ship. Realising the cubes were fleeing this deadly new race, *Voyager* explores the wreckage of the Borg battleships in order to learn more about such a formidable opponent. Discovering the Borg refer to the aliens as Species 8472, Captain Janeway is forced into an uncomfortable alliance with the Borg to save *Voyager*. This proved to be one of the series' most popular end of season cliffhangers with fans. The second episode introduced the Borg fully designated as Seven of Nine, Tertiary Adjunct of Unimatrix 01 (Jeri Ryan), the envoy between the humans and the Borg. Based on the human ship, Seven helps the crew confront Species 8472 by introducing Borg technology to the vessel. Afterwards, Seven attempts to assimilate *Voyager*, but is defeated thanks to forward planning by Janeway: having escaped the Borg, the ship now has a disconnected Borg drone as a member of the crew.

Future episodes would give Seven of Nine a poignant backstory (assimilated at the age of six, she'd grown up Borg), and explored her Spock or Data-like attempts to blend in with the human crew in sometimes serious, sometimes humorous ways. With the majority of her cybernetic implants removed, Seven still retained the appearance and manner of a Borg, a most unsettling development for those on *Voyager*'s crew who had to work alongside her (an issue not widely explored by the series). However, she would prove to be an undoubted asset in the crew's future battles with both the Borg and Species 8472 and in their eventual return home to Earth. Jeri Ryan also proved to be an asset to the show: producers emphasised her sexiness by putting her in a series of skin-tight uniforms. Ryan undoubtedly brought a degree of sex appeal to *Star Trek* that had largely been missing since the short skirts of *The Original Series*. Of course, some critics and fans saw this as nothing more than a blatant attempt to boost the ratings of a flagging show ...

*Voyager* drew further on the success of *First Contact*

by reintroducing the character of the Borg Queen. The Borg continued to be a nuisance for the crew of *Voyager* through a variety of episodes, appearing as hallucinations or holograms in a handful ('The Raven', 'Living Witness', 'One') before making proper appearances in fourth season finale 'Hope and Fear', fifth season episodes 'Drone' (exploring the life cycle of a Borg drone) and 'Infinite Regress' (exploring multiple personality disorder through Seven of Nine). A two-part tale, 'Dark Frontier', in the middle of season five saw actress Susanna Thompson take over from *First Contact*'s Alice Krige as the Borg Queen. While filling in the back-story for Seven, the episodes revolve around a daring heist by the *Voyager* crew to steal Borg technology that might allow them to speed up their return to Earth. Captured by the Borg, the Queen attempts to convince Seven that she was deliberately infiltrated into *Voyager*'s crew by the Borg, and now they intend to study her in order to devise a successful way of assimilating humanity. Janeway is able to rescue Seven, but only after the former drone suggests a way of disrupting the Queen's control. A very popular feature-length tale, 'Dark Frontier' helped give the final seasons of *Voyager* a new dramatic energy as the Borg Queen became something of a regular nemesis for the *Voyager* crew, creating an almost maternal struggle between her and Janeway for control of their wayward child, Seven.

More Borg-centric episodes followed, each exploring different aspects of the collective. 'Survival Instinct' saw Seven of Nine encounter a trio of Borg connected with her past, while 'Collective' explored the lives of a group of isolated Borg children. The two-part 'Unimatrix Zero', from the end of the show's sixth season and the beginning of the final year, returned the Borg Queen to centre stage, and introduced a utopian, rebel faction of Borg who share a realm of the unconscious called 'unimatrix zero'. Janeway and the Queen once more clash over Seven of Nine, leading to the seeds of civil war being sown in the previously united Borg collective.

All of this eventually culminated in the final double episode of *Voyager*, 'Endgame', broadcast in 2001. That the series finale should feature the Borg and their Queen can have come as little surprise to fans, given the prevalence of Borg stories throughout the second half of *Voyager*'s existence. Whereas *The Next Generation*, which spawned the Borg, featured only six Borg episodes, *Deep Space Nine* just one and the subsequent *Enterprise* also only one, *Voyager* clocked up a whopping twenty-two Borg-centric instalments. For a series that had declared its intention to set out to explore new frontiers and introduce new ideas into *Star Trek*, *Voyager* had come to rely pretty heavily on some very old concepts and characters for its storytelling.

For the finale, Alice Krige returned from *First Contact* to take over the role of the Borg Queen from Susanna Thompson. Although she didn't want to watch Thompson's take on the role, Krige did read the scripts of previous Borg Queen episodes in order to get up to speed on story developments. 'I read all of the *Voyager* episodes that the Borg Queen was in', she told startrek. com, 'but I didn't watch them. I didn't want something in my head, in my imagination. I needed my performance to happen in the moment, and I didn't even watch *First Contact* again.'

'Endgame' had an unusual structure, beginning in a future in which *Voyager* has already successfully made its way home to Earth. It's now 2404 – the tenth anniversary of the ship's return from its twenty-three-year journey back to the Alpha Quadrant. The older Admiral Janeway uses adapted Klingon technology to travel back in time to a period when *Voyager* was still lost in space, hoping to help her younger self use stolen Borg technology to speed up *Voyager*'s return home. She's trying to change the past because in her original return, Seven of Nine, Chakotay and twenty-two other crewmembers were killed while Tuvok suffered an irreversible neurological condition. The younger Captain Janeway prefers to use the technology from the future her older self has provided to destroy a major Borg transwarp hub (a kind of Borg transit station that will allow them to spread across the galaxy). In an attempt to achieve both aims – destroy the Borg and get the ship back home – Admiral Janeway allows herself to be assimilated by the Borg Queen, only to infect the

Borg with a neurolytic pathogen she has been carrying in her bloodstream (an echo of the climax of the Founders story arc on *Deep Space Nine*). At the same time, Captain Janeway uses the Borg's transwarp corridor to blast the ship back to Earth, destroying the last Borg sphere in the process.

Alongside that main story, several other characters have varying degrees of closure with the birth of a daughter for Paris and Torres, and a late-blossoming romance for Seven of Nine and Chakotay, while Tuvok continues to suffer from a degenerative brain disease. In the aborted future shown at the beginning of the episode, Harry Kim is in command of his own starship, the USS *Rhode Island*, while the holographic Doctor has finally chosen a name for himself: Joe. In an echo of *The Next Generation*, the series ends with the same line delivered by the same character that closed the pilot episode, 'Caretaker'. Captain Janeway says: 'Set a course . . . for home.'

Actor Robert Beltran was an outspoken critic of the way *Voyager* ended, and was clear where – in his view – the responsibility for the relative creative failure of the show lay. 'Frankly, I don't think [the writers] really cared what happened at the end. *Voyager* has been the ugly stepchild of the *Star Trek* family, and that's the way we've been treated. From mid-season onwards I kept waiting for them to start making a move towards wrapping up some of these story arcs, but they didn't. [This] was meant to be about nine people on the ship, trying to get through some really extraordinary circumstances. Frankly, I'm not sure what it ended up being about. [They] had a whole year to prepare, but they waited until the final two episodes to fix things. To me, that's just a symptom of their uncaring cavalier attitude towards the show.'

Although it has its followers and fans – as do all the individual incarnations of *Star Trek*, even the once-derided *The Animated Series* – *Voyager* is largely regarded as a creative failure. Ratings-wise, the show did all right and managed to support an entire network for seven years.

So what went wrong? *Voyager* quickly abandoned so much that had been set up in 'Caretaker'. The rebel Maquis faction was quickly assimilated into the crew, while the vast, unexplored region of the Delta Quadrant managed to feature many friends and foes from *Star Trek*'s collective past. Beltran was probably right to complain about the poor development of his character. Despite his rebel origins and ethnic difference, Chakotay became – in the long run – simply another Starfleet officer. In Gene Roddenberry's utopian take on the future, that was probably the right outcome, but it doesn't make for great drama when a potentially long-running series almost immediately neuters one of its more rebellious characters. A similar fate befell Tom Paris and even half-Klingon B'Elanna Torres. Unfortunately, *Voyager*'s characters were more inconsistent than those of previous *Star Trek* shows, prone to suddenly developing specialist interests just when the theme of a particular episode needed it, never to mention them again. Harry Kim was a bland character with little to do, who became increasingly annoying and irrelevant as the series progressed (like *South Park*'s Kenny, he was repeatedly killed off, but kept coming back).

None of this character underdevelopment was helped by the arrival of Seven of Nine, who came to dominate the later seasons of the show at the expense of some of the regulars who'd been around much longer. The arrival of the Borg, following the smash success of *First Contact* on the big screen, can have been no surprise, but the fact that they and Seven of Nine came to dominate the show's final three years and were instrumental in the series finale can have been part of no one's original plan for the show.

When episodes were not Borg-focused, they often replayed various concepts from other *Star Trek* series. Many *Voyager* characters seemed concerned with extending their lives or in seeking a form of immortality, such as recurring villains the Vidiians. Suffering from the genetically disruptive 'phage', the Vidiians were like biological Borg, stealing organs from other species to ensure their own survival and prolong their lives. Of course, the Borg themselves were a species who had artificially extended the lives of their individual members in the service of the overall collective.

Ron Moore quit the show after the fifth season, and was clear on why it had failed: 'It's not about anything. It is a very content-free show, not really speaking to the audience. It's very superficial, there's not really very much underneath the surface. The show doesn't have a point of view, it doesn't have anything to say really. It simply is just wandering around the galaxy and doesn't even really believe in its own premise, which is to me its greatest flaw.'

Rick Berman admitted that *Voyager* may have suffered due to a glut of *Star Trek* 'product' in the mid-1990s. He told startrek. com in an in-depth interview covering his eighteen years at the helm of *Star Trek*: '[*Voyager*] allowed us to do some new stuff, which was important. We were all aware that these things could get stale. We didn't want to do *The Next Generation* again. We were also writing and producing *Generations* and then, two years later, *First Contact*. So we were doing movies with *The Next Generation* crew, we had *Deep Space Nine* in its last three or four years, and all of a sudden we were asked to do another show, which was *Voyager*. It was a very, very busy time and it was imperative for everybody to try to keep things from getting stale and repetitive, but it got more and more difficult.'

Was there simply too much *Star Trek* in the 1990s? Certainly, *Voyager* was the first time that the fans and the storytellers involved in the various shows began to think that the *Star Trek* franchise had played out. After all, there'd been four TV series, from the 1960s to the 1990s, as well as eight successful big screen movies. The ideas and creative juices among the long-serving *Star Trek* storytellers were running dry. Yet, as *Voyager* drew to a close, Paramount was insisting that there be yet another return to the *Star Trek* well. There would be a new *Star Trek* show for the twenty-first century, and this time it really would go where no *Star Trek* show had gone before – back in time to the years before even Kirk and Spock. *Enterprise* would depict mankind's faltering first steps on his epic star trek . . .

# Chapter 11

## Yesterday's Enterprise: *Enterprise*

*'I think my eighteen years of* Star Trek *had some great highs and some definite lows. It was not a big concern of mine, if we screwed up, if things fell between the cracks [on* Enterprise*]. It was unfortunate, but we did our best. I can't imagine that there won't be a new series on television.'* Rick Berman

The fifth and to date final live-action *Star Trek* TV series was the first to dump the *Star Trek* name, initially at least. *Enterprise* would rely on the viewers' recognition of the classic starship's name. Rick Berman, co creator of *Enterprise*, noted: 'We've had so many *Star Trek* entities that were called "*Star Trek* colon something". Our feeling was, in trying to make this show dramatically different, that it might be fun not to have a divided main title. If there's one word that says *Star Trek* without actually saying *Star Trek*, it's *Enterprise*.'

The title sequence and theme tune were also radical departures from *Star Trek* tradition. Rather than the usual trip through space, *Enterprise* opened with a montage of historical flights, craft and aviation pioneers, leading up to the iconic first spacecraft to bear the title. A *Star Trek* theme tune featured vocals for the first time, from opera singer Russell Watson. The chosen song, 'Faith of the Heart' by Diane Warren, had been used previously (in a performance by Rod Stewart) in the Robin Williams movie *Patch Adams*.

This radical iconoclasm was deliberate on the part of *Star*

*Trek*'s long-serving producers, who were keen to differentiate *Enterprise* from all the *Star Trek* shows and movies that had come before – especially *Voyager*, a show widely regarded as a failure. This *Star Trek* would 'belong' to Berman and Brannon Braga, completely free of any of Gene Roddenberry's forty-year-old trappings. Even though the pair had the opportunity of putting their unimpeded stamp on a new *Star Trek* show, Berman was not initially enthused by the idea. 'You could take too many trips to the well, you could squeeze too many eggs out of the golden goose, but [it was] made very clear to me that if I did not do this they would ask someone else to.'

From the beginning, the new show failed to connect with the majority of fans and more casual viewers alike, rapidly losing almost half of the first episode's 12.5 million audience. '*Enterprise* was embraced, but by a smaller audience', admitted Berman, talking to startrek.com. 'Whoever came up with the term "franchise fatigue" was right, there was definitely some of that. There was just too much going on at the same time. By then, *Deep Space Nine* had ended, *Voyager* was still on the air, a third *The Next Generation* movie was coming out, and there was definitely a feeling that maybe we were pushing it. It was the fourth *Star Trek* series in a decade. The prequel idea was good – going back and learning something about what went on for the very first people who were stepping out into space . . . it seemed to us to be a great idea.'

When the time came to create a fifth live-action *Star Trek* series, all those involved were certainly aware that it would not be possible simply to dish up more of the same formula that had gone out under the *Star Trek* banner for twenty years. Since the debut of *The Next Generation*, *Star Trek* had grown ever more dense. This complexity of the fictional universe was a key attraction for many of the series' die-hard fans, who were deeply involved with it, but it was equally off-putting for the large, more casual viewing audience who felt it might now be difficult to understand *Star Trek* after twenty years of previously accumulated storytelling. Each subsequent series following *The Next Generation* had played to diminishing returns, with ratings falling and cultural impact lessened. It was never likely that either *Deep Space Nine* or *Voyager* would follow the first two *Star Trek* series to the big screen. Many people knew the characters of *Star Trek* and *The Next Generation* – often through the clichéd perception of their catchphrases – but few had the same knowledge of, or affection for, Sisko or Janeway and their respective crews and antagonists. Arguably, it was only the frequent appearances of the Borg on *Voyager* that had kept the show afloat for its final three years, rather than any intrinsic liking for the characters among viewers.

It was clear that any new *Star Trek* show would have to be radically different, yet would have to still retain those core elements that made it the *Star Trek* of popular perception. Neither a series featuring the adventures of Captain Sulu or the repeatedly suggested Starfleet Academy idea were deemed to have the potential popular impact required. To avoid entanglements with the rich, deep and detailed twenty-fourth century back-story, Berman and Braga decided to go back to basics, to recreate what had made the original 1960s *Star Trek* such a long-lasting cultural phenomenon. They would go one step further than simply having a starship crew in space, as *Voyager* had done. Their idea was to build a similar mix of characters as seen on the original *Enterprise*, but move the time scale further back, pre-Kirk and nearer to contemporary Earth. A show set in the near future – about 150 years from now – would be more accessible to a wider audience than the technobabble-driven tales of the twenty-fourth century. It could show the events that led to Kirk and crew embarking on their five-year mission. What came before: how did humanity progress from the strife-riven twenty-first century to the creation of Starfleet and membership of the United Federation of Planets?

Using a scene from the conclusion of the movie *First Contact* as their jumping-off point, Berman and Braga set out to explore what happened after the Vulcans made contact with humanity. This key event would launch mankind on a larger voyage, one that would take the crews of the first starships out into the depths of space where Kirk, Picard, Sisko and Janeway would eventually follow.

Radical and different were the key words for *Enterprise*. Berman considered setting the entire first season of a hoped-for seven-year run on Earth. The drama would take place in and around the first space dockyard where humanity's first ever warp-capable starship was being constructed. The main characters would include those involved in the creation and construction of the ship, as well as those in training to become the crew of the first ever ship named *Enterprise*. Eventually it was felt this approach was too far removed from what might be expected from a show within the *Star Trek* universe, so the series would start with the ship already operational, crewed and beginning to explore the universe, following Vulcan contact.

Perhaps the makers of *Enterprise* were too slavish in their attempt to recreate what had worked on the original 1960s *Star Trek*, especially when it came to the central characters. Captain Archer was certainly no Kirk, but he filled the leadership and man-of-action role in a way that no other *Star Trek* captain had since the 1960s. Casting *Quantum Leap*'s Scott Bakula in the role, following in the footsteps of Shatner, Stewart, Brooks and Mulgrew, seemed to owe as much to studio politics as to artistic choices. 'Bakula had a good relationship with Kerry McCluggage, who was running the studio at that point', admitted Berman, 'and he was the first big name that seemed to be interested. He was an actor who I'd enjoyed [and] we thought [we were] putting together something that was fresh and unique and with some wonderful new actors.'

Archer would find himself surrounded by avatars of the key characters of the 1960s *Enterprise*. There's the logical, unknowable, inscrutable Vulcan – but this time she's female, in the shapely form of T'Pol (Jolene Blalock). There's a crusty, ornery Southern character who can advise the captain, but instead of being the doctor like McCoy, he's Trip Tucker (Connor Trinneer), the ship's engineer. Linda Park as Hoshi Sato faced a task almost as thankless as that handed to Nichelle Nichols' Uhura, as the ethnic communications officer. The ship's doctor has been dramatically different on each version of *Star Trek*: Southern, female, genetically engineered, sentient hologram and now alien. Doctor Phlox (John Billingsley) would largely provide the series' comic relief as the Denebulan doctor unafraid of flaunting his alien ways. The callow youths – the equivalents of Chekov or Wesley – were Malcolm Reed (Dominic Keating) and Travis Mayweather (Anthony Montgomery). Perhaps the most interesting and dramatically different addition to the *Enterprise* cast – and something no other *Star Trek* had yet featured – was the captain's pet dog, Porthos.

Like the original *Star Trek* (and it is unclear whether this was a deliberate echo or not) *Enterprise* focused on its trio of central characters – Archer, T'Pol and Trip – at the expense of most of the others. Everyone had their storylines and occasional episodes would focus on them, but for the most part the central trio would dominate events, just as they had back in the 1960s.

*Enterprise* effectively dropped the complicated and convoluted *Star Trek* back-story by locating itself in the fertile ground before any of the previous *Star Trek* series had even happened. In doing so it set up an entirely different problem: how to make sure the stories told worked within the established future continuity of the 1960s *Star Trek* and beyond. It was an issue that would receive varying degrees of attention from the show's writers and producers, but sometimes-fanatical attention from many of the franchise's die-hard fans. Many initially regarded the latest series as a betrayal of all the *Star Trek* material that had come before it.

Well-established aspects of *Star Trek* were largely missing altogether from *Enterprise*, such as matter transporters (in their infancy and only used for inanimate cargo) and the holodeck, while others were actively explored by the series. The origins of starship force shields – intrinsic to *Star Trek* from its 1960s debut – were explored through the work of Malcolm Reed, while Captain Archer's ethical considerations about interfering with new species would lay the groundwork for the idea of the Prime Directive that would so tax Kirk and Picard.

As well as exploring old *Star Trek* ideas, *Enterprise* was wise enough to throw some brand new elements into the mix. One of the most significant was the 'temporal cold war' concept, in which a mysterious entity (only ever depicted in shadow or silhouette) from the far future of the twenty-seventh century attempts to manipulate the timeline to his advantage. The Suliban – a species new to *Star Trek* – were the pawns of this temporal manipulator whose true identity (much speculated over by fans) was never satisfactorily resolved on screen. Archer's dealings with the mysterious 'future guy' would be aided (or hindered) by another time-travelling character, Agent Daniels (Matt Winston). Having infiltrated Archer's crew, he then reappeared several times across the series. Daniels took Archer into the future to experience a galaxy without the United Federation of Planets (in first season finale 'Shockwave'), to visit a future *Enterprise-J* ('Azati Prime'), and on trips to the past (Earth in the year 2004 in 'Carpenter Street'; World War II in 'Storm Front').

Widely explored during the first season – and one reason for the prominence of T'Pol – was the relationship between humanity and the Vulcans. For almost 100 years since the 'first contact' incident depicted in the movie, the Vulcans had been nurturing mankind to become a space-faring race. While this involved offering assistance, it also meant withholding much useful knowledge, creating tension in the relationship. With the first steps into the wider universe taken by the *Enterprise*, the Vulcans never seem to be far away, seemingly keeping watch on Archer's initial explorations. This aspect created a more interesting conflict between T'Pol and the other *Enterprise* crewmembers than that depicted between the alien Spock and his crewmates, which was more often played for incongruous laughs. T'Pol was assigned to the ship explicitly to keep an eye on what the humans get up to, as well as to aid Archer in his explorations. Complicating the situation, T'Pol eventually seems to 'go native', leaving the Vulcan High Command to properly accompany Archer in his battles with the aggressive warmongering Xindi, joining Starfleet in the process.

Following an outcry from fans, and in an effort to perhaps

label the series in a clearer way, *Enterprise*'s producers decided to re-establish the *Star Trek* prefix for the show's third season. The series set out in a new direction, exploring a single season-long story inspired by the events that struck America on 11 September 2001 (when the series was shooting its first few instalments). The *Enterprise* equivalent of the attack on the Twin Towers in New York was an attack on Earth by a mysterious alien assailant, when an unknown probe cuts a deep swathe across the planet from Florida to Venezuela, killing over 7 million people (with Trip's sister a victim, giving at least one member of the *Enterprise* crew a personal connection to events). The final episode of the second season, 'The Expanse', sees the *Enterprise* recalled to Earth and refitted as a warship. The ship and its crew is now tasked with travelling through an unknown area (shades of *Voyager*) known as the Delphic Expanse to discover the home world of the Xindi, the malevolent alien race believed to be behind the unprovoked attack. This unsubtle echo of real-world contemporary events – the attack on 9/11, the invasions of Afghanistan and Iraq – was a return to the kind of direct political comment that had fuelled so many of the original *Star Trek* episodes of the 1960s and featured in many of *Deep Space Nine*'s best episodes, and it gave *Enterprise* a new sense of purpose and a clear direction. It also served to distinguish the show from the other *Star Trek* incarnations, something the producers had been keen to do from the start.

The temporal cold war storyline was effectively woven into that involving the Xindi – a distinctive alien species who did not just exhibit one distinguishing feature as so many previous *Star Trek* aliens had. Instead, the Xindi came in a variety of 'flavours', including aquatic, insectoid, reptilian, arboreal (tree-dwelling) and even an extinct avian variety. The Xindi included a primate branch that appeared more humanoid than the others. This imaginative approach to an alien species was unusual, with many other alien races falling foul of what fans had dubbed the 'bumpy forehead' syndrome in which the only distinguishing feature between species was a make-up-based cosmetic change to the forehead area.

The Xindi, it transpires, have been used by a race of time-travelling sphere-builders to attack the Earth in the hopes of preventing the establishment of the United Federation of Planets. Making Captain Archer's activities key to the future survival of the rest of the *Star Trek* universe (already depicted in the various series and movies) gave *Enterprise* a little more weight than a simple space exploration theme might have done. As the Xindi regard the sphere-builders, whom they know as 'the guardians', as gods (akin to the wormhole dwellers of *Deep Space Nine*), they are quick to act on their behalf. The season built to an event-packed finale in 'Zero Hour' in which Archer and his crew defeated the sphere-builders and destroyed the Xindi super weapon that had loomed as a season-long threat. In an unexpected development, the *Enterprise* returns to Earth only to discover the ship has somehow travelled in time to World War II – a weird, out of left-field *Star Trek* cliffhanger.

During its third season, *Enterprise* had shown a willingness to explore some strong science fiction ideas, such as the sphere-builders and the nature of the alien Xindi, an approach more often found in literary science fiction than on television. The fourth season saw this continue, but also saw the show delve much more into *Star Trek* lore under the direction of new chief storyteller Manny Coto. For the fourth year, *Enterprise* moved from its previous Wednesday night slot to Friday – long regarded as a 'death slot' for many television series, not least of which was the original *Star Trek*. Coto rapidly resolved several long-running story arcs, moving attention away from the fan-troubling (due to increasingly complicated continuity concerns) temporal cold war arc and resolving the outstanding Xindi story elements by the third episode of the fourth year.

These moves allowed Coto and his writers to introduce a new storytelling focus connected strongly with the nature and style of the original 1960s *Star Trek*. Characters, themes and concepts explored in *Enterprise*'s fourth year would draw heavily on the original tales of Captain Kirk's time period. One main area explored was that of human (and alien) genetic engineering, resulting in 'improved' people known as 'Augments'. The creation of people with genetically resequenced DNA was used to explain both the Eugenics Wars and the existence of Khan Noonien Singh from *The Original Series* episode 'Space Seed' and the movie *Star Trek II: The Wrath of Khan*, as well as the changing features of the Klingons between the 1960s TV show and 1979's *Star Trek: The Motion Picture* (covered in the *Enterprise* episodes 'Affliction' and 'Divergence'). The forehead ridge-less Klingons seen in *The Original Series* were explained away as victims of an Augment virus plague, an event that Worf in *Deep Space Nine*'s 'Trials and Tribble-ations' describes as a long story Klingons do not discuss with outsiders.

Three episodes ('Borderland', 'Cold Station 12' and 'The Augments') featured *The Next Generation*'s Brent Spiner as an ancestor of Data's creator, who is laying the groundwork for sentient androids. This was a transparent attempt to bring disenchanted fans of *The Next Generation* back to the show by featuring actors and characters they were more familiar with.

Such 'ret-conning', or retro-active continuity – providing explanations or origins of things already seen in the *Star Trek* universe – became something of a fetish during *Enterprise*'s fourth year, much to the pleasure of many fans of the franchise. The series also explored long-standing discrepancies in the ongoing depiction of the Vulcans throughout *Star Trek* history, attempting to explain variations by creating a splinter Vulcan society who follow the teachings of Surak, a mythical guru who developed the race's penchant for logic (as seen through Spock). This allowed the Vulcans of *Enterprise* to be more emotional, even war-like.

The mirror universe of *The Original Series* and *Deep Space Nine* was revisited – again, a fan-pleasing gambit. The two-part story 'In a Mirror Darkly' was a prequel to *The Original Series'* 'Mirror, Mirror' episode and saw the show sport a darker title sequence depicting the rise of the Terran Empire. The familiar *Enterprise* characters were reshaped as the most barbaric members of the evil Empire. Other episodes saw a return to the shuttle diplomacy practised by the 1960s *Enterprise*, featuring races such as the Tellarites and Andorians, drawing on *The Original Series* second season episode 'Journey to Babel' (which had also introduced Spock's parents). Although these connections were pleasing to *Star Trek* fans, it seems that was the only audience the show was reaching. This trio of episodes ('Babel One', 'United' and 'The Aenar') received the lowest Nielsen ratings for the show to date, leading network UPN to cancel *Enterprise* in February 2005. It was the first *Star Trek* show to have been cancelled by the network rather than wrapped up by its producers since the original series in 1969. The termination of *Enterprise* brought to an end eighteen years of continuous *Star Trek* on television and effectively finished off the franchise for the next four years.

Even so, Manny Coto still had to wrap up the show. The result was a final set of episodes exploring terrorism (a thematic follow-up to the real-world driven Xindi attack storyline of season three). *RoboCop* actor Peter Weller starred as the leader of an anti-alien faction attempting to use an artificially created half-alien baby (using DNA from T'Pol and Trip) to rouse alien-fearing humans living in dread since the Xindi threat. This anti-immigration storyline was ripped from the day's headlines, but was also seen by the producers as a dramatic narrative stepping-stone, taking humanity towards the utopian depiction that *Star Trek* creator Gene Roddenberry had intended in his original conception. The episodes were additionally packed with fan-pleasing references to other *Star Trek* shows, but came far too late to do anything to save the series from the ignominy of cancellation.

As the end of *Enterprise* was announced before the writing of the final episode, and with the producers' awareness that this was likely to be the last *Star Trek* seen on television for a while, the decision was taken to broadcast an unusual finale. Not only would 'These Are the Voyages . . .' be the final episode of *Enterprise*, it would also function as a franchise finale for the whole eighteen years of modern television *Star Trek*, from *The Next Generation* through *Deep Space Nine* and *Voyager* to *Enterprise*. This decision was yet another taken by *Star Trek*'s long-serving producers that would be extremely controversial with fans of the venerable franchise.

The setting of the episode was not *Enterprise*'s time period of the twenty second century – instead, events featuring the NX-01 crew were part of a holodeck recreation experienced on the *Enterprise-D* in 2370, observed by *The Next Generation*'s Riker and Troi. The events were even tagged as having taken place during a particular *The Next Generation* episode, season seven's 'The Pegasus'.

Faced with a decision about whether to make a difficult admission concerning a cover-up to Captain Picard, Riker (a returning Jonathan Frakes) visits a simulation of the final mission of the original *Enterprise*, commanded by Captain Jonathan Archer. He sees the creation of the Federation, within which all following *Star Trek* captains will operate.

Although co-writers Berman and Braga intended the episode to be (in Braga's words) 'a valentine' to the fans, its intended recipients reacted badly, especially to the surprise death of ship's engineer Trip Tucker. Fans of *Enterprise* in particular felt short-changed that their series' final episode had been essentially hijacked by *The Next Generation* to form a coda to the overall *Star Trek* television franchise. That the episode did not feature the actual characters from *Enterprise* but merely holographic re-creations on board the *Enterprise* from *The Next Generation* also rankled with loyal fans of the series. Although, across its four years on air, ratings for *Enterprise* had fallen from over 12 million to around 3 million, many fans appreciated an increase in story-telling quality across the last two seasons – mainly because the show became more *Star Trek*-like. For his part, final-year writer–producer Manny Coto regarded the penultimate episode, 'Terra Prime', as the end of the *Enterprise* story, as it wrapped up the final narrative arc he'd been producing.

As previously with *The Next Generation* and *Voyager*, the final episode ended with the same words that had opened the show's debut four years previously – 'To boldly go where no man has gone before' – concluding a montage of opening narration lines from Captains Picard, Kirk and Archer (working backwards in time, narratively).

'I would have never done it if I had known how people were going to react', admitted producer Rick Berman to startrek. com. 'We were informed with not a whole lot of time that this was our last season. We knew that this was going to be the last episode of *Star Trek* for perhaps quite some time . . . It was a very difficult choice, how to end it. The studio wanted it to be a one-hour episode. We wanted it to be special, something that would be memorable. This idea, which Brannon and I came up with – and I take full responsibility – pissed a lot of people off, and we certainly didn't mean to. Our thought was to take this crew and see them through the eyes of a future generation, see them through the eyes of the people who we first got involved [with] in *Star Trek* eighteen years before: Picard, Riker and Data. [We wanted] to see the history of how Archer and his crew went from where we had them to where, eventually, the Federation was formed, in some kind of magical holographic history lesson.

'It seemed like a great idea, [but] a lot of people were furious about it. The actors, most of them, were very unhappy. In retrospect it was a bad idea. When it was conceived it was with our heart completely in the right place. We wanted to pay the greatest homage and honour to the characters of *Enterprise* that we possibly could, but because Jonathan (Frakes) and Marina (Sirtis) were the two people we brought in, and they were the ones looking back, it was perceived as "You're ending our series with a *The Next Generation* episode." I understand how people felt that way. Too many people felt that way for them to be wrong. Brannon and I felt terrible that we'd let a lot of people down. It backfired, but our hearts were definitely in the right place. It just was not accepted in the way we thought it would be.'

Equally, in later years Braga was just as candid about what had gone wrong with the *Enterprise* finale: 'I do have some regrets: it didn't quite creatively align with the rest of the season. It had some great stuff in it and it was a cool concept, but I don't know if it fully delivered and it really pissed off the cast. Rick

[Berman] and I were involved in the franchise for years, Rick for eighteen, me for fifteen. We felt like we wanted to send a valentine to the show, but I do concur it was not a complete success.'

T'Pol actress Jolene Blalock called 'These Are the Voyages . . .' 'appalling', while Anthony Montgomery felt 'there could have been a more effective way to wrap things up for our show as well as the franchise as a whole. It seemed to take a little bit away from what the *Enterprise* cast and crew worked so diligently to achieve'. Even Jonathan Frakes recognised the folly of bringing in his character from *The Next Generation*: 'It was a bit of a stretch having us shut down [their] show.'

Critical reaction to the episode was the most negative that a *Star Trek* finale had ever received. Objections ranged from the inclusion of *The Next Generation* characters getting in the way of the *Enterprise* characters' farewell, to the suggestion that *The Next Generation* cameos simply served as a painful reminder of a time when *Star Trek* on television had simply been better than it was in the twenty-first century. The *Toronto Star* claimed that the way *Enterprise* ended robbed 'the characters (and their fans) of a significant long-term development or satisfying sense of closure'. Most critics laid the blame for the botched episode at the feet of Berman and Braga, while acclaiming Coto's popular take on the *Enterprise* prequel idea.

The unexpected death of Trip Tucker was seen as a pointless stunt that had been pulled with little impact. Again, the *Toronto Star* noted 'a major character is pointlessly killed off in service of a pointless plot device'. Even Tucker actor Connor Trinneer said he felt that the death of his character was 'forced' and was simply a device to manipulate the fan audience. In general, *Enterprise* was the most poorly regarded of all the *Star Trek* TV series, even after *Voyager*. Melanie McFarland, writing in the *Seattle Post-Intelligencer*, noted that the series 'never found the sense of uniqueness within the *Star Trek* universe that every version that came before it possessed'.

What Berman and Braga failed to recognise was that in re-creating the *Star Trek* of the 1960s, they were sticking with storytelling techniques that were slow and old-fashioned. Television – and science fiction shows in particular – had developed and changed hugely over the years, drawing inspiration from contemporary movies and science fiction literature of more recent decades. *Star Trek* had almost stopped being television science fiction and had become a period genre unto itself, with *The Next Generation*, *Deep Space Nine* and *Voyager* all being variations within that fixed, 1960s style of storytelling. For all its attempts to do something 'different', because it was still essentially Gene Roddenberry's *Star Trek*, *Enterprise* was doomed almost from the outset to contain all the positives and negatives of every other *Star Trek* TV series and movies that had come before it. It couldn't help itself, and it wasn't possible for it to be any other way. Those in charge, however, didn't seem to realise they were not making science fiction television, they were specifically making *Star Trek* television, a sub-set all its own.

According to Brannon Braga, 'If *Enterprise* had continued, we would have kept going with Manny Coto's unique vision of the show. Also, we would have explored the temporal cold war to its conclusion. We all felt that there were many more *Trek* stories to tell with that crew, and we were saddened by its premature end. Manny and I speak often about this – the show had really caught fire in seasons three and four.'

Among the ideas planned for the aborted fifth season of *Enterprise* were the origins and birth of the Federation (partly covered in 'These Are the Voyages . . .') and the first moves in the war with Romulus described in *The Original Series* episode 'Balance of Terror', with the Romulans developing as the season's major villains. Braga even hinted that he and Berman had considered making the mysterious 'future guy' of the temporal cold war a Romulan, to fit in with Coto's proposed story arc.

Following his work on year four, Coto planned to continue to strengthen the connections between *Enterprise* and the other *Star Trek* shows. One planned episode was a sequel to 'The Slaver Weapon', an instalment of *The Animated Series* featuring the alien Kzinti race, created by renowned science fiction author Larry

Niven. The construction site of the first ever Starbase and the cloud city of Stratos, previously seen in *The Original Series* episode 'The Cloud Minders', were also under consideration as settings to be further explored. An origin story for *Voyager*'s Borg Queen was also in the works, as was the revelation that T'Pol's father was a Romulan agent (perhaps tying in with the Romulan war arc). Another mirror universe story was also in preparation, perhaps to focus on Hoshi Sato in her alternate role as Empress of the Terran Empire. This may have taken the shape of a four- or five-episode mini-series spread throughout the season.

Coto even planned for an addition to the *Enterprise* crew in the form of Andorian Commander Shran (Jeffrey Combs), a recurring character who'd already appeared in ten episodes of *Enterprise*. The character might have joined the crew, in the words of Coto, as 'an auxiliary or adviser'.

The cancellation of the series meant that none of these ideas would come to fruition, although in response to the fan outcry about the death of Trip Tucker, tie-in novels were published by Pocket Books, beginning with *Last Full Measure* and *The Good That Men Do* (both by Andy Mangels and Michael A. Martin), which revealed the holographic depiction of his demise was a fabrication covering up Tucker's involvement with the shadowy Section 31 intelligence agency. According to the novels, Tucker faked his own death in order to be sent undercover to infiltrate Romulan space, aiming to prevent an interstellar war. These novels, and further follow-ups, presented an opportunity for the authors to expand upon the back-story and future of one of *Enterprise*'s most loved characters. It was an unusual example of those who police the expansion of the franchise in licensed spin-off material allowing an on-screen development to be superseded by ancillary material, a development that played well with Trip Tucker fans.

Almost immediately after the demise of *Enterprise*, Rick Berman attempted to further prolong the *Star Trek* franchise by beginning development work on a new film to take place after the events of *Enterprise* but before those of the original *Star Trek*

TV series. An executive reshuffle at Paramount put paid to Berman's efforts and he was finally removed from controlling the *Star Trek* franchise after eighteen years in charge, the most influential person on its development after creator Gene Roddenberry himself.

Berman was a television production professional, responsible for delivering hundreds of hours of technically complicated television on time and to broadcast standard over a period of eighteen years – no mean feat. He was not primarily a creative storyteller himself, but he'd been surrounded by key figures who'd used the *Star Trek* format in various ways to tell modern, meaningful stories. Key among those whom Berman had supported in their project to reshape Gene Roddenberry's universe were Michael Piller, Ron Moore, Ira Steven Behr, Jeri Taylor, Brannon Braga and Manny Coto.

The opening episode of *Enterprise* in 2001 had attracted 12.5 million viewers, but the number of people watching regularly dropped to less than 6 million very quickly. By the final season that number had halved again to under 3 million viewers, with a series low of just 2.5 million in January 2005, resulting in cancellation. Based on the number of viewers alone, the show must be considered a failure, whatever narrative achievements may have been made. It was a downward spiral Rick Berman could not deny. 'The show certainly had a great start. It got very good reviews and it had a huge audience for the first half dozen episodes and then it started to slip', he said. 'I could take the blame for it. I could put the blame into the scripts. I could put the blame into franchise fatigue. I don't know why it didn't work.' Brannon Braga suggested that the reason for the cancellation was viewer fatigue, noting that 'after 18 years and 624 hours of *Star Trek*, the audience began to have a little bit of overkill'.

It would take almost exactly four years from the transmission of the final episode of *Enterprise*, but *Star Trek* would return – not on TV, but back on the big screen once more – and it would become bigger and more successful than ever before.

# Chapter 12

## Hollow Pursuits: Unmade *Star Trek*

*'I think there is a need for the culture to have a myth. People look to* Star Trek *to set up a leader and a hearty band of followers. It's Greek classical storytelling.'* William Shatner

With the creation of so many stories for the ongoing *Star Trek* universe, it was inevitable that many often fully developed ideas for scripts would fall by the wayside. From the earliest days of the original *Star Trek* pilots through to the abandoned plans for the fifth season of *Enterprise* and beyond, to series ideas that were never progressed, storylines, characters and plots were developed that would never see the light of day. Perhaps the largest body of abandoned work came during the development of *Star Trek: Phase II* and *The Motion Picture* (discussed in chapter 5), but there have been many more untold adventures of Kirk, Picard, Sisko, Janeway, Archer (and several other captains) through the years that now only exist as scripts filed away in Paramount's archives.

There were enough abandoned episodes from the three years of the original *Star Trek* series between 1966 and 1969 to have filled two additional seasons on air. Almost sixty storylines and script ideas were developed, some not far beyond just the basic idea stage, while others were fully written storylines, meaning that writers and producers put some significant effort into trying to shape and prepare the material for production.

Gene Roddenberry's initial outline for *Star Trek* contained several episode ideas that were little more than one- or two-line concepts, some of which were developed into finished episodes (such as 'President Capone', which became 'A Piece of the Action' in the second season, and 'The Mirror', sowing the seeds for 'Mirror, Mirror').

Many of the more developed ideas that have since come to light were from David Gerrold, writer of 'The Trouble With Tribbles' and one of the co-developers of *The Next Generation*. Although he only scripted the single episode for the original *Star Trek* (and provided the story for 'The Cloud Minders'), he also supplied two scripts for the 1970s *Animated Series* and story-edited much of the first season of *The Next Generation*.

Although 'The Trouble With Tribbles' (itself developed from an idea originally called 'The Fuzzies') was his only *Star Trek* episode actually to be produced, Gerrold had worked on a variety of other ideas. Among them was a 1967 idea entitled 'Bandi', which probably influenced his Tribbles concept. The title character is a critter brought on board the *Enterprise* as a kind of mascot, but which causes much disruption among the crew due to its empathetic nature, leading to the death of a crewmember. Spock eliminates the creature and frees the crew from its malign influence. Gerrold later adapted the story for a *Star Trek* manga (Japanese comic).

Gerrold was also behind the never-produced episode 'The Protracted Man'. During an experiment to establish a faster than ever 'warp corridor', the pilot of a shuttlecraft is beamed to the *Enterprise* just in the nick of time. However, the man is 'protracted' – split in time. The concept was to be depicted by having three images of the man moving seconds apart, and displayed in the primary colours, blue, red and yellow. The affected man maintains himself by drawing energy from the *Enterprise* itself, thus becoming a threat to the ship. As the ship travels at warp speed, the man's triple images become further adrift in time from each other. Eventually, the protracted man has to be reintegrated using the ship's transporter. Gerrold claimed he had been influenced by a similar graphic sequence of images in Robert Wise's movie *West Side Story* (1961).

This was certainly a strong, original science fiction idea, but one that would have been complicated to realise on screen with 1960s television technology (although not impossible, just time-consuming and expensive). It would perhaps have been more suited to *The Next Generation* era, when scientific puzzles and easier to achieve special effects were more in vogue.

One of Gerrold's earliest outlines was a sixty-page storyline called 'Tomorrow Was Yesterday' (unrelated to the episode 'Tomorrow Is Yesterday'). Planned as a two-part tale, in order to ration the show's resources, the story saw the *Enterprise* discover a long-lost generation starship (a ship sent into space long ago in which generations of crew have grown, lived and died due to the slow pace of early space travel). Those on board have long forgotten their origins and have even lost the knowledge that they are on board a spacecraft. The idea was similar to one *Trek* writer Harlan Ellison would develop (and then disown) in the 1970s TV series *The Starlost*. Gerrold reused the idea himself several times, in his 1972 novel *Starhunt* and again in the 1980 *Star Trek* novel *The Galactic Whirlpool*.

It had always been Gene Roddenberry's intention from the beginning of *Star Trek* to involve science fiction prose authors in the creation of stories. This ideal was often hard to achieve, as many novelists were unable to adapt their ideas to the limited format of a weekly television show. However, several did get involved and made multiple, ultimately futile, attempts to crack *Star Trek*.

A. E. van Vogt had been high on Roddenberry's wish list to work on the series. He developed at least two story ideas – 'Machines Are Better' and 'The Search for Eternity' – that ended up on the shelf. There has been much speculation that van Vogt's *Voyage of the Space Beagle* from 1950 was an influence on Roddenberry when he created *Star Trek*, especially given this speech from a character called Von Grossen: 'The Beagle is going to another galaxy on an exploration voyage – the first trip of the kind. Our business is to study life in this new system'. It's

close to the opening narration of *Star Trek* as a mission statement, and the episodic novel includes a crew embarked on a
perilous exploration of unknown space. However, the author
himself found it difficult to tailor his ideas for *Star Trek*.

Philip José Farmer was another science fiction author who
contributed a variety of story ideas, but failed to get an episode
on air. His first proposal was titled 'Image of the Beast' (a title
he also used for an erotic horror novel with no connection to his
*Star Trek* idea). That, and another called 'Mere Shadows', didn't
get past the story outline stage. However, a third attempt, 'The
Shadow of Space', appears to have progressed further. Farmer's
idea saw the *Enterprise* escape the confines of the physical
universe altogether – truly going where no man had gone before.
Although the outlandish idea was rejected, Farmer published it
as a short story, stripped of all the *Star Trek* content. It appeared
in the magazine *Worlds of If* and later in one of Farmer's short
story collections. He did the same with a fourth rejected idea,
'Sketches Among the Ruins of My Mind'. According to Farmer,
his ideas were rejected as Gene Roddenberry found them 'too
sophisticated' for the general television audience. He told
*Starlog* magazine in 1990: '[Roddenberry] said his criterion is
what his little old maiden aunt in Iowa would understand, and
he said, "She would not understand these." "Sketches Among
the Ruins of My Mind" originally involved a little idol that
Captain Kirk had picked up in the ruins of a planet. It turns
out to be a device that makes you lose memory two days in a
row and you keep going backwards . . . eventually it's a year
before, and he's in a new situation . . . I don't think they could
put "Sketches" across'. These ideas, and a fifth known as 'The
Uncoiler', all remained unproduced.

Authors Norman Spinrad and Theodore Sturgeon did
succeed in getting episodes on air ('The Doomsday Machine'
for Spinrad, the Hugo Award-winning 'Amok Time' and
'Shore Leave' for Sturgeon). Spinrad's other script, co-written
with writer–producer Gene L. Coon, was titled 'He Walked
Among Us' and concerned a health food fanatic from the

Federation taking over a planet and breaching the Prime Directive by reshaping its society according to his beliefs. As the inhabitants perceive the man as a god, Kirk finds it very difficult to remove him without also disrupting the planet's society. It was an idea that would be returned to in *The Next Generation* instalment 'Who Watches the Watchers?' and the *Deep Space Nine* story 'Accession'.

Spinrad recalled he'd built the episode around an available standing set of an old village on the studio back lot. Additionally, the instalment was conceived by its co-author Gene Coon as a vehicle for entertainer Milton Berle, who would probably have fitted right in as one of *Star Trek*'s long list of would-be God-like beings, although Spinrad wasn't keen on the casting. 'I had Milton Berle and this village', he explained. 'I know that Berle can be a serious actor, but he likes weird get-ups. [Coon] rewrote a serious anthropological piece into something played for laughs.' Unhappy with Coon's rewrite, Spinrad asked Roddenberry to drop the script: 'I killed my own script rather than have it presented in that way.' He'd also eventually write a script for the aborted *Star Trek: Phase II* series.

Sturgeon's third script for *The Original Series* was to be 'The Joy Machine' (also called 'The Root of All Evil'). Although based on a story outline by Sturgeon, the full teleplay was eventually written by Meyer Dolinsky, also the writer of 'Plato's Stepchildren' and three episodes of the 1960s anthology show *The Outer Limits*. In a tale similar to 'This Side of Paradise' (which probably led to the abandonment of 'The Joy Machine'), Kirk and co visit a 'perfect' world where hard work is rewarded by a regular 'payday' session with the 'joy machine'. Induced to abandon their ship, the *Enterprise* crew are co-opted into the society of the joy machine. The unmade tale was written up as a novel by James Gunn for Pocket Books in 1996. Also outlined by Sturgeon in 1968 but never made was the self-explanatory 'Shore Leave II'.

Jerome Bixby wrote four episodes for *Star Trek* in the 1960s ('Mirror, Mirror' – introducing the mirror universe concept and a Hugo Award-winner – 'By Any Other Name', 'Day of the

Dove' and 'Requiem for Methuselah'), but even he had other ideas rejected, including 'For They Shall Inherit', 'Mother Tiger' and 'Skal', about which few details survive.

George Clayton Johnson, one of the few regular writers for *The Twilight Zone* other than Rod Serling, developed a story under the imaginative title 'Rock-a-Bye Baby, or Die!' following his initial episode, 'The Man Trap'. His second attempt at a *Star Trek* script saw a juvenile alien being enter the *Enterprise*'s computer system, where it incubated and grew to adulthood. Kirk would have become a father figure to the entity, coaching it through its life trapped within the computer. Gene Coon was not keen on the idea and it was rejected. However, both he and Roddenberry liked Johnson's 'The Syndicate' (drawn from Roddenberry's 'President Capone' idea) well enough to develop it into 'A Piece of the Action' (originally called 'Mission into Chaos' and written by Coon and David P. Harmon).

Other science fiction authors didn't fare as well. Comic science fiction writer Robert Sheckley had several ideas rejected, including 'Rites of Fertility' and 'Sister in Space', although he did write a tie-in *Deep Space Nine* novel in 1995. Larry Niven eventually wrote an episode for *The Animated Series* ('The Slaver Weapon', linked to the author's own 'Known Space' stories), but he first submitted ideas to the 1960s show. 'The Pastel Terror' concerned a 'star beast' plasmoid life form that fed off the energy of stars. The *Enterprise* was to be enveloped by the creature, which was intent on draining the ship's energy. One method of escape suggested by Spock was to separate the saucer section of the ship (a possibility built in by Roddenberry, but not seen until the 1987 *The Next Generation* pilot episode 'Encounter at Farpoint' and in the 1994 movie *Star Trek Generations*). Spock replaces Kirk and proceeds with the saucer separation, destroying the secondary hull in an attempt to wipe out the plasmoid life form. The saucer section of the *Enterprise* lands on a remote planet and the crew prepare to establish a colony. Aided by the planet's giant dragon-like inhabitants, however, they are able to return to the Federation.

Niven himself realised that the special effects required by his story made it virtually unproducable, while Spock's betrayal of the captain did not go down well with Roddenberry. The rather apocalyptic storyline puts the *Enterprise* crew in a desperate situation and virtually destroys the ship (as eventually seen in *The Search for Spock* and *Generations*). Niven's outline was eventually published in the *Star Trek* fanzine *T-Negative#17* in 1972. Niven would go on to contribute to the syndicated *Star Trek* newspaper strip, pitting the *Enterprise* crew against his own Kzinti once again.

Even those most closely involved with writing and producing the original *Star Trek* had ideas that failed to be produced. Story editor D. C. Fontana made several attempts to give Dr McCoy a daughter called Joanna, but each story was rejected. The first, simply entitled 'Joanna', was heavily rewritten to become the episode 'The Way to Eden' (an infamous episode featuring space hippies). The original outline saw McCoy's free-spirited daughter having a romantic fling with Captain Kirk, much to the horror of her father. Another Fontana script introducing Joanna McCoy and intended for the unmade fourth season of *Star Trek* was called 'The Stars of Sargasso'.

Associate producer Robert Justman tried his hand at an original story with 'The Deadliest Game', a riff on the 1932 movie *The Most Dangerous Game* about an insane hunter who pursues the most dangerous game of all: man. Justman gave the setting as a 'hell planet', with the *Enterprise* crew trapped aboard a ship like the *Mary Celeste* and on a quest for something akin to the Treasure of the Sierra Madre, which turns out to be the fountain of youth.

John Meredyth Lucas, producer of the second season of *Star Trek* from 'Journey to Babel' to 'The Omega Glory', wrote four episodes ('The Changeling', 'Patterns of Force', 'Elaan of Troyius' and 'That Which Survives') and directed three (his own 'Elaan of Troyius', plus 'The Ultimate Computer' and 'The *Enterprise* Incident'). Even with all those credits, his script for 'The Godhead' found itself stuck in development hell in the

*Star Trek* production office in 1968. It concerned the last two representatives of an ancient race out to absorb the entire universe within their brains. Another idea, 'The Lost Star', echoed the episode 'The Apple', in that an entire race of people are held in subjugation by either a priestly elite or a malfunctioning computer, as seen in several *Star Trek* episodes.

Even the cast of *Star Trek* got in on the act, developing or suggesting ideas for storylines, more often than not revolving around dramatic events concerning their own characters. Gene Roddenberry seriously entertained a few of these ideas, including one by William Shatner, another by Nichelle Nichols and one by DeForest Kelley. Shatner's 1966 idea was called 'The Web of Death' and was described in *TV Guide* of October that year as having a 'good flow'. The story outline saw the *Enterprise* discover the long-missing ship *Momentous*, encased in a web-like substance from a massive 'space spider'. The spider attacks the *Enterprise*, but is repelled by a poison developed by Kirk, who uses the dead-in-space *Momentous* as a decoy to save the *Enterprise* (a gambit later used in 'The Doomsday Machine').

DeForest Kelley's story idea was to feature him as McCoy and Nichelle Nichols as Uhura trapped on a planet dominated by a dark-skinned race who subjugated the lighter-skinned people. Kelley noted, 'there was a great racial problem, only reversed. The fact that I am a Southerner and she is black, and that we're trapped on this planet together' would provide the drama. According to David Gerrold, in *The World of Star Trek*, the script idea was 'written, rewritten, and rewritten. Either the premise was too touchy for television or nobody could quite make it work. The script never reached a form where Roddenberry or Coon wanted to put it into production.' A similar idea would be eventually explored in the conflict between the half-white, half-black and half-black, half-white Cheron race in 'Let That Be Your Last Battlefield'.

These were by no means all the unproduced ideas for the original *Star Trek*. Many did not get beyond thoughts or writer pitches that were never followed up. What they do show, though, is the depth of thought and experimentation that was going into *The Original Series*, that so many workable ideas did not progress to the screen in that initial three-year period of invention.

While there are not as many surviving unproduced story ideas for *The Next Generation* as there were for the original *Star Trek*, across its seven years on air there seem to have been at least enough unrealised ideas for an entire additional season.

Michael Piller began writing for *The Next Generation* during its second year, becoming the show's lead writer during its third. Uniquely across the *Star Trek* series he implemented an 'open door' policy, inviting anyone who thought they could write a *Star Trek* teleplay to have a go. This led to a huge number of submissions, the vast majority of which were quickly rejected. However, the policy did pay some dividends, resulting in several episodes including the very popular 'Yesterday's *Enterprise*'. Writers who got their start from Piller's policy include Ronald D. Moore (*Carnivàle*, *Roswell*, *Battlestar Galactica*), René Echevarria (*The 4400*, *Medium*, *Castle*) and Brannon Braga (*Threshold*, *24*, *FlashForward*).

One teleplay that resulted was 'Deadworld', from journalist (and *Star Trek* chronicler) James Van Hise. 'I wrote the story in 1987 at the behest of a mutual friend of Gerd Oswald', said Van Hise. 'Oswald had directed a couple of *Star Trek* episodes in the 1960s ("The Conscience of the King", "The Alternative Factor") and I'd spoken to him while he was directing an episode of the new *Twilight Zone* for CBS when I visited that studio in 1986. Oswald was looking for a story he could take to Paramount for *The Next Generation* which he could attach himself to as director. He read this outline but rejected it as being "too depressing". I told my friend that Gerd, who was then in his 70s, was obviously a man who had never come to terms with his own mortality'.

*The Next Generation* creative consultant Greg Strangis tried to get an original story of his own on air. Although much work was done on his script for 'The Neutral Zone' (unrelated to the

season one finale of the same title, although some of Strangis'
ideas did surface in 'Too Short a Season'), the episode failed to
be produced. The story featured a misanthropic, wheelchair-
bound Federation security expert called Billings, who was
charged with opening negotiations with the antagonistic
Romulan Empire. All the *Enterprise* crew who have had contact
with Romulans are assigned to the mission, including Worf, who
dislikes them. A sabotaged transporter causes tension among
the two groups, while Dr Crusher works on a cure for Billings.

Even 'the Great Bird of the Galaxy' himself had story ideas
rejected by his replacements at Paramount. 'Ferengi Gold' was
a two-part tale by Gene Roddenberry intended for the second
season of *The Next Generation*. Many of Roddenberry's tried
and tested themes featured in the draft screenplay, including an
alien world, a developing civilisation that parallels one from
Earth's history, and the ultimate perfection of the Federation.
His idea of the Ferengi posing as gods and lording it over a less
developed civilisation (an idea that would have fitted right in
with the 1960s *Star Trek*) later turned up in the third season
*Voyager* episode 'False Profits'.

Sometimes ideas or concepts defeated the combined efforts
of the writing staff of *The Next Generation*, as was the case for
René Echevarria and Jeri Taylor on 'Q Makes Two', an episode
planned to feature the mysterious Q (John de Lancie). During
the fifth and sixth seasons of *The Next Generation*, various writers on the staff wrestled with the idea. The story featured Q
duplicating the *Enterprise* crew for his own nefarious ends.
According to Brannon Braga: 'There was a sense of doom from
the moment we started "Q Makes Two". I think we broke it
[worked out the basic elements of the story] three times. René
[Echevarria] wrote two drafts and it was ultimately abandoned.
It's an interesting notion that Q comes onboard and Picard's
saying people are inherently good and we have managed to get
rid of our darker elements in the twenty-fourth century, we're
better people. Q says, "So you don't think you have dark components and you think you're better without them? Well, I'm

going to show you a thing or two." He extracts the darker components and puts them into doubles. The clean, good components suffer and so do the darker components and neither function without the other. We see that dramatically, but for some reason we made it more complex than it needed to be. The image in my mind that we never really got to was the two *Enterprise*s shooting at each other – that's what you want to see!'

Taylor described the experience as a 'nightmare', dragging attention away from important work on other episodes for which the deadlines were more imminent. The idea of dividing the starship in two later came to the screen in an episode of *Voyager* called 'Deadlock'. To some, the plot also recalled the early original *Star Trek* series episode 'The Enemy Within', which saw Captain Kirk divided into his 'good' and 'evil' halves due to a transporter accident.

Another rejected Q episode had the clever title of 'I.Q. Test'. It would have seen Q going to war with another member of the Q Continuum, drawing the *Enterprise* and her crew into the conflict. The episode would have seen the two Qs pitting their own teams in a metaphysical Olympics, putting the humans from the *Enterprise* up against the alien Zaa-Naar species. It was even hoped that *Terminator* actor Arnold Schwarzenegger would appear as a representative of the superhuman Zaa-Naar race. Although it was a story from a new writer, Michael Piller killed it off. Ron Moore later noted in an internet Q and A, 'In defence of Michael, the Q-Olympics story was ludicrous and needed to be deep-sixed.'

Actress Vanna Bonta (*The Beastmaster*) pitched a time travel story to *The Next Generation*, perhaps in the hope of being cast in a role in her own episode. The *Enterprise* receives a distress signal from a starship lost in the space equivalent of the Bermuda Triangle. This area is made up of 'energy rings', with each ring enclosing a different period of time. Travelling through the rings, the *Enterprise* crew experience different variations of their own history that include a beard-wearing Picard, Beverly Crusher's husband Jack still alive, and a married, sighted Geordi

La Forge living and working outside Starfleet. Data, as an android, is the only one aware of the different realities, and manipulates Picard into saving the ship. Crusher attempts to stay behind in one of the alternative timelines, but is persuaded to return to 'normality'.

Happy to deal with important contemporary themes, *The Next Generation* often dealt with environmental issues, including in a rejected story idea by René Echevarria. Working through many drafts, Echevarria admitted the idea 'never got off the ground'. Speaking in *Captains' Logs*, Echevarria recalled 'smokestacks [were] the cause of blindness and mutations in a tribe kept on a little island called the Island of Tears. They were hidden from view in order for the rest of the society to be able to maintain its mode of production, which was highly exploitive and environmentally unsound. The audience would have guessed at the end of the first act what was going on. What I came up with was a Federation colony that mined dilithium and they're natives to the planet. The twist was that what was causing the problems were these organisms that had evolved in the presence of electromagnetic fields of dilithium. Its removal was creating mutations.' His clever idea tied the environmental damage into a core need of the Federation, the dilithium crystals which powered starships – a clear analogy for the Western world's reliance on fossil fuels. The episode, however, did not progress any further.

So Piller's open door policy did bear fruit (other episodes that got made included Ron Moore's 'The Bonding' and 'Hollow Pursuits', which introduced the character of Reg Barclay), but it also led to a whole lot of extra work for the writing staff in sifting through thousands of submissions in search of something that would work on *Star Trek*.

After *The Next Generation*, there were far fewer rejected storylines and scripts that progressed to the stage of substantial written material. There are several potential reasons why both *Deep Space Nine* and *Voyager* had very few unused storylines. By that stage the writers and producers were far more comfortable with modern *Star Trek* and knew the kind of concepts and stories that would work, so didn't waste time and effort developing stories that did not stand a chance of reaching the screen. Also, after seven years in production, the writers had run through many of their best ideas on *The Next Generation*, so material that might previously have been rejected was heavily reworked until it actually made it to the screen.

Certainly, *Deep Space Nine* was a harder show for outside writers to break into, especially in later years when the war story arcs meant that the show became far more serialised and by necessity the majority of the writing was by staff writers. Even so, there were a couple of ideas that didn't progress beyond rough storylines, including one dealing with a day in the life of bartender Quark ('Day at Quarks') and a seventh season story dealing with Ezri Dax having the Dax symbiont removed ('Dysfunctional'). Ron Moore's fifth season episode 'Soldiers of Fortune' began life as 'Klingon Hell', a very different episode that saw Worf and the crew of the Klingon Bird-of-Prey ship *Rotarran* enter Gre'thor, the Klingon Hell where dishonoured Klingon souls are consigned. The concept lived on, later forming the basis of the *Voyager* story 'Barge of the Dead', this time with B'Elanna Torres in a near-death experience instead of Worf.

Perhaps drawing on the abandoned 'Q Makes Two', *Voyager* had in development a storyline concerning duplicates of the lost crew of that starship. The duplicates are actually the biometric life forms featured in the episodes 'Demons' and 'Course: Oblivion', and they would complete the voyage back to the Alpha Quadrant long before the real *Voyager*, arriving to great acclaim at the *Deep Space Nine* station. Jeri Taylor recalled, 'Everybody thinks *Voyager* is home and there are celebrations, and they see their loved ones . . . it turns out to be an invasion or a dark plot of some kind.' Although never fully scripted, the idea hung around through the whole of *Voyager*'s seven-year run. The closest it came to being made was as the third season finale, later replaced by 'Scorpion'. In order not to waste a good idea, it was revived again for the possible fourth season finale, but the writers couldn't make it work, feeling the return of a 'fake' *Voyager* crew would undermine the return of the real team later.

The arrival of *Enterprise* saw a return to a looser commissioning structure and so resulted in a higher number of well-developed ideas that never made it to the screen, most of them apparently coming from *Star Trek* cast members past and present.

According to Hoshi Sato actress Linda Park, her co-star Connor Trinneer proposed a story inspired by the Quentin Tarantino movie *Pulp Fiction*, told from the point of view of an alien race. The alien perspective would have been depicted through the *Enterprise* crew talking incomprehensible gibberish until a method of communication was discovered (some might say many *Enterprise* episodes were 'incomprehensible gibberish' anyway).

Following up on his story pitch of 1966, William Shatner was set to return to *Star Trek* by appearing in an *Enterprise* two-parter. Fourth season showrunner Manny Coto recalled that the plan was to feature Shatner in a mirror universe-set tale written by Shatner's friends and novel co-writers Judith and Garfield Reeves-Stevens, who were also staff writers on the final season of *Enterprise*. The story pitch came from Shatner himself over lunch with Rick Berman, Coto and Brannon Braga. The mirror universe featured a device called the Tantalus Field that disintegrated targets remotely. The writers wanted to revise this, making it instead a time travel device that sent prisoners back in time to a penal colony. The *Enterprise* discovers the prison colony, finding mirror-Kirk (called Tiberius) imprisoned. Tiberius sees the ship as an opportunity for escape, but he discovers that in this time period the mirror universe does not yet exist. Tiberius and Archer work together to investigate what creates the mirror universe, only to find that it is their own actions that bring it about. Although the ideas were well received, Berman had an alternative take from Mike Sussman, one of the producers on both *Voyager* and *Enterprise*, that would see Shatner playing the chef (perhaps riffing on his presenter role in TV

show *Iron Chef*) on board the earliest *Enterprise*, a comic equivalent to *Voyager*'s Neelix. As neither Shatner nor Paramount
could agree terms for his appearance, the ideas progressed no
further, although 'In a Mirror, Darkly' saw the return of the
mirror universe with an alternative explanation of its origins.
Coto's exploration of the links between his show and the 1960s
*Star Trek* resulted in a handful of other aborted ideas. Coto
became fixated on returning a little known character, Colonel
Green – an eco-terrorist involved in the third world war and
seen in the episode 'The Savage Curtain'. Coto planned to have
his *Odyssey 5* star Peter Weller (best known as RoboCop) play
Colonel Green in an episode that returned to some of the issues
explored in the earlier 1960s instalment. Both Weller and
(briefly) Colonel Green would appear in the *Enterprise* episode
'Demons'. That same episode featured the idea of terraforming
Mars, home of rebel separatist Paxton (Weller), which had its
origins in a Coto story dealing with the independence of the
Earth colony on the red planet. Coto envisaged an attempt to
change the atmosphere of Mars using comets that would instead
be aimed at Earth by terrorists, an incident Coto described as
the Cuban Missile Crisis in space.

Some of the more unusual unused ideas for *Enterprise*
featured Captain Archer's dog, Porthos. Stories pitched included
Porthos becoming intelligent and conversing with the crew, the
dog being the only one able to communicate with an alien
canine race and Porthos becoming captain of the *Enterprise*.
While these stories were inherently silly, the official reason for
their rejection was that the showrunners did not want Porthos
becoming the star of the show, in the way that some robotic
sidekicks of the 1970s (such as Twiki on *Buck Rogers in the 25th
Century* or robot dog K-9 on *Doctor Who*) had done. Many of
these story claims came from Andre Bormanis in a DVD extra
on the box set of *Enterprise* season four, resulting in some fans
believing he'd actually just invented them . . .

The lost voyages of *Star Trek*, from the 1960s birth of the show
to its final end (on television at least) at the beginning of the

twenty-first century, provide a secret history of the series. It's a glimpse into an alternative world – a kind of mirror universe of *Star Trek* storytelling – in which everything is not quite as we know it in the stories we experienced across four decades as *Star Trek* viewers. It's certainly a fascinating byway in *Star Trek* history.

Unmade scripts and story ideas were not the only unseen alternative *Star Trek*s: alongside and beyond the airing of *Enterprise*, several prominent creative people proposed new takes on the series' basic concepts to Paramount (which became CBS Paramount in 2006 as a result of a corporate merger) to continue the franchise beyond *Enterprise*. The fact that their ideas were quickly rejected suggests the studio focus was on bringing *Star Trek* back to cinemas rather than television. Jonathan Frakes, Commander Will Riker on *The Next Generation*, was behind one failed pitch: 'I had a *Star Trek* [series idea] that I developed for TV', Frakes told website UGO in 2011, 'and we were told in no uncertain terms that they said no to a Bryan Singer television *Star Trek*, they said no to a William Shatner television *Star Trek*. They feel at CBS Paramount that they don't want to make the same mistake that's been made before, which was watering down the brand by having a TV show and a movie [at the same time]. That's what happened with *Star Trek Nemesis*, and that's why I think *Star Trek: Enterprise* didn't last the way they expected it to. It was the classic corporate greed of "we've got something good, so let's continue to milk it" and [they] milked it so dry that the fans had no appetite for a movie. So I think what they've done by taking time off before the Abrams' *Star Trek*, and they're doing it again [with] the second one, is a much smarter business plan. Much to my chagrin! Not that I wouldn't love the *Titan*, or the *Rikers in Space*, or any of those shows on the air.'

*Star Trek: Titan* was a spin-off series of novels published by Pocket Books, starting in 2005, that drew on the fact that Riker ended *Star Trek Nemesis* as captain of his own ship, the USS *Titan*. It seems likely that Frakes' idea for a new *Star Trek* TV show was based around these further adventures of Riker.

As mentioned by Frakes, both *The Original Series* star William Shatner and film director Bryan Singer (*X-Men*, *Superman Returns*, *Valkyrie*) had also developed new *Star Trek* series ideas. Shatner's notion would have sounded very familiar to *Star Trek* movie producer Harve Bennett. Called *Star Trek: The Academy*, his proposed series would have followed the adventures of teenage versions of Kirk, Spock and McCoy. The actor had worked up his proposal with Judith and Garfield Reeves-Stevens, but this time he bypassed Rick Berman, pitching directly to Paramount chief Sumner Redstone. Once the concept was rejected, the Reeves-Stevens instead turned it into a planned two-novel series, but only the first (*Star Trek Academy: Collision Course* (2007)) ever appeared. In the novel, the first meeting between Kirk and Spock takes place in a strip club where Kirk is hiding out while Spock is trying to sell off Vulcan artefacts. Facing time in a penal colony, Kirk and Spock opt to join Starfleet Academy instead, with Kirk giving his Vulcan friend the nickname 'Stretch'.

Movie director Bryan Singer was a lifelong *Star Trek* fan who'd made a minor cameo appearance in *Star Trek Nemesis* as a Starfleet officer on the bridge of the *Enterprise*. He'd been involved in a stalled attempt in 2001 to revive *Battlestar Galactica* (a feat eventually achieved by *The Next Generation*'s Ron Moore in 2003). Singer claimed his proposed version of *Star Trek* would have been 'Big . . . it would be very big', according to an interview with iseb.net in 2005. Set just beyond the thirtieth century, Singer's proposed TV series would have been called *Star Trek: Federation*. It would have featured a less warrior-like and more political depiction of the Klingons, while Vulcans and Romulans would be pursuing their reunification away from human contact. The Federation would have spread far and wide across the galaxy, making communication a difficult and time-consuming process. Distant areas of the galaxy would therefore provide new frontiers for exploration, cut off from the support that Starfleet and the Federation normally supply (echoing the set-up of *Voyager* – although unlike *Voyager*, Singer seemed

intent on exploring genuinely new and unknown worlds).
Singer's *Star Trek* essentially proposed a fresh start for the franchise, devoid of any connections with the previous series, while
also being a back to basics, 'starship facing the unknown' show.
It would have one clear connection to *The Original Series*, the
*Star Trek* founding myth. The sole survivor of the USS *Sojourner*
(a victim of the mysterious 'scourge') would have been Lt
Commander Alexander Kirk, co-opted onto the crew of an all-
new *Enterprise* (the first in 300 years), sent out in search of the
unknown malevolent enemy. Other crewmembers would have
included The 76th Distillation of Blue, a gaseous alien who uses
a 'motion suit' to interact with humans and goes by the name
Diz, and M.A.J.E.L., the ship's sentient computer (named after
Roddenberry's wife – and voice of the *Enterprise* computer –
Majel Barrett).

A proposal document for the series was drawn up after a
lengthy dinner conversation between Singer, writer Christopher
McQuarrie (*The Usual Suspects*, which Singer had also directed)
and Robert Meyer Burnett (director of *Free Enterprise*). The
document recognised that television storytelling had changed
since *Star Trek* had originally been created, promising 'more
complex, serialized stories ... compelling stories about our
world today. Let *Star Trek* breathe. Let's grapple again with the
issues of the day – diversity, government power, gender fric-
tions, a controversial war on foreign soil'. The proposal sets out
to 'acknowledge what's come before, [but] turn the *Star Trek*
universe upside down'.

Burnett claimed the first draft outline was never submitted
to Paramount as the J. J. Abrams movie was announced instead.
'It was meant to be a jumping off point for further discussion',
he told website i09, 'not to ever be sent anywhere, certainly not
to any network. There are things in the pitch I still quite like. I
wanted to see more "hard" sci-fi concepts addressed directly
in *Trek*.'

There was another big-name, more fully developed *Star
Trek* pitch dating from 2004. *Babylon 5* creator J. Michael

Straczynski and UFO-conspiracy series *Dark Skies* creator
Bryce Zabel co-authored an unsolicited TV series pitch entitled '*Star Trek*: Re-boot the Universe'. The fourteen-page
document was sub-headed 'A Proposal For Re-Imagining the
First Five-Year Mission'.

The pair had met when sharing a flight between Los Angeles
and Vancouver (where many American TV shows are shot).
Later, when working together on an ultimately unmade TV
mini-series called *Cult*, their conversation turned to the current
state of *Star Trek*, as *Enterprise* was reaching its final stages. 'We
wanted to start over, use Kirk, Spock and McCoy and others in
a powerful new origin story about what it was that bonded them
in such strong friendship, and show them off as you'd never
seen them before. It was, admittedly, pretty audacious', Zabel
later wrote on his website.

In their resulting document – after singing the praises of *Star
Trek* as a concept – the authors then lamented the state of the
franchise in 2004. 'There's trouble in the *Star Trek* universe.
Ratings have declined, demographics have stagnated . . . Can
*Star Trek* be saved?' The difficulty of telling new stories within
the overgrown, complicated, established *Star Trek* universe was
summed up with the following responses to proposed story
ideas: 'It's been done, it's being done or it would never be done'.
The most recent *Star Trek* spin-off shows were characterised as
'a copy of a copy of a copy', and the blame for *Star Trek*'s decline
lay with the fact that 'the all-too-reasonable desire to protect the
franchise may now be the cause of its stagnation'.

The answer proposed by Straczynski and Zabel? 'The best
solution is to go back to the original and start again. It's time to
re-boot the *Star Trek* universe.' Their concept for twenty-first-
century *Star Trek* was a return to the 1960s setting and characters
but combined with 'the kind of storytelling that audiences of
2004 are used to seeing in modern prime-time television. Hard-
hitting. Exciting. Character-driven. Innovative.' Straczynski had
demonstrated his undoubted ability to achieve all of that with
the groundbreaking *Babylon 5* during the latter half of the

1990s. Now he wanted to apply those storytelling techniques to *Star Trek*.

His starting point would have been 'the three best things in the *Star Trek* universe: Kirk. Spock. McCoy'. These three characters would be reimagined and sent off on a brand new five-year mission to explore strange new worlds and new civilisations, free of all the baggage that *Star Trek* had built up over almost forty years. 'It is time to go boldly back to the original', the authors wrote, 'reborn and retooled for a new millennium'.

Straczynski and Zabel firmly believed that audiences would be happy to accept new actors playing the much-loved classic characters of Kirk, Spock and McCoy in new television adventures, characterising the trio as 'the warrior, the priest, the doctor'. The plan was also to reinvent the second-tier characters from *The Original Series*, with new takes on Scotty, Sulu, Uhura and Chekov.

The 'creative plan' for the series proposed an opening two-hour pilot TV movie depicting the meeting of the central trio (no strip clubs here), their discovery of a lost city on an uncharted world and their encounter with the ancient advanced race who had built it (shades of Philip Kaufman's *Planet of the Titans* movie project). The pilot would end with Kirk (the youngest starship captain in the Federation), Spock and McCoy aboard the *Enterprise*, poised at the edge of known space and ready for exploration.

A revamp of *Star Trek*'s technology, such as the communicators and tricorders, was proposed, although the classic silhouette of the *Enterprise* would be retained. More complex and adult relationships would drive the drama on a more human level, while action-oriented plots would form the core of the series.

Straczynski and Zabel's proposed series would have an ongoing narrative arc at its core: throughout the series, Kirk and crew would be seeking the ancient race encountered in the pilot. They would not be the only ones searching for the aliens' ancient knowledge, though, with 'forces of darkness' also on the hunt. Buried deep within the DNA of all species is a mathematical code, an 'artist's signature' that could not have occurred by chance. The series' new Prime Directive would be 'to do whatever is necessary to find this long-lost race and discover the truth about the common origin of life'. These – and other mysteries – would be woven into the story of the week episodes of the proposed series. Although individual episodes of the proposed show would stand alone, 'these explorations do not exist in a vacuum, there's a reason and a mystery behind it all'.

The document criticised the existence of the holodeck in modern *Star Trek*, stating that *The Original Series'* characters had no need of such artificial distractions as there were more than enough adventures and more than enough excitement in their real world. The series was planned to run for exactly five seasons, with the overall story having a beginning, a middle and an end (just like Straczynski's *Babylon 5*). At the end of the five-year story arc, the *Enterprise* and her remaining crew would return to Earth, allowing any follow up series to 'move the franchise into new territory'. The writers proposed returning to one of *Star Trek*'s earliest habits – buying in short stories from top science fiction authors to adapt to the *Star Trek* format. The modern equivalents to Richard Matheson, Robert Bloch and Norman Spinrad were (according to Straczynski and Zabel), Neil Gaiman, Dean Koontz and Stephen King.

Straczynski and Zabel's document proposed that all pre-existing *Star Trek* material should be relegated to 'Universe A', permitting their rebooted *Star Trek* to be free of previous continuity ties and dubbed 'Universe B'. This would allow for 'the unshackling of all the pent-up talent and ideas that are precluded from expression by virtue of what has gone on before'.

The series would simply be called *Star Trek* and would be a 'bold new interpretation . . . a fresh start'. Symptomatic of this fresh start was the suggestion that in this version, Scotty should be a woman (a similar tactic had been used by Ron Moore in 2003's *Battlestar Galactica*, recasting the role of Starbuck as female).

The document included a sparse breakdown of a proposed

first season, mainly a structure with rough story points promising a mix of stories adapted from *The Original Series*, tales from
well-known writers and stand-alone original stories, all serving
the larger mystery arc of the long-lost ancient race. The writers
promised this series would spark an all-new wave of *Star Trek*
excitement, something they dubbed 'the coming buzz'. The
search for actors to fill the iconic roles of Kirk, Spock and
McCoy would be a major showbusiness story in itself, while the
prospect of an all-new five-year mission for those classic characters would generate broad audience re-engagement with the
legend of *Star Trek*.

'No one can ever compete with Gene Roddenberry's original
series', the writers concluded. 'We can, however, stand on his
shoulders and see things from a different perspective.'

While developed with good creative intentions, the *Star Trek*
reboot proposed by J. Michael Straczynski and Bryce Zabel
went nowhere. 'We held back from putting everything we were
thinking into [the document] because, if we did, what would be
the point of hiring us? So we suggested and prodded and
explained and held some of the point-by-point work back for a
meeting or an opportunity that never came', Zabel wrote.

When the team of writers Roberto Orci and Alex Kurtzman
and director J. J. Abrams were faced with the same challenge of
reinventing *Star Trek* in 2007, their lengthy considerations led
them to very similar story solutions to those proposed by
Straczynski and Zabel almost three years earlier.

The challenge after *Enterprise* was how to return *Star Trek* to big
screen popularity without either the cast of *The Original Series*
or that of *The Next Generation*. There was no appetite (even
among fans) for *Deep Space Nine*, *Voyager* or *Enterprise* to
become movies, but studio executives at CBS Paramount
believed there was still life in *Star Trek*, despite the relative failures of *Voyager* and *Enterprise* on television. Indeed, there was
still much fondness among the wider general cinema-going
public for *Star Trek*, especially the simpler, less complicated

days of Kirk, Spock and McCoy. It was also true that those original *Star Trek* characters continued to be the most impactful, with the widest recognition factor globally, even after the success of *The Next Generation*.

The *Star Trek* movie franchise appeared to have died with the amazingly poor box office performance of *Nemesis*, while on television the franchise had also ground to an ignominious halt. Was *Star Trek* over by 2005? Rick Berman didn't believe so, and in the wake of the failure of *Enterprise* he began exploring new possibilities for a *Star Trek* movie unconnected to either *The Original Series* or *The Next Generation*.

With the support of CBS Paramount's new studio executives, Berman developed a movie to take place in the one unexplored area of the *Star Trek* timeline, between the end of *Enterprise* and the period of *The Original Series*. He saw the film as both a sequel to the most recent TV series and a prequel to everything else that would come after.

Writer Erik Jendresen, riding high on the success of the Steven Spielberg-produced *Band of Brothers* TV mini-series, was brought in to write the new *Star Trek* screenplay. The result was a 121-page script delivered with the working title *Star Trek: The Beginning*, echoing the successful 2005 Christopher Nolan-directed blockbuster reboot *Batman Begins*.

Jendresen set his story in 2159, chronicling the origins of Starfleet and the launching of the first warp-eight-capable starship, the *NX-Omega* (the previous *Enterprise* managed just warp five). Essentially a space war movie, the story sees an antagonistic Romulan fleet heading for Earth with only rookie pilot Tiberius Chase and his untested crew standing in their way. An added twist sees Chase come from a long-standing Earth isolationist family, fearful of alien contamination. Extending this theme, the Romulans are demanding that the Earth give up its population of Vulcans, who they regard as an illegitimate offshoot of the Romulan race. Chase steals a ship – the USS *Spartan* – and he and his space cadet friends confront the approaching threat.

'The notion was to do a prequel to *The Original Series*', explained Jendresen. '[We would] fill that void with a trilogy which would all deal with Kirk's progenitor. We wanted to reveal the actual cause of the [Earth–Romulan war], which was surprising to all involved at the time. We simply wanted to reveal the truth behind that startling incident.'

The inspiration for the tone and approach of this new *Star Trek* were the movies *Top Gun* and *Starship Troopers*, making it more of a military adventure in space than ever before, something Gene Roddenberry had never been keen on. While the screenplay hit many of the *Star Trek* touchstones (the name Tiberius, the Romulans, Vulcans, Andorian Commander Shran from *Enterprise* and so on), it told the story in a very free-flowing and decidedly un-*Star Trek*-like way. This was exactly what Berman was looking for: a fresh take on the core *Star Trek* ideas, in the hope of attracting a new audience to the long-running franchise.

Jendresen's script had strong support from CBS Paramount studio president Donald DeLine, but fell out of favour with the studio brass when he exited the project to be replaced by Gail Berman (no relation to Rick). Jendresen blamed a 'classic case of Hollywood regime change' for the death of his 'big and epic' *Star Trek* movie: 'A project is greenlighted [sic] by one regime, and by the time it is delivered there's a coup d'etat.' Even before the screenplay was dropped, Rick Berman had confirmed studio reservations that the new *Star Trek* outing featured no established *Star Trek* characters.

Even though *Star Trek: The Beginning* proved to be a false start, the name of Chase recurred as the lead character in another unseen *Star Trek* project. Believing that the cost of any new live-action TV series or movie was holding back the development of a new *Star Trek* outing, a trio of professional fans, David Rossi, Doug Mirabello and comic book artist José Muñoz, proposed a new animated *Star Trek* series. CBS Paramount declared some interest in the project and allowed the trio to develop concept artwork and write scripts for five 'mini-episodes'. The idea, under the title *Star Trek: Final Frontier*, pushed the *Star Trek* timeline further forward into the future, post-*Star Trek Nemesis*. A new *Enterprise* was to be captained by Alexander Chase, embarking on a new mission to 'seek out new life and new civilisations' in an unknown region of space. An entire crew complement, complete with artwork representations, was developed for the proposed series. The idea was shelved, however, when studio head Gail Berman declared her preference for a radical new *Star Trek* movie – and this one would genuinely go back to the beginning . . .

# Chapter 13

## Future Imperfect: *Star Trek* (2009)

*'Gene [Roddenberry was] asked, "What's going to become of* Star Trek *in the future?" He said that he hoped that some day some bright young thing would come along and do it again, bigger and better than he had ever done it. And he wished them well.'* Richard Arnold, Gene Roddenberry's assistant

Among the three biggest science fiction entertainment franchises of the twentieth century, *Star Trek* had the shortest time out of production, cumulatively. The four-year wait between the end of *Enterprise* and the arrival of J. J. Abrams' 2009 movie was surprisingly short compared to those endured by fans of *Doctor Who* and *Star Wars*.

The earliest, *Doctor Who*, began in 1963 in the UK and ran uninterrupted until 1989. A one-off TV movie followed in 1996 before a full ongoing TV series started in 2005. The gap between the original series and its continuation was sixteen years.

*Star Wars* began with a trilogy of movies between 1977 and 1983. A series of bestselling novels by Timothy Zahn in the early 1990s relaunched then-dormant *Star Wars* fandom and led to the release of CGI-upgraded special editions of the original trilogy in 1997, with a brand new prequel trilogy of movies released between 1999 and 2005. Those were followed in 2008 by a hugely successful weekly CGI-animated TV series, *The Clone Wars*.

*Star Trek* had a mere ten-year break (with the exception of the short-lived *The Animated Series*) between the last episode of *The Original Series* and the arrival of *The Motion Picture* in 1979. From then until 2005 *Star Trek* was in continuous production, either as movies or TV series.

In the first decade of the twenty-first century, prequels to existing film and television entertainment properties were in vogue, especially in the worlds of science fiction and fantasy. The first use of the term 'prequel' in movies is connected to the sections of Francis Ford Coppola's 1974 film *The Godfather Part II*, which were set before the events of the previous film. The 1979 movie *Butch and Sundance: The Early Days* was a prequel, but it was the work of filmmakers George Lucas and Steven Spielberg that was to popularise the concept and cause Hollywood to indulge wholesale in the prequel process.

Lucas and Spielberg used the term 'prequel' to chronologically position the second *Indiana Jones* movie, *Indiana Jones and the Temple of Doom* (1984) before the first movie in the series, *Raiders of the Lost Ark* (1981). It was with the *Star Wars* prequel trilogy, however, that the concept really entered the mainstream of blockbuster filmmaking. The urge to go back and explore the origins of characters or events already seen was the narrative driving force behind many sequels (such as *Red Dragon* (2002) and *Hannibal Rising* (2007), both prequels to 1991's *The Silence of the Lambs*), while several sequel films since the year 2000 numerically tagged as '2' were looks back at events before those of the first movie (*Vacancy 2*, *The Scorpion King 2*, *Internal Affairs II* . . .). Following *Star Trek: Enterprise*, *Caprica* (setting up the rebooted *Battlestar Galactica*) and *Spartacus: Gods of the Arena* were prequel TV series. Origin stories or major franchise reboots would also provide fertile ground for sequels and reimagining, especially of comic book characters, as in *Batman Begins* (2005).

For his part, Gene Roddenberry had first mentioned the notion of making a film that took place before his *Star Trek* TV series as early as 1968, at the World Science Fiction Convention.

*Star Trek* movie producer Harve Bennett had repeatedly promoted the idea of an origin story for Kirk, Spock and McCoy as part of his Starfleet Academy concept. Although a *Star Trek* prequel idea (with all-new characters) had come to fruition in the *Enterprise* TV series, it had been deemed a failure. The idea of setting up the universe fans were familiar with was still seen as fertile ground, though, with Rick Berman pursuing development of Erik Jendresen's *Star Trek: The Beginning* script.

Most of these concepts had steered clear of the most obvious *Star Trek* prequel concept of them all, one most likely to have popular appeal to mainstream audiences: the reinvention of Kirk, Spock and McCoy (as boldly suggested in J. Michael Straczynski and Bryce Zabel's *Star Trek* 'reboot' concept for television from 2004). It had taken a long time for the executives at Paramount to accept that the time was right for this approach, but with the failure of *Enterprise* they almost immediately embarked upon the search for a new creative team who could reinvent classic *Star Trek* from first principles as a blockbuster movie.

By 2006, due to corporate takeovers and restructuring, the rights to make new *Star Trek* were held by two different companies. Essentially, Paramount Pictures (owned by Viacom) retained the movie option, while CBS now controlled the *Star Trek* television franchise. Paramount chief Gail Berman decided that the right place for a dramatic reinvention of *Star Trek* – despite the failure of *Nemesis* – was on the big screen, not on television, following the declining fortunes of *Voyager* and *Enterprise*. Part of her approach was to remove the control of big screen *Star Trek* from those who'd been making the television version. Her aim was to turn over Paramount's valuable property to experienced blockbuster moviemakers, rather than exhausted television producers. Berman negotiated with CBS to give Paramount a clear eighteen-month run at developing a new *Star Trek* feature film before the television company could even think about developing a new television series (as part of the deal, CBS retained all *Star Trek* merchandising rights). The question was, what kind of film would the new *Star Trek* be and who could Berman task with creatively driving the project?

Writer, director and producer J. J. Abrams already had strong connections with Paramount, having directed 2006's *Mission: Impossible III* to great critical acclaim and box office success. Abrams had a track record creating cult TV series that also had broad mainstream appeal in spy-thriller *Alias* (2001–6) and the mystical island castaway drama *Lost* (2004–10). Abrams had previously written screenplays for the movies *Regarding Henry* (1991), *Forever Young* (1992) and *Armageddon* (1998), as well as an unproduced *Superman* script in 2002. He'd followed *Mission: Impossible III* with the weird science TV series *Fringe* (from 2008). To Gail Berman, Abrams was just the right kind of maverick left-field talent needed to bring new life to the moribund *Star Trek* franchise.

Abrams himself was a casual *Star Trek* fan. He was born in June 1966, just two weeks after the final draft script for Harlan Ellison's acclaimed episode 'The City on the Edge of Forever' had been completed. For Abrams, *Star Trek* was Kirk, Spock and McCoy – the core characters he'd grown up watching during syndication reruns throughout the 1970s and into the first series of *Star Trek* movies in the early 1980s. He regarded everything else as 'separate space adventures with the name *Star Trek*'

Abrams felt that the later incarnations of *Star Trek* had turned inwards. 'At a certain point it seems like *Star Trek* stopped trying to reach a bigger audience', he said to *SFX* magazine. 'They decided, "let's just cater to our fans". This movie is not meant to be a continuum of that way of thinking, this is very much "let's start over".' The director had also admitted to a strong preference for the action-adventure format of the first *Star Wars* trilogy to *Star Trek*'s more cerebral content. Abrams signed on as producer of the Paramount *Star Trek* reboot, turning over the development of the script to his team of *Lost* and *Fringe* writers Roberto Orci and Alex Kurtzman (who'd also scripted *Mission: Impossible III* and *Transformers* (2007)).

According to Abrams, his interest in *Star Trek* came from the fact that it was 'about exploration of the stars, not about conquering worlds, but discovering them, exploring them and understanding them'. He told *Empire* magazine, '[*The Original Series*'] problem was they had a space adventure, but never had the resources to actually show the adventure. Doing this movie with the resources we had and the technology that exists now gave us the chance to make something fast-paced, full of action and visually stunning, but also tap into what made *Star Trek* great.'

All concerned felt that the best approach would be a 'clean' reboot of *Star Trek*, returning to first principles as outlined by Gene Roddenberry in his creation of *The Original Series*. However, as fans of the original show, Orci and Kurtzman knew how important actors like Shatner, Nimoy and the late DeForest Kelley were to *Star Trek* fans. With that in mind, they set out to develop a reboot of *Star Trek* that would allow for the re-invention of the classic Kirk–Spock–McCoy trio for a new twenty-first-century audience, but would also in some way manage to incorporate all that had gone before. They were not prepared to simply dump over forty years of storytelling.

For Abrams, the characters were key to his reinvention of the franchise. '[There's a] feeling of broken and interesting characters in Kirk and Spock', he told *SFX* magazine. '[We show them] coming together in a way that is unexpected and ultimately throw them into a massive adventure. The approach was to take inspiration from what was in *The Original Series* and then filter it through what is relevant and vital for now. The goal was not to make it cool or different, but to make it real, with characters that feel true and emotional, like there's a piece missing from them and they're up against something significant and the stakes are high. It was fun to figure out a way to make the relationship between Spock, Kirk and Bones [McCoy] come to life.'

The writers hoped that the possible involvement of someone from *The Original Series* would put the seal of approval on the new *Star Trek* for many sceptical fans. From the original key trio, due to the death of Kelley in 1999, Orci and Kurtzman were left with Shatner and Nimoy, and they felt that Spock was the more iconic and useful of the two remaining characters. The presence of the character they dubbed 'old Spock' or Spock Prime would also tie into Nimoy's last appearance on *The Next Generation* in the two-part 'Unification' story from 1991, although Nimoy himself professed not to recognise the connection. That storyline had also featured the Romulans, now chosen by Abrams as the villains for the new film in preference to the Klingons, whom he considered overused as well as problematic due to their non-villainous status from *The Next Generation* onwards. At that point Abrams was unaware that the Romulans had featured as the major villains in the most recent *Star Trek* movie, *Nemesis*, and that the film had been a huge box office failure. He claimed he'd been 'disconnected' from the franchise when that movie was released.

According to Abrams, the casting of Leonard Nimoy was 'critical if we're going to look at reintroducing these characters . . . [this film must] both please the fans and those who have never seen *Star Trek*. Having Leonard in the film shows that this film exists in a continuum of *Trek* history, as opposed to an absolute page one reinvention.' Nimoy, who had retired from acting in 2000 to pursue photography, claimed he was happy to play Spock once more as he admired the work of Abrams and the film offered an 'essential and interesting Spock role'. Re-energised by his work on the movie, and continuing to work with Abrams and his team, Nimoy would go on to guest star regularly in the pivotal role of William Bell on Abrams' *Fringe*.

Although it had been much used throughout *Star Trek*, the writers of the new movie decided that time travel would be the best device they could use to begin a new story built around Kirk, Spock and McCoy and yet involve a character from *The Original Series*. Time travel would bring Spock Prime into contact with younger versions of Kirk, Spock and McCoy, allowing the old and new storylines to connect, and could then be forgotten in any subsequent films which would follow the adventures of the new characters without any overt connections to the past. 'One of the reasons we wanted to break with the original *Star Trek* timeline was it felt restrictive', Abrams told MTV.com. 'The idea, now that we are in an independent time-line, allows us to use any of the ingredients from the past – or come up with brand new ones – to make potential stories.'

Orci and Kurtzman drew inspiration from many elements of past *Star Trek* in working out their new approach, including spin-off novels not always thought of as canon by fans. Knowing that the continuity of *The Original Series* had itself been incon-sistent, the writers set out to cherry-pick the elements they felt they needed to launch a new version of classic *Star Trek* without necessarily being slavish to established details. For example, it had long been established that the *Enterprise* had been constructed in Earth orbit, but the movie would instead depict the ship being built on the ground in Kirk's home state of Iowa.

In order to appeal to a mainstream audience perhaps un-familiar with the detailed universe created over many decades, Abrams and his creative team deliberately set out to simplify *Star Trek*, stripping out the technobabble of *The Next Generation* and replacing it with the action-adventure appeal of the first *Star Wars* movie. Humour and sex appeal were also key to Abrams' recreation of *Star Trek*, elements that had been missing from some of the spin-off shows. The central characters – Kirk, Spock and McCoy – were reduced to archetypes, almost fulfill-ing the popular clichés that resided in the mainstream imagination. The characters of these new versions of the core *Star Trek* trio were easily delineated through their chief charac-teristics, summed up by their well-known catchphrases used in the 1987 novelty song 'Star Trekkin'' by The Firm.

The question was, who could play these iconic characters? Which modern film stars or character actors could fill the well-worn roles of Kirk, Spock and McCoy and stand the comparisons with Shatner, Nimoy and Kelley – especially as whomever was playing young Spock would be acting directly opposite the original. While it wasn't quite the big show-business event predicted by Straczynski and Zabel's reboot proposal, there was much media interest in the casting process for the all-new *Star Trek*.

'It was hard in ways I didn't anticipate', said Abrams to *SFX* magazine of casting the movie. 'I thought [finding the right actor for] Spock would be impossible, yet he was the first person we cast.' Although the film would feature three versions of Spock (including Jacob Kogan as child Spock and Nimoy as Spock Prime), the focus was heavily on actor Zachary Quinto, who secured the task of reinventing the half-human, half-Vulcan *Enterprise* science officer. Quinto, who'd come to prominence as Sylar in the superpowers TV series *Heroes*, came to Abrams' attention thanks to an interview in which he expressed interest in the role. Many commentators had pointed out Quinto's curious physical resemblance to the young Nimoy. Quinto wore a blue shirt (reflecting Spock's usual outfit on *The Original Series*) and flattened his hair to more resemble Spock for his audition. He was aided in taking on the persona of Spock by make-up and hair tricks that emphasised his Nimoy-lookalike characteristics, although he did claim, 'There's no question I was born to play the Spock role'. The only other actor who'd been publicly connected with the part was Oscar winner Adrien Brody.

The most prominent candidate to inherit William Shatner's role as the captain of the *Enterprise* was Matt Damon, who met with J. J. Abrams to discuss the role. Deciding that Damon was too old for the role of Kirk as written, the pair discussed having him play Kirk's father in the opening section of the film, a part that Damon turned down and went to *Thor*'s Chris Hemsworth instead. The new Captain Kirk was to be played by Chris Pine, then best known for romantic comedies like *The Princess Diaries 2* (2004) and *Just My Luck* (2006). Abrams had not seen Pine's initial audition for the part (a performance Pine had described as being awful), so re-auditioned him alongside Quinto (by now already cast as Spock). Quinto and Pine already knew each other as they frequented the same Los Angeles gym. Having won the role, Pine sought (and obtained) the approval of Shatner, and then immersed himself in studying *Star Trek* history. He finally gave up researching and watching old episodes, as he feared his performance would become an imitation of Shatner's when what he wanted to do was explore Kirk's 'humour, arrogance and decisiveness', while bringing a touch of Tom Cruise and Harrison Ford to the character.

One of the last parts to be filled for the movie was the final piece in the puzzle of the central *Star Trek* trio, Dr McCoy. Among those considered for the role were Oscar-nominated Gary Sinise, who, like Damon, was eventually deemed too old for the role. Abrams chose *The Lord of the Rings* star Karl Urban, who'd previously worked with writers Orci and Kurtzman on the TV series *Xena: Warrior Princess*. Urban had been a fan of *Star Trek* all his life, setting out not to provide a 'carbon copy' of DeForest Kelley's McCoy but instead to honour Kelley while 'bringing something new to the table'. For Abrams, Urban was a man of previously hidden talents: 'Karl Urban surprised the hell out of me by coming in and being crazy good and funny in a way I never thought or knew he could do and blew my mind. He is far more versatile than anyone knows.'

The second tier of characters was filled by a range of actors, including Zoe Saldana as Uhura (she'd never seen *The Original Series*, although her mother was a fan, and the actress had played a *Trek* fan in *The Terminal* (2004)); English writer–actor Simon Pegg as Scotty (who based his Scottish accent on that of his Glaswegian wife); Asian-American John Cho as Japanese Sulu (his casting was approved of by George Takei as he said Sulu represented all of Asia on the *Enterprise*); and Anton Yelchin as Russian Pavel Chekov (whose character hadn't appeared on the *Enterprise* until the second year of *The Original Series*). The villain of the piece was Romulan Nero, played by Eric Bana heavily disguised under a series of facial tattoos.

*Star Trek* opens with the Federation starship USS *Kelvin* investigating a 'lightning storm' in space. The vessel comes under attack by the Romulan mining ship Narada, which emerges from the spacial disturbance. During the battle, first officer George Kirk replaces the dead captain, evacuates the ship and loses his life taking the ship on a collision course with the Narada, just as his son – James Kirk – is born aboard an escaping shuttle.

Years later, troubled Jim Kirk joins Starfleet at the urging of Captain Pike, who challenges him to live up to the example set by his father. Kirk falls in with half-human, half-Vulcan Spock, cantankerous medical man McCoy and languages specialist Uhura. A distress signal sees an under-prepared *Enterprise*, led by Pike, embark on a mission to investigate a new space 'lightning storm'. Recognising the phenomena from the time of his birth, Kirk finds his way onto the ship. The *Enterprise* discovers the Romulan ship attacking Vulcan. The planet is destroyed, killing most of the population, including Spock's mother. An argument sees Kirk marooned on Delta Vega, where he encounters Spock Prime. Both he and the Narada have travelled from the future, where Nero's planet Romulus was destroyed before Spock could prevent a supernova. Blaming Spock and the Federation, Nero is out to change the future and save his planet. Picking up Scotty, Kirk returns to the *Enterprise*, takes command and with Spock's help attacks the Narada and defeats Nero. Kirk is unexpectedly promoted to captain of the *Enterprise*, and he, Spock, McCoy and the rest of the crew are ready for new adventures . . .

Shooting on the movie – under the dummy title *Corporate Headquarters* – took place between November 2007 and March 2008, with J. J. Abrams taking up the option to direct as well as produce (*Spider-Man*'s Sam Raimi had been considered by Paramount as a possible alternative director). Designing a new *Enterprise* for the twenty-first century proved a challenge. Abrams appointed Scott Chambliss, his production designer on *Alias* and *Mission: Impossible III*, to envision the new starship. Given that so much modern technology had apparently either been inspired or influenced by that depicted on *The Original Series* – such as mobile phones, computers and iPads – it was

going to be difficult to come up with a new idea for the future
of the twenty-third century while still staying true to 1960s *Star
Trek*. New communicators were designed with the help of
mobile phone manufacturer Nokia, while medical tricorders
were made smaller and more portable and the phasers were
designed with revolving barrels that could switch from 'stun' to
'kill' settings.

The biggest challenge was the bridge of the *Enterprise*. While
the original layout was retained, the whole space had a brighter,
whiter feel, drawing inspiration from the 1968 Stanley Kubrick
film *2001: A Space Odyssey* and modern high-tech retail environments, like the Apple stores. This new *Enterprise* bridge was
built on gimbals, meaning that when the ship was attacked the
actors would not have to try so hard to fake being thrown from
side to side, as had often been the case on the *Star Trek* TV
shows. The ship's engine room had a very different feel, being
filmed in a real Budweiser factory in Van Nuys rather than built
from scratch in a studio. The film was shot on a variety of locations in and around Los Angeles, but one of the main ones was
the infamous Vasquez Rocks formation featured in several
episodes of *The Original Series* ('Shore Leave', 'Arena', 'The
Alternative Factor', 'Friday's Child') as well as episodes of *The
Next Generation*, *Voyager* and *Enterprise*, and also *Star Trek VI:
The Voyage Home*. The jutting rock formation has become known
as 'Kirk's Rock', thanks to this frequent use, and was featured in
the movie as Spock's home planet of Vulcan.

Wrapping on the film, Abrams told *Empire*, 'I've come to
know these characters through working on this movie, and I've
come to understand what the world of *Star Trek* is. It's not so
much that I feel that I've bought into a pre-existing world as
much as I've come to know and appreciate personalities and
history I didn't even remember. The [TV] series just assumed
you cared, but I never felt that until now.'

Although originally intended for release on Christmas Day
2008, J. J. Abrams' *Star Trek* was delayed until 8 May 2009 as
Paramount believed the film would find a larger audience during

the summer blockbuster season than the Christmas holiday period. It was a reflection of the wider appeal the studio executives believed Abrams and his team had brought to the reinvented *Star Trek*.

The first public screening was a surprise sneak peek at the Alamo Drafthouse theatre in Austin, Texas on 6 April 2009. Billed as a screening of *Star Trek II: The Wrath of Khan* with a ten-minute preview of the new *Star Trek* movie, the print of the earlier film appeared to melt after a few minutes, followed by an appearance by Leonard Nimoy, who asked the audience if they wouldn't rather see the new *Star Trek* movie. The official premiere of the film took place at the Sydney Opera House on 7 April. Following a request from astronaut Michael R. Barrett, the movie was uploaded to the International Space Station for a screening on 14 May.

*Star Trek* took $4 million at the US box office on its opening day, clocking up a total opening weekend figure of $79.2 million in the US and another $35.5 million internationally. The film topped *First Contact* as the biggest opening *Star Trek* movie and would go on to become the highest grossing *Star Trek* film to that date, with an overall US box office take of $257.7 million (making it the seventh highest grossing film of 2009 and beating *The Voyage Home*'s $109.7 million). International takings of $127.7 million brought the overall worldwide total to $385.5 million.

The reviews for the new *Star Trek* movie were hugely positive, with the film having largely succeeded in the tricky task of bringing a new audience to the classic *Star Trek* characters of Kirk, Spock and McCoy, while also pleasing the majority of the franchise's long-term fans. *Entertainment Weekly* called J. J. Abrams' *Star Trek* 'clever and infectious', while the *Boston Globe* dubbed the movie 'ridiculously satisfying'. While most critics accepted the new film in the style of a Hollywood summer blockbuster, the *Chicago Sun-Times*' Roger Ebert worried that Gene Roddenberry's more thoughtful *Star Trek* had 'been replaced by stories reduced to loud and colourful action'. Some reviewers came to the conclusion that this reintroduction to *Star Trek* lacked some of the ideas-driven narratives that had frequently been featured in the best TV episodes and films in *Star Trek*'s past. Many held out the hope that free of the need to relaunch the concept, any sequel films would be better able to introduce an element of the cerebral *Star Trek* so central to Gene Roddenberry's original conception of the show.

Among the strong points of J. J. Abrams' *Star Trek* was the emotional core in the relationship between Kirk and Spock. Kirk has a strong personal reason for tackling Nero and his Romulan band: they were responsible for the death of his father on the USS *Kelvin*. Having been born into conflict, Kirk has grown up with a huge challenge hanging over him – could he ever live up to the example set by his father? It's what Pike uses to lure Kirk into signing up with Starfleet. Of course, Nero's presence in this universe is due to the activities of Spock Prime in the original *Star Trek* universe.

Spock faces a similar series of emotional challenges. His home world is attacked by Nero in revenge for Spock Prime's failure. Attempting to rescue several Vulcan leaders, Spock witnesses the death of his mother as the planet is vaporised. As seen in the young Spock scenes, the Vulcan has long struggled with his human emotions, so the loss of his human mother further complicates his struggle between logic and emotion.

Kirk and Spock are connected by more than just being in Starfleet, and finding themselves aboard the *Enterprise* at a moment of crisis. They've both lost parents in violent incidents, and both parental deaths were caused by the same antagonist: Nero. Spock's role is to counterbalance Kirk's rash nature and over-emotional involvement in events, while Kirk's passion serves to temper the Vulcan's cold logic and allows him to see the value of human feelings. It is only through pushing Spock to display his anger that Kirk gains the captaincy of the *Enterprise* at the crucial moment. It all faithfully harks back to the positioning of the original characters in *The Original Series* along an emotional continuum.

Both characters have older mentors who guide them in their actions: Pike for Kirk and Spock Prime for both Kirk and Spock – they are both essentially surrogate parental figures. The third wheel – Dr McCoy – is an enabler for both characters. It is McCoy who brings Kirk aboard the *Enterprise*, a ship he is not supposed to be on, but it is also McCoy who challenges some of Kirk's planned actions.

These characters and the emotional connections between them were wrapped up in a cracking plot that was simple for audiences to understand and engage with, with a series of action set-pieces (the opening battle, an assault on a drilling platform, an attack on Nero's ship) that impressed more casual viewers. While the movie set out to appeal to non-*Star Trek* fans, it was equally loaded with touchstones that reached out to fans of all of *Star Trek*'s previous incarnations. The use of Vasquez Rocks was a prominent visual shout-out to *The Original Series*, but there were many more, covering much of the *Star Trek* canon. During the opening bar fight, Kirk uses a bottle of Saurian Brandy as a weapon. The Kobayashi Maru test sequence (lifted from *Star Trek II: The Wrath of Khan*) sees Kirk eating an apple, something Shatner's Kirk is seen doing in *The Wrath of Khan* when he confesses how he beat the same test – although this apparently came about as Pine simply happened to be eating the apple during a break in filming. There are other *Khan* references, such as Spock quoting Sherlock Holmes and Spock Prime telling Kirk he 'has been and always shall be' his friend. Sulu was able to put his fencing training into practice during the assault on the mining rig – he was also seen displaying his fencing skills in the early *Star Trek* episode 'The Naked Time'. The same sequence sees the unfortunate Chief Engineer Olsen wear a red-tinged space suit, dooming him to die during the fight (a necessary event, so Scotty can take over). A tribble even turns up, purring contentedly in Scotty's workshop. And there's some love for Porthos, Captain Archer's dog in *Enterprise*, when Scotty references 'Admiral Archer's beagle' as an unfortunate victim of a transporter prank. By the film's finale, Pike is confined to a wheelchair; however, it is not as high-tech (nor is he as disfigured) as his counterpart in the two-part *The Original Series* episode 'The Menagerie'. Most of these references would have been unnoticed by the majority of casual viewers – many of whom were content with the big character moments reinforcing the idea that this Kirk, Spock and McCoy were the same as those they recalled. That audience was happy just to hear the well-worn catchphrases and character comments, such as Scotty's 'I'm giving it all she's got', McCoy's 'I'm a doctor, not a physicist' and his 'Are you out of your Vulcan mind?' However, for fans of the series, these little in-jokes and throwaway moments showed a reverence (and knowledge) of the long-running *Star Trek* franchise on the part of those who'd made the 2009 movie.

'The themes that got me excited honestly had less to do with *Star Trek* and space and more to do with optimism and humanity, of finding your purpose through unity', said Abrams of his first *Star Trek* film. 'It ends up being a guiding principle of the movie – it needed to be faithful to the optimism that Gene Roddenberry wrote with during a time of fear and hate and suspicion. He was writing of our future where we were not just surviving it, but by cooperating and collaborating, we actually thrived. That to me is, more than ever, a relevant idea.'

Given the huge box office numbers of *Star Trek*, a follow-up film was inevitable. All the major cast members were already signed up for at least two sequels, but given the triumphant reinvention of the whole *Star Trek* franchise, it is possible there may be many more. The second movie was scripted during 2010–11, with shooting following towards the end of 2011. Release was set for the summer of 2012. This *Star Trek* was set to go on for a while . . .

Former *Deep Space Nine* and *Voyager* writer Bryan Fuller had publicly talked about his desire to bring *Star Trek* back to television since at least 2008. Fuller followed his *Star Trek* experiences with his own series – *Dead Like Me* and *Pushing*

*Daisies*, and a role as consulting producer on *Heroes* – but felt that *Star Trek* belonged on television, even with the J. J. Abrams film then entering production. 'I would love to return to the spirit of the old series', Fuller told *iF Magazine*. '[The later series] seem to have lost the 1960s fun and I would love to take it back to its origin.'

Of course, that's exactly the approach taken by Abrams with his movie, although Fuller wanted to feature *Men in Black II* and *Sin City* actress (and well-known Trekkie) Rosario Dawson as a lead in his proposed TV show. Even if he might not be the one to do it, Fuller remained convinced that *Star Trek* would eventually return once more to its natural home on television. 'I think after the second [J. J. Abrams] *Star Trek* movie comes out, they will start to have serious conversations again about a TV show. I think *Star Trek* always has a home on television. It is the defining piece of science fiction for the United States, [as] *Doctor Who* is for the UK. It's all about the vision of the storyteller.'

# Chapter 14

## Legacy: Can *Star Trek*
## Live Long and Prosper?

'*Why does* Star Trek *continue to survive, to touch people, to intrigue? One of the major reasons is that* Trek *is a meritocracy. It doesn't matter who or what you are, your colour or race. None of that matters.*' Leonard Nimoy

*Star Trek* has been a pop cultural phenomenon for over forty-five years, given new life by the huge success of the 2009 movie. That reinvention – and its sequels – succeeded where the later television series had failed, by returning to *Star Trek*'s iconic characters and thrilling storytelling.

Although the original show finished in 1969, the continual airing of episodes in syndication and the reappearance of the original cast in movies meant that the first incarnation of *Star Trek* was ever present. The new ensemble cast of characters of *The Next Generation* had to establish themselves alongside the originals for much of the time. It was only the later trio of spin-offs – *Deep Space Nine*, *Voyager* and *Enterprise* – that were not overshadowed by the iconic characters of Kirk, Spock and McCoy. That's when the rot set in . . .

*Star Trek* had three hugely successful periods before its re-invention by J. J. Abrams: *The Original Series*, the 1980s original cast movies and *The Next Generation*. Ask the average television viewer who they remember from *Star Trek*, and the answer will invariably be Kirk, Spock and McCoy, with a smaller but significant number remembering the bald Captain Picard and Data, the yellow-faced android – and even those two characters were arguably versions of Kirk and Spock.

Gene Roddenberry developed all three successful incarnations, but many of the best individual instalments of *Star Trek* came after he had stopped having any creative involvement. *The Original Series* was his brainchild, seen in its purest form in the failed pilot 'The Cage'. This was *Star Trek* as the Great Bird of the Galaxy saw it, unadulterated by the concerns of networks, sponsors or fandom – yet it failed to sell. It was the more action-adventure based second pilot – Roddenberry's *Star Trek* filtered through writer Samuel A. Peeples – that sold the series to NBC, launching the first flight of the *Enterprise*. And it was only when other storytellers (like Fontana, Gerrold and Coon on *The Original Series*) got their hands on Roddenberry's *Star Trek* that the concept truly came alive.

A decade after that show's cancellation, when the storytellers had all but departed the show, Roddenberry once again had the chance to realise his version of *Star Trek* – this time for the big screen. *The Motion Picture* is a slow-moving, lumbering film that dazzles with its visuals, but fails to engage on a human level – ironic, given that the marketing slogan was 'The human adventure is just beginning'. But once again, the successful and satisfying original cast movies only came after Roddenberry's forced departure, involving Harve Bennett, Nicholas Meyer and Leonard Nimoy in their creation: *The Wrath of Khan*, *The Search for Spock*, *The Voyage Home* and *The Undiscovered Country*. The movies that failed were *The Motion Picture* (under Roddenberry) and *The Final Frontier* (largely the creation of Kirk actor William Shatner).

Finally, there was *The Next Generation*. Roddenberry's new take on *Star Trek* for the 1980s – in which he hoped to achieve a better representation of his original intentions for the 1960s version – was most fully achieved during the show's rather inert, lacklustre and undramatic first season. *The Next Generation* debuted in syndication and managed to survive due to a unique business arrangement. In order to persuade the independent stations of the syndication network across the United States to run *The Next Generation*, Paramount made taking the new show a condition of renewing the right to rerun *The Original Series*, Paramount's 'seventy-nine jewels'. Even in the late 1980s, the original *Star Trek* was still a significant show for many stations. The deal guaranteed *The Next Generation* a safe environment in which to debut. It is doubtful the series would have survived its first rocky couple of seasons as a network show. But it did survive – and outlived its creator – only to really flourish in the third year, which culminated with the invasion of the Borg in 'The Best of Both Worlds'. That 1990 cliffhanger gave dramatic new life to *Star Trek*, although it is arguable whether Roddenberry would have recognised that storytelling as true to his perception of *Star Trek*. Yet, this two-parter is one of the series' best remembered, over two decades later, and one of scripted dramatic television's true events.

Gene Roddenberry failed to create anything as successful as *Star Trek*. He spent much of the 1970s making one failed pilot TV movie after another and his attempts to break into film were unsuccessful. His biggest post-*Star Trek* television successes came with *Andromeda* and *Earth: Final Conflict*, shows sold by Majel Barrett Roddenberry, using her husband's name prominently, long after his death. Roddenberry seemed more content as a figurehead for *Star Trek* fandom, revelling in his Great Bird of the Galaxy status, promoting his own myth and the legend of his creation of all-things *Star Trek*. Only much later did it become clear that he was not above shamelessly exploiting those same fans (in the 1960s and 1970s his Lincoln Enterprises sold copies of *Star Trek* scripts, without authorisation from either the individual writers or Paramount). For a man whose utopian vision of the future did not include cash, it was often money that was his main motivation, not propagating a future-focused philosophy. 'I had to get some money from somewhere', Roddenberry said of his claim to half the royalties on sales of Stephen Whitfield's 1968 *The Making of Star Trek* book and

Alexander Courage's theme tune (to which Roddenberry wrote unneeded lyrics). 'I'm sure not going to get it from the profits of *Star Trek*!' This Great Bird had feet of clay.

Until the 2009 movie, nothing in *Star Trek* was ever again as successful as *The Next Generation*. The Borg-based *First Contact* was a huge blockbuster, but the other movies featuring *The Next Generation* cast failed to capture the same energy and intensity. *Deep Space Nine* embarked on an interesting anti-*Star Trek* experiment in hard-hitting storytelling and serialisation – and it succeeded, especially when executive attention was elsewhere with the launch of *Voyager*. The space station series was probably the furthest removed from Roddenberry's view of *Star Trek*, escaping quite decisively from Michael Piller's concept of 'Roddenberry's box' of storytelling limitations. Producer Rick Berman ensured that Roddenberry's utopian vision of the future was faithfully adhered to in all the follow-up series, with both *Deep Space Nine* and *Voyager* faithfully following *The Original Series*' liberal humanist creed, featuring an African-American and a woman as their leading characters. However, with *Voyager* (and the final series, *Enterprise*), a step backwards was taken in an attempt to recreate elements of *The Original Series* within the template of *The Next Generation*-style *Star Trek*. Now the original cast was gone from cinemas, the new television shows could cannibalise the past to recreate what had worked in terms of characters and stories. *Star Trek* was continuing without the original icons of Kirk, Spock and McCoy or Picard and Data, those that had successfully emerged from *The Next Generation* into popular consciousness. The last years of *Voyager* and *Enterprise* attempted to draw upon the past, without the character archetypes that had captured the world's imagination.

*Star Trek* could now be ruthlessly satirised due to its creative stagnation. There had always been comedy skits and sketches making fun of Spock's pointed ears and the danger of donning a red shirt. However, 1999's *Galaxy Quest* was of a different order. This mainstream movie affectionately spoofed the on-screen icons of *Star Trek*, the reported behind the scenes squabbles among both cast members and fans, while also delivering a great comedy science fiction adventure story in its own right. For this movie to succeed it required the audience to be familiar with *Star Trek*'s image, but also for that image to be fixed and unchanging. The failure to innovate within *Star Trek* itself opened the door for *Galaxy Quest* to exist.

As the producer of *Star Trek* for eighteen years between 1987 and 2005, Rick Berman used the term 'franchise fatigue' to describe what happened to *Star Trek* after *Deep Space Nine*. That show had run in parallel with *The Next Generation* and *Voyager* for its seven-year duration, meaning that there were always two *Star Trek* shows on air between 1993 and 2001. That period also saw the release of three big screen movies – *Generations*, *First Contact* and *Insurrection* – only one of which was creatively successful. After *Voyager*, and with *Enterprise* in a lacklustre second season, *Nemesis* made its abysmal debut at cinemas in 2002, killing off the *Star Trek* movie franchise for seven years.

Berman saw the problem as simply too much *Star Trek*, with movies and television shows exploring the same concepts and with similar characters competing with each other. Not only was the new product saturating the market, the old series and movies were widely available, first on VHS tape, then on DVD, as well as in endless television reruns around the world. If current *Star Trek* wasn't to your liking, then your favourite show or movie from the series' long history was easily available to you at the flick of a switch.

That issue may have been a factor, but there is no denying that *Star Trek* had become trapped within a static formula: its later years were missing characters that audiences could believe in and storytelling they found accessible. Berman and his various creative teams were struggling with how to create not only new science fiction television shows, but also new *Star Trek*, with all that the concept implied.

With the end of the original cast movies and the arrival of the Borg, *The Next Generation* had finally found itself and successfully created a new way of telling *Star Trek* stories that succeeded with a mass television audience. After that, it was a case of rapidly diminishing returns. Each new series would debut to huge viewing figures as a curious public were seduced into checking out what the latest version of *Star Trek* was like. They then discovered each show and its new characters simply didn't match up with their vivid memories of the originals or *The Next Generation*. Without exception, every series after *The Next Generation* suffered a catastrophic fall in viewing figures across each full run, culminating in the ignominy of cancellation for *Enterprise* in 2005. The franchise had turned inwards and begun to service only the die-hard fans – often with very well-told stories – but it failed to reach beyond the fan base. Each subsequent series featured either characters from *The Original Series* or *The Next Generation* in an attempt to bring back the mass audience and appeal to fans of those individual shows. *The Next Generation*'s Worf became a regular on the later seasons of *Deep Space Nine*, while the Borg (and even Sulu) appeared on *Voyager*, and *Enterprise* fell back on regular appearances by Klingons and Vulcans (and even controversially concluded with a story built around *The Next Generation*'s Riker and Troi).

Television science fiction had changed in the 1990s, following the success of *The Next Generation*. The show had opened the doors to a new breed of darker science fiction and fantasy shows such as *The X-Files*, *Buffy the Vampire Slayer*, *Babylon 5*, *Farscape*, *Stargate SG-1* (and its spin-offs, *Atlantis* and *Universe*), *Firefly* and *Battlestar Galactica*. Many of these shows successfully reacted against the edicts of *Star Trek* storytelling (in the way that *Deep Space Nine* had attempted) and fitted much better with television in the 1990s and 2000s when stories became darker and serial television was much more willing to deal in long-running story arcs. Characters would change and develop, often in dramatic ways. *Star Trek* told great stories, but apart from in *Deep Space Nine*, few of the long-running characters were very different at the end of a series than they had been at the beginning. The result was that the later *Star Trek* shows – especially *Voyager* and *Enterprise* – began to look old-fashioned, like something from the 1960s, in fact. That echoing of the past may have worked well for fans in the final season of *Enterprise* (showrunner Manny Coto said he felt the fans were all that was left watching, so why not cater to them?), but it failed to engage the mass audience needed to keep such an expensive show on network television. Without the archetypal characters they remembered, and with many other better choices available, audiences began to desert new *Star Trek*.

Once seen as the saviour of *Star Trek*, Rick Berman was – by the time of the cancellation of *Enterprise* – enemy number one to fans. The perception was he'd destroyed the franchise he'd done so much to create and shepherd – after all, eighteen years of continuous television production of very complicated shows is not to be discounted. He seemed to believe that serving up more of the same, sometimes modelled on the character dynamics and dramatic situations from *The Original Series*, would be enough to see the lucrative franchise continue. Berman was wrong, and by 2005 *Star Trek* on both the big and small screens was dead, slowly strangled by a failing formula and killed by creative complacency. The *Star Trek* franchise had simply not adapted – Borg-like – to the twenty-first-century television environment, and so it ultimately failed.

There was one lesson to be learned from all this: *Star Trek* worked as an event. *The Next Generation* had succeeded as a series with mass appeal, drawing an average of 10–11 million viewers per season, but none of the other series enjoyed the same success. Yet, each had begun with massive viewing figures. *Deep Space Nine* had drawn almost 12 million viewers to its spectacular debut episode, but had ended its seven-year run with less than 4.5 million watching regularly. Similarly, *Voyager* had begun with around 8 million but concluded its seven years on air with fewer than 3.5 million tuning in to see if the ship got home or not. *Enterprise* had an even better start, surpassing *Deep Space Nine* numbers with around 12.5 million, such was the attraction of a *Star Trek* prequel. The show was cancelled, however, because those bothering with the adventures of

Captain Archer and crew had collapsed to a low of 2.5 million. Those 'first nights' demonstrated one thing – a mass audience would come to new *Star Trek* as a one-off event, but only a core of dedicated fans and other open-minded casual viewers of around 3 to 4 million would stick with an ongoing TV series.

That's why J. J. Abrams' dramatic back to basics reinvention of *Star Trek* in 2009 was a movie that celebrated the iconic original triumvirate and the rest of the original *Enterprise* crew. To the mass audience, these lovingly remembered characters *were Star Trek*, and that's why the movie was a huge success.

There is no doubt that *Star Trek* has been influential beyond just television and movies. Nichelle Nichols tells a famous story of how she was persuaded to stick with the show when Dr Martin Luther King Jr explained how important her appearance on mainstream television was. 'You changed the face of television for ever', he told her, 'you are a role model for everyone'. *Star Trek*'s racial diversity and (mostly) positive depictions of women in important roles of responsibility was part of the show's positive view of the future.

The technology of *Star Trek* has led to the look and feel of many of today's gadgets, used daily by millions of people. The incredibly popular Apple iPhones and iPads bear more than a passing resemblance to *Star Trek*'s communicator and *The Next Generation*'s PADD (Personal Access Display Device). Kirk and many of the crew of the first *Enterprise* were often seen using small hand-held computing devices. Similarly, Bluetooth in-ear phones match with Uhura's oft-mocked communication device. Five years after the show was cancelled, Ed Roberts launched the build-it-yourself Altair 8800 computer, named after a galaxy featured on *Star Trek* (and its progenitor, *Forbidden Planet*). That machine in turn inspired Steve Jobs and Steve Wozniak to improve upon Roberts' innovation with their own Apple computer, launching a computing empire that led to the iPhone and iPad.

*The Original Series* featured other devices that have since become reality. Tricorders – portable scanning devices that assess the local environment – don't quite exist in that form, but many personal phones are now mini-computers, which through GPS technology can provide information on nearby shops, museums or other attractions. The medical tricorder and sick bay monitors are much closer to reality with the rapid development of medical technology, to the extent that a modern ER can be a very high-tech place. Even more extreme technology, such as tractor beams, the holodeck, warp speed and deflector shields, are seen now as less like science fiction and more realistic in the future due to advances in the understanding of quantum physics. Work in the robotics and artificial intelligence fields is moving closer to a Data-style android.

While *Star Trek* itself was inspired by the 1960s space race between the United States and the Soviet Union – it was the reason NBC decided to go with the show – many modern scientists have in turn been inspired by *Star Trek* to go into science. One such was the Jet Propulsion Laboratory's Steve Matousek, who was involved in the 1990s Mars Pathfinder mission, among others. '*Star Trek* gives you a way to see ahead, to look into the future', he told Jeff Greenwald in *Future Perfect*. 'I wanted to be an aerospace engineer because I knew that they were the ones that designed the things that went out into space.' Of the 6,000 who worked at JPL, Matousek estimated that up to 75 per cent had been inspired by *Star Trek*. In 1996, physicist Lawrence Krauss wrote an entire book devoted to the science of *Star Trek* and its real-world impact in *The Physics of Star Trek*. The first NASA prototype space shuttle – which unfortunately never journeyed to space – had even been named *Enterprise*, thanks to fan pressure.

While waiting for scientists to invent the future, most fans thought the only way they'd ever get to live the *Star Trek* experience would be to visit the studio sets at Paramount in Los Angeles where the episodes were made. Indeed many fan-journalists, a few privileged guests and a handful of competition winners got to do just that. Even so, many fans did get a chance to experience a little of the twenty-third and twenty-fourth centuries, *Star Trek*-style. Interactive exhibitions, including recreations of the *Enterprise* bridge, props and costumes, toured the world, touching down in Edinburgh, Berlin, and the Science Museum and Hyde Park in London. A more extensive venue was the *Star Trek* Experience, located in the Las Vegas Hilton Hotel for a decade between 1998 and 2008. This provided a much more immersive encounter, allowing fans to fully enjoy as much of *Star Trek*'s visionary future as could be recreated here on Earth. A steady stream of spin-off novels and a variety of computer games fed fans' imagination and participation in the worlds of *Star Trek*.

*Star Trek* has been a pervasive part of the cultural environment worldwide for over forty-five years. It has developed and changed, prospered and failed and become part of the identity of millions of people. The return of the archetypal *Star Trek* trio of Kirk, Spock and McCoy has given the concept new life in new stories on the big screen. *Star Trek* has always prospered when true storytellers have been able to make the series their own. Now, a new generation of storytellers is charged with re-vitalising the series' iconic characters and ensuring that *Star Trek* will truly 'live long and prosper'.

# Bibliography

Alexander, David, *Star Trek Creator: The Authorized Biography of Gene Roddenberry*, New York: ROC, 1995

Asherman, Allan, *The Star Trek Compendium*, London: W.H. Allen, 1983

Ellison, Harlan, *Harlan Ellison's Watching*, Novato, California: Underwood Miller, 1989

Ellison, Harlan, *Harlan Ellison's The City on the Edge of Forever: The Original Screenplay That Became the Classic Star Trek Episode*, Clarkston, Georgia: White Wolf, 1996

Engel, Joel, *Gene Roddenberry: The Myth and the Man Behind Star Trek*, New York: Hyperion, 1994

Geraght, Lincoln (Ed)., *The Influence of Star Trek on Television, Film and Culture*, North Carolina: McFarland, 2008

Gerrold, David, *The World of Star Trek* (revised edition), London: Virgin Books, 1996

Greenwald, Jeff, *Future Perfect: How Star Trek Conquered Planet Earth*, New York: Penguin, 1998

Gross, Edward and Mark A. Altman, *Lost Voyages of Trek and The Next Generation*, London: Boxtree, 1995

Gross, Edward and Mark A. Altman, *Captains' Logs: The Unauthorized Complete Trek Voyages*, New York: Little Brown, 1995

Hark, Ina Rae, *BFI TV Classics: Star Trek*, London: Palgrave Macmillan/BFI, 2008

Hughes, David, *The Greatest Sci-Fi Movies Never Made*, London: Titan Books, 2008

Jones, Mark and Lance Parkin, *Beyond the Final Frontier: An Unauthorised Review of the Trek Universe on Television and Film*, London: Contender, 2003

Meyer, Nicholas, *The View From the Bridge: Memories of Star Trek and a Life in Hollywood*, New York: Penguin, 2009

Nimoy, Leonard, *I Am Spock*, London: Century, 1995

Reeves-Stevens, Judith and Garfield, *Star Trek: Phase II – The Untold Story Behind the Star Trek Television Series That Almost Was*, New York: Pocket Books, 1997

Shatner, William with Chris Kreski, *Star Trek Movie Memories: The Inside Story of the Classic Movies*, London: HarperCollins, 1994

Solow, Herbert F. and Robert H. Justman, *Inside Star Trek: The Real Story*, New York: Pocket Books, 1996

Whitfield, Stephen E. and Gene Roddenberry, *The Making of Star Trek*, London: Titan Books, 1991

**Additional resources**

All the *Star Trek* TV series and movies, from *The Original Series* to 2009's *Star Trek* are available on DVD (and increasingly on Blu-ray).

Online episode guides are available at fan site Memory Alpha (www.memory-alpha.org) and the official site www.startrek.com

An invaluable resource – and highly recommended – is the official *Star Trek Magazine*, edited by Paul Simpson (titanmagazines.com/t/star-trek/)

# Index